Development
in Infancy

A Series of Books in Psychology

EDITORS: Richard C. Atkinson
Jonathan Freedman
Richard F. Thompson

Development
in Infancy

T. G. R. Bower

University of Edinburgh

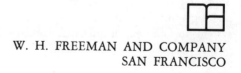

W. H. FREEMAN AND COMPANY
SAN FRANCISCO

Library of Congress Cataloging in Publication Data

Bower, T G R 1941-
    Development in infancy.

    Bibliography: p.
    1. Infants. 2. Cognition (Child psychology)
I. Title. [DNLM: 1. Child development. 2. Cognition
—In infancy and childhood. 3. Perception—In infancy
and childhood. WS105 B783d   1974]
BF723.J6B623   155.4'22   73-19995
ISBN 0-7167-0777-2
ISBN 0-7167-0776-4 (pbk.)

Printed in the United States of America

9 8 7 6 5 4 3 2 1

Contents

Preface

I think it is generally agreed that infancy, the period before language, is one of the most critical segments of human development. During infancy the basic human motor skills are established, perceptual development is virtually completed, and the roots of the cognitive skills that will grow into a human intellect are laid down. Despite this, it is only comparatively recently that infancy as a field of study has truly burgeoned. In the last ten years our methods for the study of infants have become much more precise. The questions we can ask of infants have become much more detailed, and the answers we received have surprised many of us. Infants are capable of many things we would not have expected and at the same time show incapacities we would never have suspected. In this book I have tried to present the methods currently used to get information from infants as well as some of the results obtained through using these methods. I have tried to show how infants can be capable of things we thought beyond them. I have also tried to elucidate the processes whereby infants develop those capacities they must develop, particularly cognitive capacities. My concern throughout has been to show the importance of the psychological environment of the developing infant in speeding up or slowing down his attainment of fundamental cognitive skills. I believe that infancy is the critical period in cognitive development—the period when the greatest gains and the greatest losses can occur. Further, the gains and losses that occur here become harder to offset with increasing age. If this book can stimulate some practical work on these problems, I shall feel well rewarded. I also hope that students who read this book will gain insight into the dynamic interactive process that is called development in infancy. I hope it will stimulate readers to ask new questions and get new answers. Only with the help of new questions and answers can we finally come to comprehend development.

September 1973   *T. G. R. Bower*

**Development
in Infancy**

one /

Introduction

Psychology, during most of its history, has been primarily concerned with studying the origins and development of human knowledge and skill. The early philosopher/psychologists who posed many of the problems that still concern us tried to explain how certain kinds of knowledge were acquired in the course of development. Being philosophers more than psychologists, they did not trouble to examine human development but rather preferred to assume that the newborn human infant knew certain things but not others, or perhaps knew nothing at all. They then tried to see if they could plausibly convert their invented infant into a human adult like themselves. With little constraint on speculation, it is no wonder that theories about the nature of the human infant abounded and gave rise to fierce controversy that was quite innocent of any empirical constraint. The main controversy was between the *nativists* and the *empiricists*. Nativists argued that human knowledge and human skill were built into the structure of the organism. Knowledge could be compared to the arrangement of our ribs—it was something we had because we were human beings rather than fish. Skill could be compared to breathing—it was something that happened inevitably, given the structure of human brains and bodies. Empiricists, by contrast, argued that human knowledge developed selectively as a result of specific encounters with certain types of environmental events. Human skills developed as behaviors were modified through successes or failures in coping with problems posed by the environment. These two theories of development, which could hardly have been more different, had very different social philosophies associated with them. Nativists tended to be pessimistic as far as the perfectability of man was concerned. The unskilled and ignorant were held to be so simply because they were born unskilled and ignorant. Their lack of competence was held to be a characteristic comparable to eye color or skin color. Competence or incompetence was something peculiar to a person's native endowment and quite beyond the reach of any human intervention. Empiricists, to the contrary, would say that the unskilled and ignorant were unskilled and ignorant because their environment had denied them the opportunity to develop skills and knowledge; if environments were sufficiently modified, ignorance would disappear and the whole community could share a general high level of competence. To this day these social philosophies heat the emotions to the extent that rational discussion becomes a near impossibility.

The philosopher/psychologists who began the debate on the origins of human knowledge did not do experiments, partly because they thought experiments were unnecessary. Even after psychology had become an experimental science, the study of development still remained nonexperimental for many years; this was particularly true of the study of development in infancy. Furthermore, most early techniques of psychological investigation depended heavily on verbal instructions and verbal reports from subjects. It is only in the last fifteen years or so that the techniques necessary for studying nonverbal humans—infants—have been brought to a level where we can begin to ask and answer questions bequeathed to us three centuries ago.

In the meantime the debate has not stood still. There has been a recent series of attempts to argue from indirect evidence that human knowledge and human skill are inherited and that environmental intervention can hardly change the developmental process at all. For example, there has been a somewhat acrimonious debate about IQ scores. IQ tests are made up of items such as those shown in Figure 1.1. It has been proposed that scores on such tests are primarily determined by inherited factors. The evidence in favor of this view is derived from statistical manipulations of the IQ scores of individuals who are more or less closely related; the details of these procedures are given in numerous readily available sources and need not be discussed here. The point to emphasize is that, on the basis of IQ test scores taken from adults and older children, it is argued that the IQ differences shown among individuals are entirely a function of inherited structural differences and have nothing to do with life histories. This hypothesis about development claims that different experiences make no difference in IQ scores. This hypothesis, however, cannot be tested without actually studying the course of development. Since relevant experiments have simply not been done, arguments over the hypothesis are premature at this point. The nativist hypothesis cannot be accepted or rejected with the information presently available.

A second line of research which is of a much higher caliber has also been cited to give some indirect support to the nativist hypothesis. The recent explosion of knowledge in genetics has shown how information that is coded in molecular structures within the fertilized egg controls the sequence of chemical events that will result in the development of a complete, complexly differentiated organism. Development under genetic control is now understood as a physical process controlled at the molecular level. According to this line of thinking, development is a complex *physico-chemical* process, requiring no reference to any concepts more abstract than those of physics and chemistry.

As long as geneticists stuck to simple physical structures, there was little in their work to disturb psychologists, most of whom have always felt that theories of knowledge, skill, and intelligence were safely beyond the compass of physics and chemistry. The growth and success of genetic studies on mental retardation, however, have shown that this is not necessarily the case. There have been many attempts to help mentally retarded children by giving them special training and special help and experiences; many environmental modifications based on diverse psychological theories have been tried in an attempt to solve the problem of mental retardation. However, the most successful modification yet discovered did not stem from psychology but rather from a discovery in biochemical genetics. This discovery concerned a type of mental retardation known as phenylketonuria or P.K.U. Persons afflicted with P.K.U., one

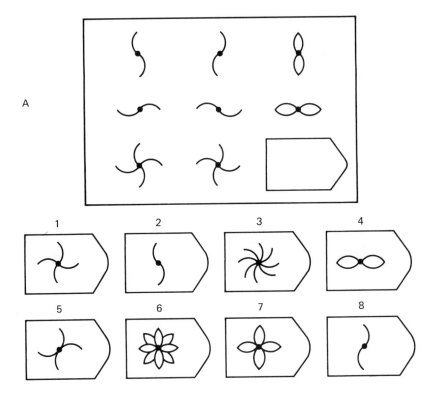

FIGURE 1.1
Sample IQ items. (A) Raven's progressive matrices: The subject must choose the missing part from the eight given alternatives. (From The Raven Progressive Matrices, 1958, Set E. Reprinted by permission of the Executors of the late Dr. J. C. Raven.) (B) Seguin Form Board: This is a performance test in which the subject must replace the pieces in the correct holes as quickly as possible. (C) Stanford-Binet Intelligence Scale: The items shown are included in the nine-year-old test items. (Reproduced by permission of the publisher, Houghton Mifflin Co.)

of the most severe forms of mental retardation, used to become imbeciles, unable to care for themselves. Special training did nothing for P.K.U. afflictions. It was then discovered persons with P.K.U. lack the enzyme that converts phenylalanine, a protein, to tyrosine, a slightly different kind of protein. In the absence of the required enzyme, phenylalanine is converted to phenylpyruvic acid; the build-up of phenylpyruvic acid is associated with the occurrence of mental deficiency. If a child who lacks the proper enzyme is given a diet low in protein and therefore low in phenylalanine, there is no build-up of phenylpyruvic acid. As a consequence,

B

C

(a) Bill Jones' feet are so big that he has to pull his trousers on over his head.

(b) In an old graveyard in Spain, they have found a small skull which is believed to have been that of Christopher Columbus when he was about ten years old.

there is no mental deficiency, and the child's development is approximately normal. This minor biochemical modification produces significant benefits that no environmental modification had ever been able to produce.

Some environmentalists may be tempted to argue that such a modification is indeed an environmental modification. This is true if *environment* is used in a broad sense, but to psychologists *environment* means the psychological environment, the world as experienced, a world of successes, failures, attempts to comprehend, emotional changes, and the like; in the traditional arguments between nativists and empiricists, *environment* has not meant the physicochemical environment. To pretend otherwise is simply dishonest.

The empiricist position has had to suffer other embarrassments. Perhaps the major obstacle to any development of the empiricist theory was the inability of developmental psychologists to demonstrate that human infants could learn at all. It is central to empiricism as a general philosophy that development be accomplished by learning, as a result of the organism's successes and/or failures in coping with its environment. It seemed a direct contradiction to empiricism that infants should develop manifestly while showing no change in behavior that could be related to the success or failure of the behavior. Learning—the adjustment of behavior in accord with its success or failure—seemed to be beyond the capacities of infants in their first year; infants nonetheless develop an enormous amount during the course of their first year. The apparent fact of development with no possibility of learning directly contradicted the empiricist point of view that development can only be generated by learning. That fact of course is a fact no longer: it has been demonstrated that infants on the first day of life can learn. Indeed it has been claimed that humans can learn better in infancy than at any later age (Lipsitt, 1969). This advance, however, has not been accomplished without some cost to the general empiricist point of view. Learning in infants now appears to be a much more complex process than ever seemed likely before.

Psychologists use very simple paradigms to study learning. In the standard paradigm the experimenter establishes a contingency between one of the behaviors of the organism and some event in the world around it. In the most famous of all learning situations the organism, a pigeon, pecks on a key. As a result of circuitry built in by the experimenter, food is presented for a short time after the pecking behavior occurs. Pecking is called the *conditioned response* or *CR*. The food is referred to as the *reinforcement*. If the organism learns in this situation, the rate of occurrence of the CR increases.

There are various possible ways of presenting reinforcement. If reinforcement is presented every time the CR occurs, we have a *continuous reinforcement* or *CRF* schedule. We might also have a schedule in which every *n*th response, say the fifth or tenth, is reinforced; this is referred to as a *fixed ratio* or *FR* schedule. Analogous to the FR schedule is the *fixed interval* or *FI* schedule in which reinforcement is made available only at fixed time intervals, say every thirty seconds. Responses made during the fixed interval produce no reinforcement. There are also *variable ratios*, or *VR* schedules, in which the number of responses required to elicit reinforcement varies from reinforcement to reinforcement. In addition, there is the *variable interval*, or *VI* schedule, in which the interval during which reinforcement is not available varies from reinforcement to reinforcement. These schedules have different effects on the rate of occurrence of a CR. The measure taken with all of these schedules is a *rate measure*. If the rate of occurrence of a CR is higher when the CR-reinforcement contingency is operating than when it is not operating, then we have evidence that the animal has detected the contingency and learned that its response produces the reinforcement. Our evidence of learning thus depends on performance of the CR, which obviously depends on the animal being motivated. If an animal is not hungry, we would not expect it to perform for a food reinforcement. In animal learning experiments, it is usual to ensure performances by starving the animal to 80 percent of its normal body weight prior to the experiment. Any such manipulation is obviously out of the question in the case of human infants. A few studies have used food reward supplementary to normal diet as a reinforcement with infants. However, a more standard practice has been to use exciting visual events to motivate performance.

The effectiveness of reinforcement is obviously critical in experiments like these. If the reinforcement is not effective in motivating the baby, there is no possibility of demonstrating that the baby can learn. Accordingly, experimenters vied with one another to devise exciting visual events, human jack-in-the-boxes, Times Square light displays, and other complex events which were presented as reinforcements; in most cases, however, these efforts were to little avail. Even CRF, the simplest of all schedules, produced learning in only a few cases in a few laboratories. Analysis of these successful cases does not indicate any obvious common factor in the reinforcements used. Experiments using a single flashing light were as successful as experiments using a human jack-in-the-box or something equally complex. However, a closer analysis of the successful experiments does show a common factor. The more successful experiments either did not use CRF at all or quickly shifted from CRF to a more complex schedule, regardless of whether the infant had learned during the CRF phase. This is puzzling since it seems to imply that the schedule rather than the reinforcement is the motivating factor. The nature of the reinforcement was seemingly unimportant, whereas the nature of the schedule was important. What is it about a schedule of reinforcement that can be more motivating than a reinforcement itself? The answer seems to be that the schedule can pose problems to the infant, and the problem solving is the true motivation for human infants in a learning situation. Problem solving seems a most unlikely form of motivation to attribute to infants; however, there are a number of experiments which make this conclusion inescapable.

Consider an infant in the situation described by Papousek (1969). The infant can turn on a light by moving his head to the left. Most infants of two to three months will succeed in turning on the light several times within a quite short time. Their rate of leftward head turning will then drop back to a level which is insufficient to serve as a criterion of learning. The rate will not pick up again so long as the left-turn-light-on contingency is operative. Suppose the experimenter changes the contingency to right-turn-light-on. Sooner or later the infant will make a left turn and the light will not go on. We then see a burst of leftward head turns, followed by detection of the right-turn-light-on contingency, as shown by a brief, high rate of right head turns, which will then subside. This second rate will also stay low if the contingency is unchanged.

If the contingency is changed again to a left turn followed by right turn to switch the light on, the rate of right turning will increase after the first trial on which the light does not go on; the rate of left turning will also increase, and finally the infant will produce a left turn followed by a right turn and switch the light on. After a brief burst of left-rights the rate will subside, until the contingency is changed. The change produces a burst of activity, ending when the correct combination of movements is discovered. In such procedures, infants have been brought to master quite complex series of movements, such as right-right-left-left. Every time the contingency is changed the activity rate of the infant goes up. Examination of the behavior shows that the activity is not random. The infant seems to be testing hypotheses and trying out sequences of movement in order to discover which one operates at the moment. When the correct sequence is discovered, it is tested a few times and then dropped. Behavior, or hypothesis testing, only picks up again when the previous sequence is shown to be inadequate. It is quite obvious from the behavior of the infants that the light source is not the motivating factor.

While hypothesis testing is going on, even after the first success, the infant barely looks at the light. A scant glance is made to check whether the light is on or not. After the confirmatory glance, the infant may manifest behavioral signs of pleasure and joy, but these signs are displayed with no attention to the light, which is obviously not the cause. It thus seems that the pleasures of problem solving are sufficient to motivate behavioral and mental activity in young infants. If a learning situation is interactive, the infant will demonstrate that he can learn; if the infant's only motive is the prospect of reward, then he will not demonstrate that he can learn. Many of the original experimental failures must thus have resulted because of failures to engage the motivational system of the infant adequately. The parameters of this motivational system have not been fully explained. We do not know, for example, whether the infant will continue to work at an insoluble problem or how successes in problem solving affect motivation in solving other problems. These questions are still to be answered.

This solution to the problem of learning in infants does nothing to bridge the gap between nativists and empiricists. If anything the gap is sharpened. One can see the possibility of some relationship between hunger and biochemical processes in the brain. Problem solving is something else, however, with no conceivable molecular equivalents at this point in intellectual history. At this time, problem solving is a factor in a psychological environment that cannot be reduced to a physicochemical environment. At the same time, demonstrations of learning in infants as complex as those recently carried out should not bring pure joy to the heart of a dedicated empiricist. Learning at this level requires a great deal of information that must be built into the structure of the organism as surely as is the structure of its hands. Consider tl.e experiment of Lipsitt and Siqueland (1966) which was carried out with infants in their first day after birth. The researchers were able to establish a head-turning response to one side when a buzzer was sounded and a head-turning response to the other side when a bell was presented. Thus, as bell and buzzer alternated, the infants came to make a head turn in the appropriate direction only. After that discrimination was made, the experimenters reversed the contingencies; if an infant had learned bell-left buzzer-right, he was now required to forget that and learn bell-right, buzzer-left. All of the infants were able to make this discrimination reversal in very short order. Indeed they did it with a facility unsurpassed by any nonhuman primate. Consider, then, what this implies in terms of information that the infant must bring to the learning situation. First of all the infant must be able to discriminate between bell and buzzer. He must be able to identify a bell and

TABLE 1.1
Contingencies in Siqueland and Lipsitt's (1966) Experiment

Stimulus	Response	Condition
Bell	Left head turn	Not reinforced
Bell	Right head turn	Reinforced
Buzzer	Left head turn	Reinforced
Buzzer	Right head turn	Not reinforced

identify a buzzer so as to know which is being presented on any trial so that he can perform the appropriate response. He must likewise be able to discriminate and identify head turns to the right and head turns to the left. Further he must be able to detect the relationship among stimulus (bell or buzzer), response (turn to right or left) and reinforcement. This is complicated enough as Table 1.1 shows, but these experimentally induced complications are not the only complications in the situation. Suppose an infant is in a bell-right-buzzer-left situation. Suppose that after the bell sounds the infant turns his head to the right and is then reinforced. At the moment the bell sounds, it is highly likely that the infant is aware of other stimuli, such as the room lighting, the texture of his diapers, outside noises, the clicking of equipment, and various other stimuli that must be present. When the infant turns his head to the right, he probably also turns his eyes left; also there are probably foot and hand movements going on before, after, or simultaneously with the head movement. One might ask why the bell and the head turn should be linked with the reinforcement event, rather than with any of the other stimuli or responses occurring prior to the reinforcement? The infant must have extremely precise selection mechanisms to allow this detection to occur as rapidly as it does. The parameters of the selection mechanisms, however, are relatively unexplored in infants. It seems likely that the major constraint is temporal; only those stimuli and responses which occur within a short interval before the reinforcement enter into the selection process. Beyond that limit, the infant must use analysis over time. Thus, if an infant has the set of events shown in Table 1.1 entered for selection, he could find out which one produced reinforcement simply by testing each combination in the list. The fact that something like this does go on is attested by the high rate of activity customary at the beginning of con-

A

Head

Left   0°

Right

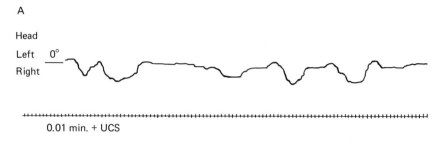

0.01 min. + UCS

B

Head

Left

0°

Right

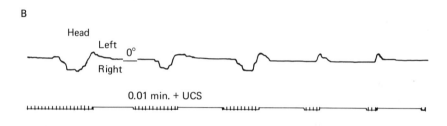

0.01 min. + UCS

C

Head

Left 0°

Right

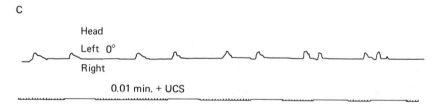

0.01 min. + UCS

FIGURE 1.2
(A) The rate of activity at the beginning of a conditioning session. (B, C)
As the session progresses, activity becomes increasingly differentiated; the
gross movements of the early stages drop out and are replaced by very
precise movements. (Papousek, 1969; courtesy of Developmental Science Trust.)

ditioning sessions. (See Figure 1.2.) It is as if the infant tests out all
possible responses for their potential efficiency. All of these capacities—
stimulus identification, response identification, stimulus-response selection
—must be built in before learning takes place. These capacities must have
developed, without benefit of learning, in the intrauterine environment
before the infant's actions had any consequences.

Since learning depends on such a complex of innate capacities and since as we have seen it is reversible and apparently does not lead to any permanent changes, there is a tendency to see learning as a consequence of development rather than as a causal factor in development. Processes of development produce the possibility of learning, but learning itself does not produce development; the effectiveness of the organism in a learning situation is seen as depending on innate mechanisms which cannot be modified by events in a psychological environment. On the surface there is some measure of support for this since learning ability seemingly declines with age. Apparently, it becomes progressively more difficult to demonstrate learning in infants as they grow older. If the infant becomes less able to learn during the process of development, it seems unlikely that learning can be the causal mechanism in development. In opposition to this view, Watson (1966) has argued that the observed decline in learning ability is a function of prior learning experiences.

> Imagine a living thing whose behavioral repertoire is such that it provides no possibility of eliciting rewards from the external world. Rewarding stimulus events could be experienced but could not be produced. With the provision of a benevolent environment, the organism would survive but not learn in the sense of acquiring behavioral adaptations which produce rewards. I propose that in certain ways this situation is descriptive of the human infant's first three months of life. Furthermore, these first few months might well be termed a period of "natural deprivation" of learning experiences, the elimination of which may have desirable long-term intellective consequences. [Watson, 1966]

Watson argues here that the observed decline in learning ability results from lack of opportunity to learn. In pursuit of this hypothesis, Watson has carried out experiments where infants were given early learning opportunities in hopes that their later learning would be greatly facilitated. Papousek (1967) has conducted similar experiments which support the hypothesis that early learning opportunities affect later learning. (See Table 1.2.) Such studies suggest that learning ability, initially shaped via innate mechanisms, can decline if it is not exercised. The development of learning ability thus seems to depend on an interaction between an innately generated set of mechanisms and the opportunity to use these mechanisms in a psychological environment—an environmental effect that is not learning in the strict sense. We shall see this pattern repeated again and again in development.

TABLE 1.2
Comparison of the Conditionability of Two Groups of
Infants at Approximately the Same Age (Group A =
Infants subjected to conditioning procedures from birth;
Group B = Infants subjected to conditioning procedures
from the age of 3 months. Comparison shows that early
learning opportunities greatly facilitate later learning.

Group	Mean Age in Days at Beginning of Test	Mean Trials to Criterion
A	107.54	94.63
B	105.92	176.23

Source: Papousek, 1967.

There are other changes in infant learning patterns which do not fit with such an analysis. Young infants seem able to detect and utilize a contingency between any response and any reinforcement event. This is not true of older infants. Thus it has been demonstrated that young infants will suck a pacifier or turn their head to switch on a display light. Nine-month-old infants are very reluctant to do this, but they will push the display with their hand. This seems to indicate a change in the parameters of the response-reinforcement selection mechanism; there is the addition of a spatial constraint so that response and reinforcement must be spatially as well as temporally contiguous. Similar changes seem to occur in the stimulus-reinforcement selection mechanism: infants begin to ignore stimuli that are spatially unconnected with the reinforcement. These changes go on throughout the first year or longer and change the possibilities of learning. Whether these new constraints are endogenously generated like those operative immediately after birth, or whether their acquisition is dependent on interaction with the psychological environment, is something we cannot decide at the moment. It is hoped this book will elucidate the nature of the built-in constraints, their relation to learning, and the relation between learning and development.

In the following chapters we shall look at the development of some of the precursors of learning; we shall begin with the mechanisms of stimulus detection, localization, and identification. The central theme to which we shall constantly return is the role of experience in development. The two generalized hypotheses, nativism and empiricism, have already been introduced. We have already looked at learning as a prototypal mechanism for the empiricist and found this approach wanting. Learning seems to depend on very elaborate mechanisms that are not themselves the result of learning; further, learning is itself subject to environmental modification by way of some process other than learning. These observations are reason enough to call into question any extreme nativist position, just as the unlearned constraints on learning must restrict any extreme empiricist position.

two /

Space Perception

Few topics in the history of experimental psychology have excited as much interest and controversy as has the origin of space perception. For a long while, the topic of space perception was the battlefield where the empiricists and nativists confronted one another with their respective theories. The battle was fought at a very general level; data on human adults was set against data from newly hatched chicks. It is no wonder that Boring (1942) dismissed the controversy as sterile; it produced nothing—not even, as we shall see, a clarification of the developmental problem of space perception.

Human adults live and move in an organized world of three dimensions. We can locate the distance of objects, detect their radial direction or position to our right or left, and determine their height relative to our

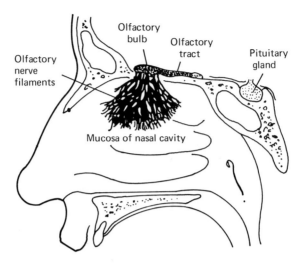

FIGURE 2.1
Drawing of the nasal cavity and olfactory structures.
The nose is to the left and the back of the mouth
to the right. The diagram exposes the interior of
the nasal cavities and shows roughly how the
olfactory membrane is spread out in the mucosa of
the cavity. (From E. Gardner, *Fundamentals of
Neurology*, W. B. Saunders Co., 1947.)

own. We do this primarily with our sense of sight, which can register all
of these variables. Radial direction, however, can also be picked up by
ear and even by the nose, though crudely.*

The perception of radial direction by the nose exemplifies the problems of space perception. If we take a blindfolded observer and place an
odoriferous source object in front of him, he can tell us whether the object
is straight ahead, to his right, or to his left, and can indicate its precise
position with an accuracy of 3.5°. This seems commonplace enough until
one inquires into the processes involved in making the judgment. The
molecules that produce the sensation of smell diffuse in all directions
from the odoriferous source. They impinge on the sense receptors inside
the nostrils whenever air is drawn through the nostrils. (See Figure 2.1.)
The nose is well supplied with odor receptors, distributed fairly evenly

---

*Both of these senses can also be used for distance perception. The abilities involved
have been studied very little in adults and not at all in infants; they will therefore not be
discussed here.

over its internal surface. The process thus far seems simple enough, but the problem begins when we ask where is the right-left-straight ahead dimension in the nose? What is the structure that registers the rightward or leftward position of the stimulus source? Indeed there is none. All of the receptors in each nostril are stimulated equally when air is drawn over them; the position of the source of stimulation makes no difference to the process of stimulation within each nostril. The nose therefore has no right and left of its own. How then do we register right-left position with our noses?

The crucial clue, suggested by Mach (1885) nearly 100 years ago is that, although we have but one nose, we have two nostrils, side by side in the radial plane. This anatomical fact has some interesting consequences for the process of odor localization. Consider the situation shown in Figure 2.2a. A subject is facing an odor source which is straight ahead of him. The molecules producing the sensation of odor are diffusing from the odor source. When the subject breathes in, a large number of molecules is simultaneously displaced, with an increasing concentration passing through each nostril over time. At each point in time the concentration in each nostril is the same. Contrast this situation with Figure 2.2b where the stimulus source is on the right. The right nostril is nearer the stimulus source than is the left nostril. When inhalation begins an increasingly intense concentration of molecules again passes through each nostril; but in this case a given intensity of concentration is reached in the right nostril before it is reached in the left nostril. Since there is a threshold below which no odor is sensed, this means that the right nostril is effectively stimulated before the left nostril. In the reverse case where the stimulus source is placed on the left, the left nostril would be stimulated before the right nostril. Unless the source object is straight ahead, one nostril will be stimulated before the other. The order in which stimulation occurs (right before left or left before right) corresponds, of course, to the position of the source object (to the right or to the left). The amount of the difference between stimulation specifies the separation of the object from the straight ahead position; the greater the separation, the longer the time lag between stimulation of each nostril. The time of onset of stimulation in each nostril can thus specify the position of the object.

The question arises as to whether this stimulus specification is used by subjects. An ingenious experiment by von Békésy (1969) shows that it is. Békésy used tubes to deliver odors to each nostril separately. The

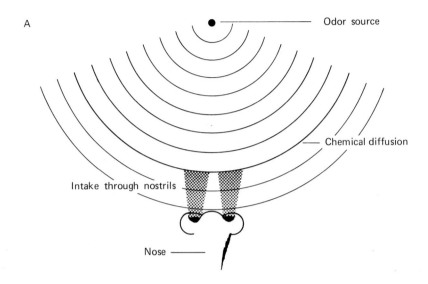

A   ●——————————— Odor source

————— Chemical diffusion

Intake through nostrils ——

Nose ———

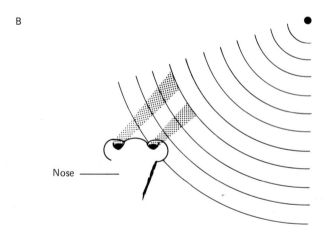

B

Nose ———

FIGURE 2.2
(A) Odor source straight ahead. At any one time, the concentration of
molecules passing through each nostril is the same since both nostrils are
equidistant from the odor source. (B) Odor source on the right. Because
the right nostril is nearer to the odor source than the left nostril, the
concentration in the right nostril at any one time is greater than the
concentration in the left nostril.

arrival time at each nostril could be varied. When the odors arrived simultaneously, subjects indicated that the perceived position of the odor source was straight ahead. When the right nostril was stimulated first, the subjects localized the odor source on the right; the greater the lead of right over left, the further the odor seemed to be from a straight-ahead position. When the left nostril was stimulated first, the odor source seemed to be on the left. Békésy thus demonstrated that differences in the time of stimulation of each nostril is the stimulus dimension which specifies for adult subjects the position of an olfactory source.

The student of development will perceive the problems that are associated with this demonstration. Does the time-difference dimension specify position of an olfactory source to the infant? Or does the infant, stimulated in the right nostril and then the left, simply perceive a double odor source with no particular spatial position attached? This is a specific question, but it is representative of the general question of whether infants perceive the world in distal terms or whether they perceive the proximal processes (the processes at the sense organ) that mediate the distal perception in adults.

Olfactory localization in infants has attracted relatively little attention from investigators, but some relevant data have been gathered in the course of studies of olfactory preference. Young infants can apparently turn away from unpleasant odors, smoothly and efficiently. They do not go left when the stimulus is on the left or right when it is on the right. Such observations have been made on infants in the first day of life—indeed in the first hours of life—and it would seem that the capacity to locate position on the basis of olfactory time differences is probably built into the structure of the organism (Engen et al., 1963). The *proximal/distal transduction rule* would seem to be incorporated at an age at which learning could hardly have affected the requisite structural modifications. We are therefore justified in concluding that the capacity to localize the positions of olfactory sources is innate.

Auditory Localization. Our auditory system, from the point of view of space perception, is similar to our olfactory system. We can locate the radial direction, the position to the right or the left, of a sound source. We do this despite the fact that there is no right and left within the ear. (See Figure 2.3.) The solution to the problem, as we might expect, lies in the fact that we have two ears. Sound is carried from a source by waves of

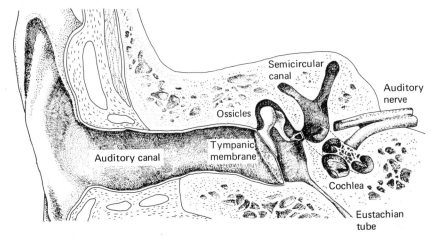

A

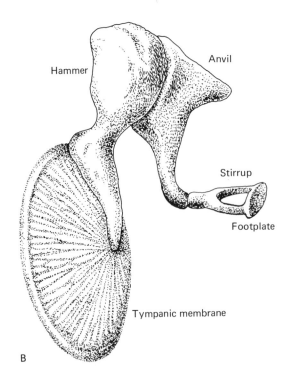

B

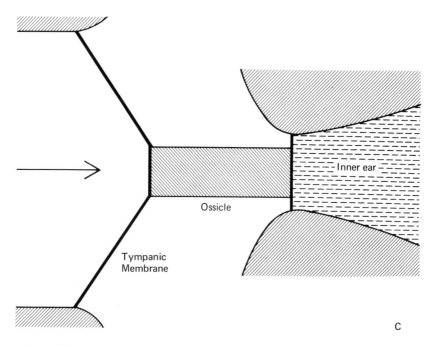

C

FIGURE 2.3
The ear. (*Top left*) Parts of the ear are illustrated in this somewhat simplified cross section. Between the eardrum (tympanic membrane) and the fluid-filled inner ear are the three small bones (ossicles) of the middle ear. The auditory nerve endings are in an organ (not shown) between the plate of bone that spirals up the cochlea and the outer wall of the cochlea. (*Bottom left*) Three ossicles transmit the vibrations of the tympanic membrane to the inner ear. The footplate of the stirrup, surrounded by a narrow membrane, presses against inner-ear fluid. (*Above*) How ossicles act as a piston pressing against the fluid of the inner ear is indicated by this drawing. Pressure of the vibrations of tympanic membrane are amplified 22 times. (From G. von Békésy, "The Ear." Copyright © 1957 by Scientific American, Inc. All rights reserved.)

pressure change. Consider what occurs when one sound source is placed straight ahead and one is placed to the right. (See Figures 2.4a and 2.4b.) Sound waves from the straight ahead source will reach both ears simultaneously; the waves from the source on the right will reach the right ear slightly before they reach the left ear. There is thus a *time difference* in the onset of stimulation at the two ears. The more a sound source deviates from the straight ahead position, the more one ear will lead over the other, thereby relaying precise information about the location of a sound source.

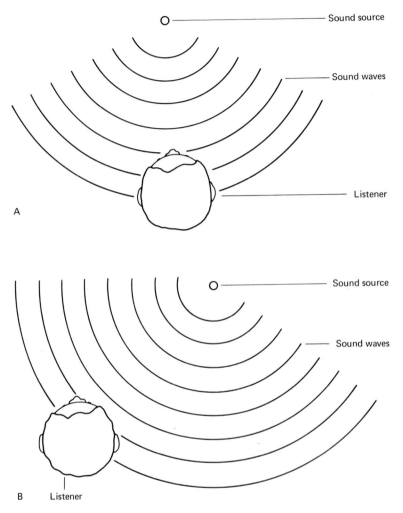

FIGURE 2.4
(*Top*) Sound source straight ahead. Sound reaches both ears simultaneously.
(*Bottom*) Sound source on right. Sound reaches right ear first.

(See Figure 2.5.) This information is supplemented by two other dimensions of stimulation—*phase differences* and *intensity differences*. Phase differences are a special kind of time difference; sound is propagated as a series
of pressure changes, which have a characteristic variation in intensity over
time as they pass a fixed station point. Simple sounds have a characteristic
wave shape. (See Figure 2.6.)

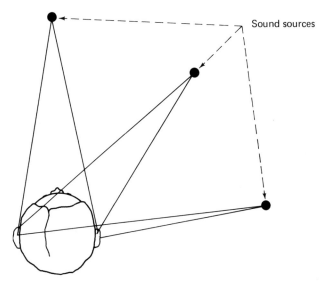

Sound sources

FIGURE 2.5
The more a sound source deviates from the straight ahead
position, the greater is the time difference in onset of
stimulation at the two ears.

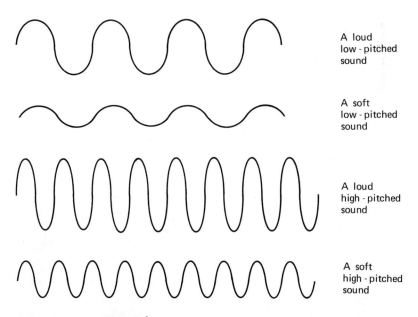

A loud
low - pitched
sound

A soft
low - pitched
sound

A loud
high - pitched
sound

A soft
high - pitched
sound

FIGURE 2.6
Characteristic wave shape of simple sounds.

A sound source which is straight ahead is equidistant from the two ears. This means that the momentary pressure change at any one point in time will be the same at the two ears. This is not so if the sound source is on the right or left. If the source is on the right, for example, the left ear will be receiving the input that the right ear received fractions of a second earlier. This phase difference between the two ears is precisely correlated with the amount of deviation from the straight ahead position.

There are limitations on the utility of phase differences. Sounds differ in frequency. This means that the rate at which the pattern of pressure changes repeats itself varies from sound to sound. High pitched sounds repeat their characteristic wave with a high frequency; low pitched sounds repeat with a low frequency. The consequences of this phenomenon for the detection of phase difference at two fixed points (our two ears) are shown in Figure 2.7. Some high frequency waves will be in the same phase at the two ears when the source is far from straight ahead. In adults it has been found that phase differences are only reliable up to 600 hertz, a range which corresponds quite well to the distance between an adult's ears (Stevens and Newman, 1936).

Intensity differences are produced whenever a sound source is located to the right or left. There are two causes for the intensity difference. The first is simply that intensity decreases with distance. The intensity at the ear farther from the sound source will of course be weaker than the intensity at the nearer ear. The second cause of intensity difference is the presence of the head, which blocks off some of the sound that would reach the farther ear, thereby enhancing the intensity difference. Intensity differences increase with deviation from the straight ahead position and reach a maximum when the sound source lies on an imaginary line drawn through the two ears.

In summary, then, there are three dimensions of stimulation at the ears—time differences, phase differences, and intensity differences. These vary with the position of a sound source and thus specify the position of the source to a perceiving organism. There is ample evidence that adult humans can and do use all of these variables to locate sound sources (Stevens and Newman, 1936). We can now ask whether the same is true of infants.

Before looking at the experimental data, such as it is, we must consider the additional problem of growth. As mentioned, the distance between the ears is critically important in determining the amount of the time, phase, and intensity differences produced by sound sources in various

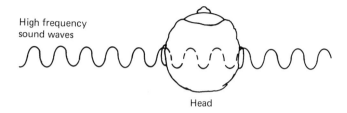

High frequency
sound waves

Head

Here, the sound wave is in the rising phase on arrival at both ears

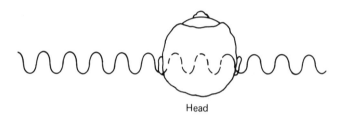

Head

Here, the sound wave is in the falling phase at both ears.

FIGURE 2.7
High frequency waves may be in the same phase upon reaching
both ears even though they originated from a point well
off the straight-ahead position.

locations. The distance between an infant's ears is not the same as the
distance between an adult's ears. Interear distance approximately doubles
between birth and adulthood, which has some considerable consequences
for auditory localization. Location of a sound at the straight ahead position—specified by zero time difference, zero phase difference, and zero
intensity difference—is of course unaffected.

Direction of differences specifying position to one side or another
are likewise unaffected. A sound on the right will stimulate the right ear
first and will be louder at the right ear, regardless of interear separation.
A sound on the left, likewise, will stimulate the left ear first and will be
louder at the left ear, regardless of interear separation. However, the size
of the differences specifying precise position off the straight ahead are
very much affected by the interear separation. The time difference produced at the infant's ears by a sound in any given location will be less
than that produced at the adult ears by a sound in the same location.
(See Figure 2.8.)

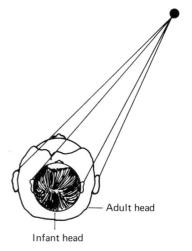

FIGURE 2.8
Because of the difference in head
size, the time difference in arrival
of a sound at the two ears is less
for an infant than for an adult.

—— Adult head

Infant head

What does this imply about the development of auditory localization?
The first implication is that the newborn infant probably cannot localize
a sound source in any and every position. To do so, the infant would have
to be equipped with structures to translate the time differences produced
by his head size into distal locations. These structures would, however,
become useless as the infant's head grew and would have to be continuously recalibrated during growth. It would seem uneconomic to build
in structures of such limited utility. It is not impossible that such structures and such a pattern of development could have evolved, but it seems
rather unlikely. On the other hand, it would seem quite likely that the
newborn is equipped with sufficient structure to tell him when a sound is
straight ahead. Such a structure could remain *invariant* during growth
since the proximal information specifying straight ahead is not affected
by growth. The same structure could serve at any age, since the information it would have to pick up (zero difference between the input at
the two ears) would not change during growth. For the same reasons, it
seems quite likely that the infant knows when a sound source is on the
right or left. The qualitative information specifying sound on the right
or sound on the left remains invariant throughout growth. If the infant
has these two capacities, then the missing quantitative information could
be calibrated in quite easily. This process would require: (1) the ability
to recognize when a sound is straight ahead—an ability which could be

built in; (2) the ability to detect when a sound is on the right or left, which could also be built in; (3) the ability to turn the head so as to bring sound sources which are off to one side into the straight ahead position; (4) some source of metric information about the extent of head movements; and (5) sufficient learning ability to associate the stimulation received prior to head movement with the amount of the head movement required to center the sound source. This is a fairly formidable list of abilities. If all were present, the infant could learn to calibrate the position of sound sources by making the appropriate precalibrated head movements.

The two positions outlined so far have attributed to the infant some or a great deal of built-in structure. If is of course possible that the infant could be born with no built-in structure. In this case the newborn would presumably hear two identical sounds when presented with a straight ahead sound source and two different sounds when presented with a sound source to the right or left. Before any other development could take place, the infant would have to discover that the two perceived sounds come from one source. How the infant would do this is by no means clear. After this discovery, learning mechanisms—possibly similar to those described above—could fill in the missing capacities.

How would one test these three hypotheses? Each hypothesis makes different predictions about the behavior one can expect from a newborn infant who is presented with sound sources in various locations. What would the last hypothesis (the extreme empiricist hypothesis) predict about the behavior of a newborn infant presented with a sound to its right? Should the infant turn toward the sound, look toward the sound, or make any other localizing responses? On the empiricist hypothesis, the baby might as well turn or look to the left as to the right, and it might well do neither. The empiricist hypothesis makes the same predictions exactly in the case of a sound presented on the left. Indeed, the predictions are the same for a sound presented in the midline. The empiricist hypothesis predicts that there should be no differences in behavior that are correlated with differences in the site of stimulation.

By contrast, the modified nativist position (the second hypothesis presented above) makes quite specific predictions about differential behavior correlated with differences in the location of a sound source. The modified nativistic hypothesis claims that the newborn knows when a sound source is straight ahead and when a sound source comes from the right or left;

the infant does not know, however, how far to right or left the source may be. When presented with a sound on the right, the modified nativistic hypothesis predicts that the infant should make his localizing responses to the right only. Localizing responses to the left should occur only for sounds on the left; sounds from the straight ahead position should elicit localization responses to the straight ahead position. According to this hypothesis, the localizing responses to any position except the straight ahead position should be imprecise in the newborn and should gradually become more precise with experience. In contrast to this modified approach, the extreme nativist hypothesis (the first hypothesis we described) predicts that localizing movements should be precise from the outset.

Before reviewing the rather scanty experimental data that is currently available, we must make two methodological points. The first concerns the conclusions we could draw from one possible outcome of the experiment outlined above. Suppose the distribution of localizing responses to varying sound sources was essentially a random one; in other words, responses to the right occurred just as frequently when the stimulus was on the left or straight ahead as when it was on the right. This outcome would be in accord with the predictions made by the extreme empiricist hypothesis. We must then ask whether such an outcome could be taken as proof of the empiricist hypothesis and a disproof of the two nativistic hypotheses? As stated, the answer must be no. If such an outcome were observed, nativists could still hold to their position by arguing that the observed response patterns resulted, not from any deficiencies in the auditory system, but from deficiencies in the response system. They could argue that the infant knows where a sound is but does not know how to get his head or eyes or hands to it. This is a plausible argument and certainly cannot be dismissed a priori. What experimental modification would allow one to dismiss it? If we could show that the motor system was precisely controllable, we would wipe out the objection. If it could be shown that localization of visible targets was precise, while localization of audible targets was not, one could not take refuge in arguing hypothetical looseness in the motor system, since such looseness would necessarily result in imprecise motor behavior in the visual situation. Thus to validate the claim that auditory localization is imprecise, two *converging* experiments would be necessary.

The problem outlined above is one that will recur. Any experiment that relies on precise motor behavior to index perceptual function in infants runs into the problem that infant motor behavior is not precise. The motor system is subject to growth processes more than is any perceptual organ. It is a wonder (a wonder to which we will return) that the infant's motor responses are as accurate as they are. Why then do we do experiments that involve this fragile system? Why not make use of discrimination methods, as Munn (1965) has recommended? One could surely teach an infant to make a conditioned response to a sound source presented on his right; after the response was established, one could then introduce a nonreinforced sound source on the left. If both sound sources were presented successively in random order, with only responses to the sound on the right being reinforced, the infant could learn to respond only to the sound source on the right. We know that infants can form such conditioned discriminations. Surely this way of studying the perceptual capacity would be more satisfactory than relying upon the necessarily unreliable motor localizing responses. One could even use an *habituation decrement* experiment. (See Figure 2.9.) One could present a repetitive sound source on the right, wait until the infant showed no more response to the sound, and then shift the sound to the left and see whether the habituation was reversed. We know that small infants show habituation to some stimuli and recovery from habituation when the stimuli are changed. If these effects could be demonstrated with change of position of a sound source, would this not indicate the capacity we want to study?

Unfortunately the answer to both these questions must be no. Neither the conditioned discrimination nor the habituation decrement experiment can, by their very nature, tell us anything about auditory *localization*. Suppose an infant could form a conditioned discrimination between a sound on his right and a sound on his left. What would this tell us? It would tell us that the infant could differentiate between a sound on the left and a sound on the right, *on some basis*; it does not tell us what the basis is. The baby could differentiate on the basis of spatial position, which is what we are interested in, or it could differentiate equally well on the basis of the succession of sounds at its two ears, with no localization at all. Discrimination experiments cannot tell us the *basis* of a discrimination; they can only tell the fact of a discrimination. They do not tell us whether the discrimination is made on the basis of the distal stimulus differences (which is what we are interested in) or on the basis of the mediating proximal stimulus differences. (See Figure 2.10.) If we are interested in the distal perception, in this case the location of a sound source, we must use a distally oriented response—in this case a localizing response.

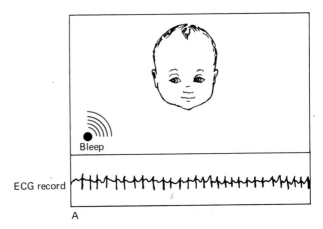

ECG record

A

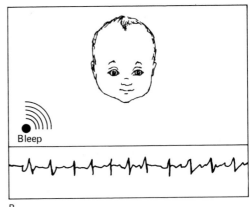

B

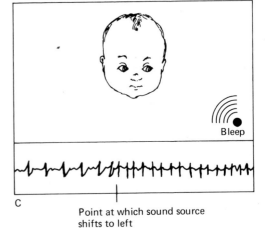

C

Point at which sound source
shifts to left

FIGURE 2.9

Habituation decrement experiment: (*Top*) Introduction of a repetitive sound source on the infant's right causes him to look to the right. His heart rate also increases. (*Center*) After a time, the infant becomes *habituated* to the sound; he ceases to look in its direction, and his heart rate is normal. (*Bottom*) If, however, the sound source is shifted to the left, the infant shows renewed interest and heart rate again increases. This recovery from habituation has been taken by some to be evidence of ability to localize sound. This assumption is questioned in the text.

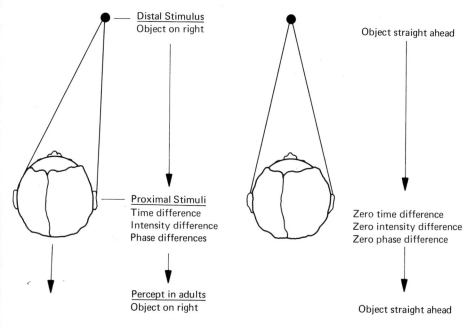

FIGURE 2.10
An infant could discriminate between these two distal presentations on the
basis of the proximal stimuli (time difference, intensity difference, and/or phase
differences) without being aware of the object being to the right or straight
ahead. If all we have is a discriminatory response, there is no way we can
determine whether it is made on the basis of perception of the distal or
proximal stimulus differences.

This is not to say that discrimination methods have no place in the
investigation of localizing reponses. Suppose we found by the use of
localizing responses that infants could not localize sound sources. This
could result from inability to pick up the proximal stimulus difference, as
E. J. Gibson (1969) might argue, or from an inability to interpret or de-
code the perceived proximal stimulus differences. At this point a discrimination experiment would be appropriate and would decide between
these two positions.

The points covered in this lengthy digression from auditory localization are important and will recur. Let us see if they illuminate the existing
data on auditory localization. The first experiment outlined above has
actually been done; moreover it was done with an infant subject who was

less than two minutes old by the end of the experiment. Michael Wertheimer (1961) was fortunate enough to obtain access to a delivery room to carry out his experiment. His subject was delivered without anaesthesia (an important point), and the birth was free from trauma. Having thus obtained an optimal subject, Wertheimer presented a series of sounds, randomly to the right or left of the subject. Over the initial period, before boredom set in, the subject correctly looked in the direction of the sound source. Recall the predictions made by the various theories outlined above. The empiricist theory predicted random localizing attempts; this position is therefore refuted by these results. There can be no doubt that the initial localizing attempts of this infant, tested almost at the moment of birth, were nonrandom and were in fact accurate in direction. Were the responses accurate enough to decide between the extreme and the modified nativist positions? The author does not tell us how accurate the localization was. Other workers have studied the accuracy of auditory localization in older infants, however. Gesell (1934) claims that visual orientation to an off-center sound source is not perfectly accurate until the age of five months, a result that would seem to support the modified nativist hypothesis. However, the qualifications on any result indicating inability must be borne in mind. Gesell did not show that the lack of accuracy prior to five months is due to lack of accuracy within the auditory system; the inability could just as well have resulted from deficiencies in the visual-motor orienting system, particularly since the auditory target in Gesell's experiment was visible.

These objections do not apply to a more recent experiment demonstrating essentially the same developmental effects. In this experiment the same infants were run in two conditions (Bower and Wishart, 1973). In one condition the infants, in full illumination, were presented with an object either straight ahead or 30° to left or right. The infants were allowed to reach for this visible target. Their hit rate in each position gave a measure of the accuracy of visual-motor coordination. In the other condition the infants were run in complete darkness. An object was presented in the same three positions; this time it was a noise-making object. Hit rate here gave a measure of the accuracy of auditory-motor coordination. The motor coordination required in both cases was the same. If the auditory system is less precise than the visual system in registering the position of objects, auditory-motor behavior should have produced a lower hit rate than visual-motor behavior. Since the same motor behavior is required in

TABLE 2.1
A Comparison of Auditory-motor Localization and
Visual-motor Localization in Infants Below Six Months

Object Position	Success Rate (%)	
	Auditory-motor	Visual-motor
30° Left	48	100
Middle	92	96
30° Right	33.5	100

both conditions, lesser auditory-motor accuracy could not be explained away by postulating sloppiness in the motor system. The results showed that, at positions off the midline, auditory-motor accuracy was less than visual-motor accuracy below the age of six months (See Table 2.1.)

What little data there is on auditory localization would thus seem to support the hypothesis that detection of a straight ahead sound source (specified by stimulation that is invariant during growth) is an unlearned ability of the human infant. Positions to the right or left (also specified by stimulation that is invariant during growth) similarly seem to be present before any learning could have occurred. Precise localization to right or left (which can only be specified by variables whose precise "meaning" is changed during growth) is not present at birth and seems to develop during infancy. We cannot say at the moment whether it is calibrated in the way outlined above. Despite its easy accessibility and despite the classic nature of the problems posed by auditory localization, there is just not enough data available to allow us to describe the development precisely. We can hope at least that this situation will soon be remedied.

three /

Radial Localization by Eye

The problem of eye movements • Inflow and outflow theories of position constancy • Problems with the outflow theory • Autokinetic movement • Induced movement • Subject-relative and object-relative movement • Growth problems in position constancy • Perception of the self in position constancy • Dynamic stimuli specifying position • Infants' ability to perceive position

---

The complexities of localization by ear and nose fade into insignificance when compared with the complex localizing capacities of the eye. The human eye can pick up location in three dimensions, with a precision beyond that of the other senses and with a set of structural peculiarities that would seem to contradict any precision in localization.

At first sight, the problem of right-left or radial localization would seem to be less for the eye than for the ear and nose. The eye has an extended, two-dimensional, sensitive surface—the retina—and a focusing structure—the cornea and lens—which ensure that the ordinal relations between objects are preserved in their projection on the retina. As Figure 3.1 shows, an object on the right is projected onto the left half of the eye, an object straight ahead is projected into the center of the eye and an object on the left is projected onto the right half of the eye. The relationship in the external world—right-center-left—is preserved on the retina,

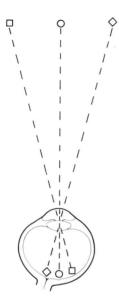

FIGURE 3.1
Ordinal relations between objects
are preserved in their projection on
the retina. Of course, the retina is a
two-dimensional surface; the
projections of the objects are
represented as three-dimensional for
ease of identification.

albeit in reverse order, as left-center-right. Where then is the problem of radial localization? The problem begins as soon as we begin to wonder how an observer can localize the radial position of an object relative to himself rather than relative to other objects. If we assume that the eye is fixed in the head, there is obviously no problem. An object that stimulates the center of the retina is straight ahead of the observer's face; an object that stimulates the left portion of the retina is on the observer's right; and an object stimulating the right half of the retina is on the observer's left.

A mechanism for translating position of stimulation on the retina into position in the external world would not be at all complex, if such conditions held. The mechanism would merely have to assign fixed labels to retinal positions in order to identify the external directions corresponding to these positions. A very simple neural structure, such as that described by Sperry (1959) for the frog, would suffice. Unfortunately the human eye is not fixed in the head. It can move. Figure 3.2 shows what happens on the retina when the eye turns from fixating the straight ahead object to fixating the object on the observer's right. After the eye movement has taken place, the object on the extreme right stimulates the center of the retina, while the other two objects (the one that is physically straight ahead and the one that is physically on the left) stimulate the right half of the

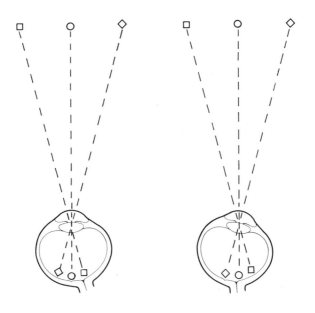

Eye fixating center object   Eye fixating object on extreme right

FIGURE 3.2
The results on the retina of a change in fixation.

retina. If a mechanism to assign fixed labels were in operation, the observer should see the object which is actually on the right but which
stimulates the center of the retina as being straight ahead; the object which
is actually straight ahead would be seen on his left; and the object which
is actually on the left should be seen at his extreme left. This, of course,
does not occur in human adults. Objects are seen to stay in the same fixed
position when the eye moves—a phenomenon referred to as *position constancy*. Position constancy is the primary problem for theorists of visual
perception of radial direction. It is obviously a very significant problem;
yet this problem has received almost no theoretical or experimental examination in this century. The experimental sources usually cited in connection with position constancy date from the 1860s. Indeed, the accepted
theory of position constancy must be the most durable piece of theory in
psychology. In essence this long-lasting theory states that position constancy is attained by combining retinal-position information with eye-
position information. For every site of retinal stimulation there is a distal,

external direction which is specified by the position of the eye at the moment of stimulation. Thus an object which stimulates the fovea, the zone of clearest vision located in the center of the adult eye, will be seen as straight ahead as long as the eye position is registered as straight ahead. An object which stimulates the fovea while the eye is turned 10° to the right will be seen as lying 10° to the observer's right. (See Figure 3.2.) An object which stimulates a retinal site 10° to the left of the fovea when the eye is turned 10° to right will be seen as lying straight ahead. Since the position of objects is not given by a system of fixed retinal labels alone, but rather by a combination of retinal labels and eye position information, changes in eye position (provided they can be registered) will not result in changes in the perceived position of objects.

This theory of position perception and position constancy depends on the combination of two separate sources of information—information about site of retinal stimulation and information about eye position. The majority of writers on the subject have taken information about site of retinal stimulation (and its labeling) as a given, as something that required no further explanation. The topic that really excited the nineteenth century investigators of position perception was the nature of our source of information about eye position. Two opposing hypotheses were put forward. One argued that we are aware of eye position as the result of feedback from stretch receptors in the eye muscles. The other hypothesis argued that we are aware of the output to the eye muscles, or the innervation signals that produce movement. The two theories are illustrated in Figure 3.3. At first sight the two theories would seem to produce identical predictions in any situation. One assumes awareness of innervation for movement; the other assumes awareness of the consequences of movement. Since innervation for movement is normally followed by movement and its consequences, there would seem to be no way of differentiating the two theories. Mach (1885), however, created an artificial situation (Figure 3.4) to clarify the matter:

> Let the eyes be turned as far as possible towards the left and two lumps of moderately hard putty firmly pressed against the right side of each eye-ball. If, now, we attempt to glance quickly to the right, we shall succeed only very unperfectly, owing to the unperfectly spherical form of the eyes, and the objects will suffer a strong displacement to the right. Thus the mere will to look to the right imparts to the images at certain points of the retina a larger "rightward value," as we may term it for brevity. [Mach, 1885]

A second critical experiment is even easier to try. Simply look at a scene and gently move your eye with a finger. As you push your eye from side to side with your finger (thereby changing its position and changing the feedback from position receptors in the eye muscles, if such exist), objects in the world lose their position constancy and seem to move in a direction opposite to that of the eye. The element that is missing in this case is the normal innervation signal to the eye muscles. Feedback there

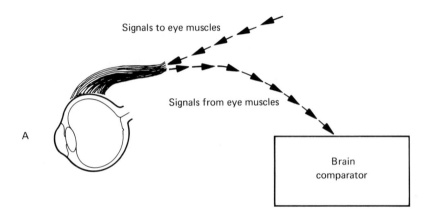

Signals to eye muscles

Signals from eye muscles

A

Brain comparator

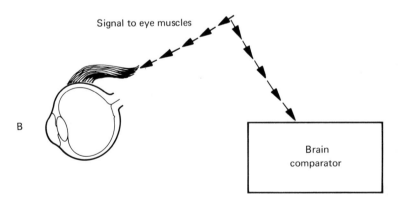

Signal to eye muscles

B

Brain comparator

FIGURE 3.3
Two theories (A and B) of perception of eye movement. (From E. Mach, 1885; reprinted 1959.)

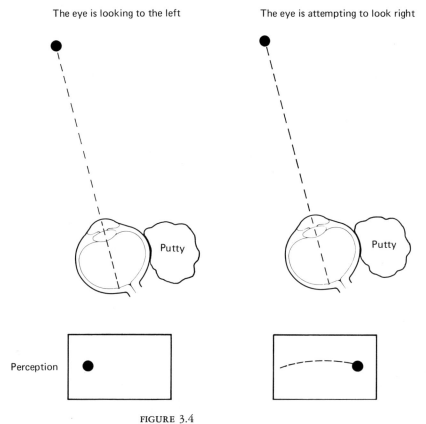

FIGURE 3.4
Mach's experiment (see text).

may be; but innervation is certainly missing, and in its absence, position constancy is lost. (See Figure 3.5.)

These two experiments have been taken as convincing proof that eye position is specified by the efferent command signals to the eye. Object position is thus supposedly specified by a combination of afferent information (coming from a specific site on the retina) and information derived from the efferent signals controlling the position of the eyes. Because of this, the theory is sometimes called the *efference-copy theory* of position perception, which is taken to include both position constancy and perception of position change (movement). Again, the theory is of considerable antiquity, hardly having been challenged during its one

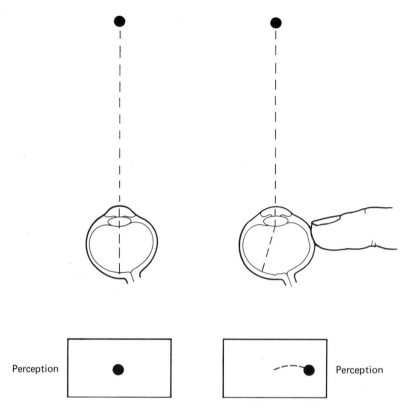

FIGURE 3.5
Passive movement of the eye results in loss of position constancy.

hundred-year sway. Despite its durability, however, the efference-copy theory is certainly completely incorrect, both in detail and overall outline. Of the predictions one can derive from the theory, almost none have been verified by experimental tests. For example, on the basis of the efference-copy theory one would predict that an observer with his eyes stationary staring at a stationary spot of light in the dark should perceive the spot of light as being stationary. If the light does not move and the observer's eyes do not move, surely the observer should have no difficulty seeing the light as stationary. This, in fact, does not happen. A stationary spot of light viewed in darkness seems to move quite dramatically to a rather large extent. This is the well-known autokinetic effect. An observer can be asked to point to the light in darkness and follow its "movement" with his finger. When the lights are switched on, the observer may be pointing by as much as 40° in the wrong direction.

It was thought at one time that unnoticed eye movements were the cause of the autokinetic effect. The hypothesis was that the eyes moved without the efferent signal being registered; thus, the resulting change in site of retinal stimulation was interpreted as resulting from movement of the object. Note how this hypothesis weakens the efference-copy theory. If the system can miss movements of 40°, how can the theory explain position perception and position constancy under normal conditions, where accuracy is better than 1°? In any event, the hypothesis has been directly disproved. Guilford and Dallenbach (1928) recorded eye movements during autokinetic movement and found that such movements effectively did not occur; eye movements that did occur were uncorrelated with either the direction or the amount of autokinetic movement. More recently Gregory and Zangwill (1963) have exploited the selective color vision of the center of the retina to demonstrate that eye movement is not the cause of the autokinetic effect. These researchers presented observers with a spot of red light surrounded by an annulus of blue light. The observers were instructed to fixate the red spot. The center of fixation, the fovea, is quite insensitive to blue light; as long as the observers continued to fixate, they could not see the blue annulus. If their eyes moved so that the spot and annulus would stimulate another part of the retina, the annulus became immediately visible. All observers reported autokinetic movement yet did not report seeing the annulus—a neat proof that true eye movements are not the cause of the autokinetic effect.

To explain these results, Gregory speculated that there must be some random discharge of efference-copy signals without any corresponding efferent signal; the central correlator would be signaled to expect an eye movement, without an actual eye movement being produced. Since there is no eye movement, the site of retinal stimulation does not change; since the central correlator thinks an eye movement has taken place, the non-change on the retina is interpreted as movement of the stimulus source. Again the explanation, designed to preserve the efference-copy theory, actually weakens the theory. If the system is so susceptible to random discharge, how can it attain the accuracy observed in normal life, where we never think the world has taken a 40° jump to one side or the other? If Gregory's explanation of the autokinetic effect were correct, we would be quite likely to suffer from autokinetic movement of our whole environment, something which never occurs.

The first prediction that we derived from efference-copy theory—that a stationary light viewed with stationary eyes should be seen as stationary

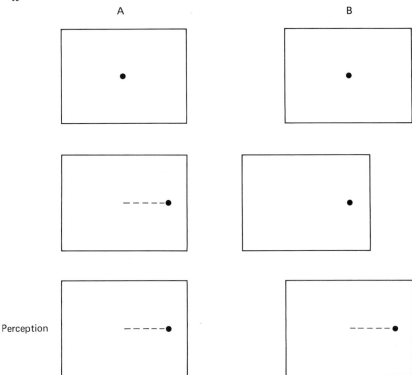

A B

Perception

FIGURE 3.6
Duncker's experiments on induced movement. (A) Spot moves to right. (B)
Frame moves to left.

—is thus not confirmed. The autokinetic effect demonstrates that there
are circumstances in which we perceive change of position when no actual
change of position, no change in site of retinal stimulation, and no eye
movement occur. A different set of experiments leading to the same conclusion has shown that there are circumstances in which actual movement
will not be perceived. In fact, there are circumstances in which an observer
consistently misjudges which of two objects (one stationary, one moving)
is actually changing its position. Figure 3.6 outlines some of the elegant
experiments conducted by Duncker (1929) on induced movement. Suppose we have a luminous frame surrounding a luminous spot. The spot
moves to the right. What does an observer see? He sees the spot moving
to the right. So far, so good. Now suppose the frame moves to the left.

What does the observer see? He sees the spot move to the right within the perceptually stationary frame! In other words the actual motion of the frame is not detected, and the change in relative positions of spot and frame is attributed to movement of the spot. The effect is quite independent of whether spot or frame is fixated. If the stationary spot is fixated, the observer thinks that the spot and his eye are moving. If the moving frame is fixated, the observer thinks that the frame and his eye are stationary. A number of complex variations of this experiment have been carried out without changing the basic conclusion; that is, when a small object or its frame moves (regardless of which one actually moves), the motion will be attributed to the small object. In other words, there are circumstances in which perception of position and change of position are determined not by site of retinal stimulation and changes therein, but by relationships between stimuli which can overcome or reverse the simple effects of retinal stimulation.

Another classic effect casts doubt on efference-copy theory; this effect pertains to the threshold for perception of change of position. Change of position like every other perceived event has a threshold value below which the change is too small to be perceived. Efference-copy theory would lead us to believe that the determinant of the threshold is the amount of change of position, its speed, the site of retinal stimulation, and nothing else. In fact, this is completely in error. The major determinant of the threshold for change of position is the presence or absence of another stationary object. Wallach (1968) has shown that the eye is one hundred times as sensitive to change of position when another stationary object is in the field as when a solitary object is in the field. Wallach has argued that the visual system can detect the change of position of one object relative to another—a phenomenon he calls *object-relative* movement. When the moving object is alone in the field, its change of position is a change relative to the viewing subject only; Wallach calls this situation *subject-relative* movement. Wallach argues that his results show observers are much more sensitive to object-relative movement than to subject-relative movement. We shall subsequently argue against this position. For the moment, however, the point to be remembered is that these experiments, like the experiments of Duncker, show that the stimulus array is much more important in determining perception of position and change of position than are site of retinal stimulation and eye position at the moment of stimulation.

A more striking negation of the efference-copy theory is found in the work of Stoper (1967)—a negation which is all the more convincing since Stoper's experiments might have been tailored to demonstrate the validity of the theory. Stoper designed a situation to measure the accuracy of position constancy—the very phenomenon efference-copy theory is supposed to explain. His situation was stripped down so that only those subsystems assumed by efference-copy theory (site of retinal stimulation and eye position) could be effective; all other sources of information were removed. At the same time, Stoper recognized that he must have a response measure which would be unaffected by the reduced conditions of viewing. A pointing response, as used in the autokinetic effect, could not be used since accurate pointing might require sight of the hand, which is not possible under conditions of reduced vision. (This objection does not apply to Duncker's or Wallach's experiments. However, with adults as with infants (see p. 28 in Chapter 2), one must be certain that the response used to index a perceptual process is as accurate as the perceptual process itself and is unaffected by variables controlling the perceptual process.) Stoper solved this problem in a very elegant way. His subjects were asked to track a spot of light slowly moving in a horizontal plane.

After the beginning of an excursion, a second spot of light was flashed on for 25 milliseconds. The second spot was flashed on again 250 milliseconds later. The position of the flashed spot could be varied between its first and second appearance. At one extreme it could reappear in exactly the same distal position; its position relative to the observer's head was thus unchanged, while its position relative to the moving spot was different. Its position on the retina, therefore, was also different, since the eye had rotated in the interval between the two flashes as it followed the moving spot. We will refer to this extreme as *distal constancy*. At the other extreme, the flashed spot could appear in the same position relative to the moving spot, thus stimulating the same site on the retina on both of its appearances but changing its position relative to the observer's head. This extreme will be called *retinal constancy*. (See Figure 3.7.) Any position between distal constancy and retinal constancy could also be obtained. The subject was asked to say when the flashed spot appeared in the same position on both occasions that it was presented. If the subjects had been able to obtain position constancy in this situation, they would have reported that the spot appeared in the same position only under the distal-constancy presentation condition. In fact this is precisely what did not occur. Subjects reported that the spot appeared in the same position only

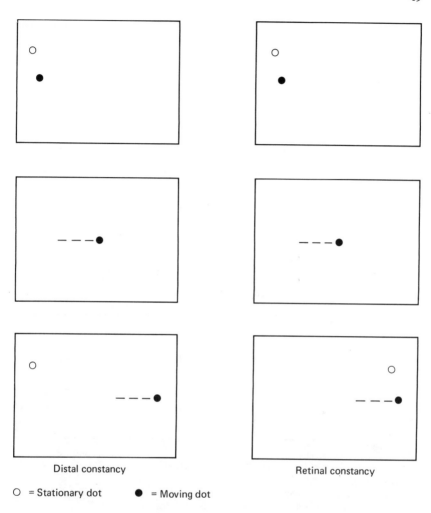

Distal constancy   Retinal constancy

○ = Stationary dot   ● = Moving dot

FIGURE 3.7
Illustration of Stoper's 1967 experiment.

in the retinal-constancy presentation condition. In other words, in this experimental situation designed to fulfill all of the conditions required by the efference-copy theory, position constancy simply is not obtained.* Stoper carried out various other versions of this experiment (see Figure

*Recently Mack and Bachant (1969) have published data which they believe contradict the results of Stoper.

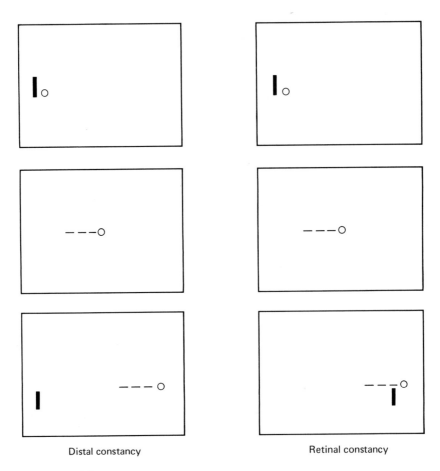

Distal constancy   Retinal constancy

FIGURE 3.8
This is the same situation as the one shown in Figure 3.7, except that a
stationary bar of light is flashed instead of a dot of light.

3.8), all of which point to the same conclusion. Where the only information about position is provided by eye position and site of retinal
stimulation, position constancy disappears. These results, taken together
with the other data presented above, show conclusively that the efference-
copy theory of position perception and position constancy cannot be
correct. If the only information provided to the perceiver is that deemed
necessary by efference-copy theory, then the whole system of position
perception breaks down completely.

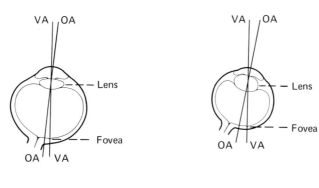

OA = Optical axis
VA = Visual axis

ADULT EYE   EYE AT BIRTH

FIGURE 3.9
Schematic diagram of adult eye and eye at birth, seen
from above.

The evidence indicates that efference-copy theory as a whole is wrong, but we are not told specifically where it is wrong. Obviously, the perceptual system does not combine information about site of stimulation with information about the efferent commands to the eye muscles. This could be a result of the visual system's inability to combine the information or a result of the unavailability of one or the other or both sources of information. From the results so far discussed, it would seem likely that the perceptual system has no information about eye movements. It seems equally likely that there is no system of retinal labeling—no way of knowing which part of the retina is being stimulated. It is here that the special problems of the development of position perception can provide some useful leads on a possible basis for a theory. The problems found on examining position perception in adults are greatly compounded when we examine the infant eye. The infant eye is quite different from the adult eye, as Figure 3.9 shows. The eye has about the same optical power; but it is much shorter, and it has a different radius of curvature. Most importantly, the fovea is in a different place relative to the optical axis of the eye. A beam of light passing through the center of the optical system of the infant eye will not strike the fovea, but rather a point 10° to 15°

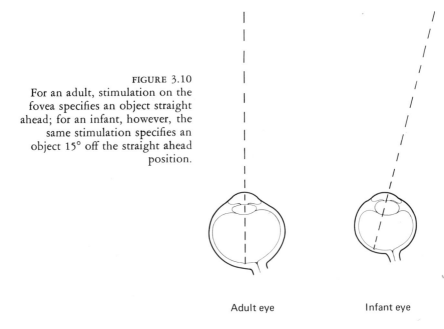

FIGURE 3.10
For an adult, stimulation on the fovea specifies an object straight ahead; for an infant, however, the same stimulation specifies an object 15° off the straight ahead position.

Adult eye   Infant eye

on the nasal side of the fovea (Mann, 1928). As the eye grows, the fovea rotates around until it reaches the adult position relative to the optical axis of the eye. Obviously, if simple efference-copy theory were correct, infants would have a wildly inaccurate system for position perception. For example, in the adult it is roughly true that, when the eyes are straight ahead and stimulation is on the fovea, the position of an object straight ahead of the observer is specified. In the case of the infant eye, this conjunction would specify the position of an object 15° off the straight ahead position. (See Figure 3.10.) Obviously, if there were a built-in rule of this sort, infants would be unable to locate the position of objects relative to themselves with any accuracy at all (until the fovea had rotated to the adult position). As we shall see, this is not the case. Infants show accurate radial localization long before this time. What this means is that, even if eye position is signaled and registered, there can be no way of combining this information with retinal-site information to yield an invariant which could be correlated with any specific position relative to the observer. The same combination of retinal-site and eye-position information would mean different external positions in the course of development.

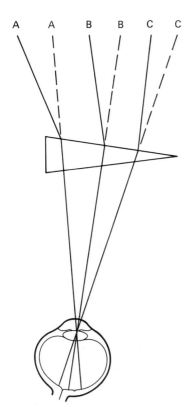

FIGURE 3.11
The distal position specified by
the retinal-site–eye-position
combination is changed by this
wedge prism.

One obvious way out of this impasse is to posit some sort of calibration mechanism that can tune or correct the inaccuracies resulting from growth processes. Some authors (Held, 1965; Kohler, 1964) have argued in favor of such a process on the basis of experiments with adults; in these experiments, the distal position specified by a retinal-site-eye-position combination is changed by an optical device, such as a wedge prism. (See Figure 3.11.) When adults utilize such devices their radial localization is initially inaccurate to some extent but gradually becomes accurate again. There is a mountain of literature on these corrective processes, which argues for the relative importance of various mechanisms in the process of correction. Some authors (Kohler, 1964; Held, 1965) have explicitly asserted that similar corrective processes must be involved in the development of the perception of radial position in infants. I would disagree and argue instead that the mechanisms proposed are not even involved in the adaptation to prisms in adults! It is a curious fact that, although adaptation to prisms is usually described as a protracted process, 75 percent of total correction occurs instantaneously, as soon as the device is put on and before any of the proposed mechanisms could operate (Rock, 1966). A more convincing proof that distal position is *not* specified by a retinal-site-eye-position combination could hardly be devised!

Some clues to the true mechanism of position perception can be found among the data already reviewed. Stoper found that position constancy could be obtained in his experimental situation by adding a permanent stationary frame to the field. When this continuous stationary frame was added, the subjects' judgments of the "same" position approached the distal constancy extreme. This recalls Wallach's finding that observers are much more sensitive to object-relative movement than to subject-relative movement. In Stoper's situation, object-relative position judgments were accurate, whereas subject-relative position judgments (those obtained with no stationary frame in the field) were of course totally inaccurate. The autokinetic effect also occurs under conditions where position can only be judged relative to the perceiving subject. Under these conditions, as we have seen, position perception becomes wildly inaccurate. One might wonder whether the autokinetic effect, like Stoper's illusion, is reduced by the addition of other points of light to the classic single point. This experiment has been tried, with negative results (Royce et al. 1962). As many as sixty dots will go into autokinetic motion together. Their position relative to one another does not change, but their position relative to the observer seems to change by large amounts.

The important point is that their position relative to the *observer* seems to change; their position relative to one another, specified in the pattern of light on the retina, does not change. In Stoper's situation, the illusion disappears as soon as the subject can make a position judgment that is relative to a visible, stationary object. When position must be gauged with reference to the observer himself (an invisible, stationary object), position perception and position constancy disappear. The key word in this description of the reference anchor or observer is *invisible*. All of these experiments where position perception breaks down take place in darkness; the observer himself is not projected onto his own retina, in normal everyday perception where position is accurately localized, the observer is represented on his own retinas; this occurs inevitably without any mediating behavior of looking at hands or feet. As Gibson (1950) pointed out, the observer's nose occupies a large area of both retinas (Figure 3.12).

FIGURE 3.12
This drawing represents the visual field of the right eye; the nose, lip, and part of the cheek are visible on the left; the body of the viewer is at the bottom. (After E. Mach, 1885; reprinted 1959.)

Under normal conditions of illumination, an observer asked to judge the position of an object relative to himself can see both the object and himself. By contrast, under conditions where position perception breaks down —conditions of darkness with luminous objects—the observer can only see the objects. We would not expect an observer to locate the position of an invisible object relative to himself. Likewise, we should not expect an observer to be able to locate the position of an object relative to himself when he is himself invisible.

We are arguing that the location of objects relative to the observer is possible only if the observer can see himself and the object to be located. We are saying that the retinal projection of the nose and orbit specify the observer's position to himself. If this information is available, position perception will be accurate. If it is not available, position perception will be inaccurate. In the standard autokinetic situation (a luminous spot in

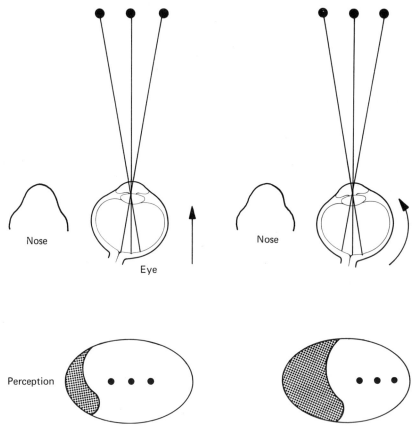

FIGURE 3.13
The relative positions of objects and nose remain the same when the eye is turned.

darkness), the observer cannot see himself, and his position perception is extremely inaccurate. In the converse case of a black spot viewed in homogeneous light by an observer who can see himself, the autokinetic effect vanishes; position perception remains highly accurate (Schweizer, 1858). Stoper's illusion occurs when the observer cannot see himself. That it does not occur when he can see himself is a matter of common observation, and some experimentation (Mack and Bachant, 1969).

Many of the problems associated with position perception simply disappear when it is admitted that the observer must see himself as well as

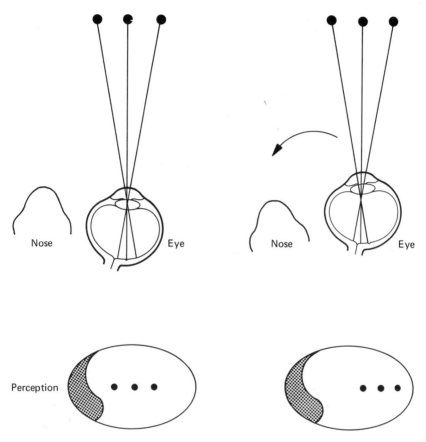

FIGURE 3.14
Only the projection of the nose retains the same retinal position when the head is turned.

the object and that the information for perception of change of position is a change in the relative position on the retina of observer and object. Consider the problem of position constancy. When the eye turns, every object is projected onto a different retinal site, *including the projection of the observer*, but there is no change in the relative position of the retinal projections of objects and observer; and therefore there is no information for change of position. (See Figure 3.13.) Position constancy is therefore the only feasible outcome. Consider the case where the observer turns his head (Figure 3.14). There is a change in the retinal projection of every

FIGURE 3.15
Although it is the room that is moving toward the man, he perceives himself as falling forward.

object except the projection of the observer. If you recall the description of induced movement given in connection with Duncker's experiments, you will predict that it is the observer who should be *seen* to move; indeed, this is what occurs. The same principle can account for the phenomenon of induced movement of the self. If one is stationary in a moving environment, the environment stays still and the observer perceives himself as moving (Figure 3.15).

How would this system cope with perception of specific directions, such as straight ahead? The direction "straight ahead of the observer's head," as we have seen, has no specific retinal correlate. However, the self, which is straight ahead, is continuously projected onto the retinas and could serve as an anchor point for that direction. As Figure 3.16 shows, all objects that are straight ahead are symmetrically projected onto the retinas with respect to the projection of the nose and regardless of eye position. All objects that are not straight ahead are asymmetrically projected with respect to the nose. The relative symmetry of the projection of an object could thus serve as the stimulus to specify straight ahead.

This reformulation of the specification of direction (in terms of projection on to the retina relative to the projection of the nose rather than in terms of absolute site of retinal stimulation) solves certain problems that are absolutely incomprehensible in terms of the traditional theory. The problem of instantaneous adaptation to prisms is no problem as soon as one realizes that the retinal projection of the self is displaced in the same way as other objects outside the body. There is retinal displacement in absolute terms but not in relation to the projection of the nose and orbit. The problem of squint can also be handled by the proposed reformulation. In cases of squint, one eye is permanently at an angle to the other

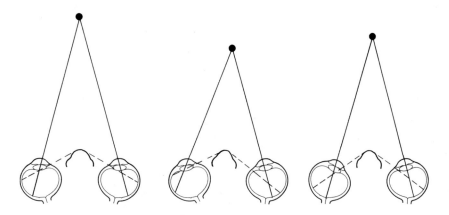

Objects straight ahead

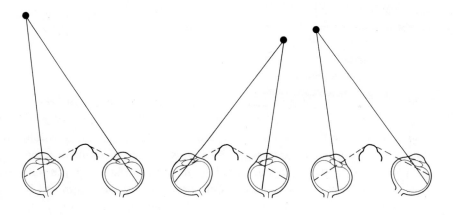

Objects not straight ahead

FIGURE 3.16
Regardless of the position of the eyes, the retinal projections of objects that are straight ahead are symmetrical with respect to the projection of the nose on the retina. Retinal projections of objects that are not straight ahead are not symmetrical with respect to the projection of the nose on the retina.

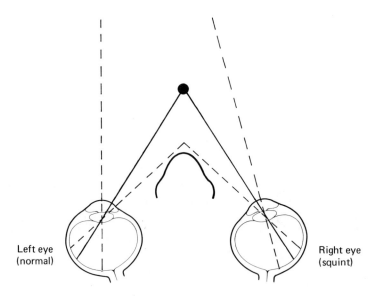

FIGURE 3.17
A case of squint. The foveas of the eyes are permanently pointed at different places. The retinal projections of an object fall on different parts of the retinas of the two eyes, as do the projections from the nose.

(Figure 3.17), which means that the foveas of the two eyes are permanently pointed at different places in the world. Despite this the two eyes see the same objects in the same directions—something quite impossible unless the information specifying distal position is site of stimulation on the retina relative to site of the retinal stimulation produced by the self.

The hypothesis proposed here can even account for the two most beloved demonstrations of the proponents of efference-copy theory. Consider the effects of passive movement of the eye. First, I defy anyone to produce a passive eye movement that is at all like an active eye movement in its visual effects. A normal eye movement is a rotation and produces no change in the relative projected positions of self and objects. As you can discover for yourself, passive eye movements do produce changes in the relative projected position of the self and other objects, which is the condition for perceived movement according to the hypothesis presented here. As for the results of obstructed movement, I cannot improve on the words of William James:

I regret to say that I cannot myself make it succeed—I know not for what reason. But even where it does succeed it seems to me that the conditions are much too complicated for Professor Mach's theoretic conclusions to be safely drawn. The putty squeezed into the orbit and pressure of the eyeball against it must give rise to peripheral sensations strong enough, at any rate (if only of the right kind), to justify any amount of false perception of our eyeball's position, quite apart from the innervation feelings which Professor Mach supposes to co-exist. [James, 1890].

Psychologists tend to think of the self as either a meaningless abstraction or a weighty problem deserving deep thought. The reduction of the self to the visual projection of the nose on to the retina is usually greeted with hilarity. Even Gibson (1950) who did more for the nose than any other psychologist did so with a kind of defensive flippancy. I would like to insert a few words in defense of the nose at this point. Among those species with chambered eyes, there is not one whose eyes do not pick up a projection of the nose or some other body part. Among those species that have evolved panoramic vision, the panorama is interrupted by a projection of the animal itself. Among those predatory species with maximum frontality and maximum binocular overlap, there is always a projection of the self. This cannot be a biological accident. The projection of body parts on to the eye must be of functional importance to have been preserved in so many differently evolved forms. Indeed, the hypothesis about position perception presented here has the merit of making sense of what would otherwise be a continuing biological error (Walls, 1942). (See Figure 3.18.)

The stimulus information described so far is of course not the only information that can specify straight ahead position. Gibson (1950) has described the stimulation consequent to the forward movement of an observer toward an object and the stimulation consequent to the movement of an object toward the observer. Consider an observer gazing at a textured wall like that shown in Figure 3.19. As the observer is moved toward the wall, the image projected on his retina will change systematically as shown in Figure 3.19.

With forward movement, all of the spots are displaced save one—the one that is straight ahead of the observer. This locus of nonmotion, or center of expansion, defines a position straight ahead of the observer's body. The eyes or the head and eyes can turn to fixate some point that is not straight ahead, without affecting the specification of straight ahead

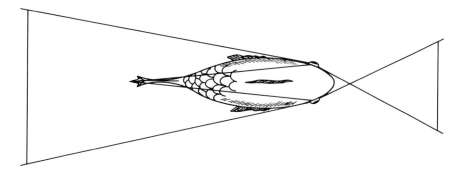

FIGURE 3.18
The visual field of various animals. The owl (*far left*) has a visual angle of 110°
with binocular overlap; its eyes point straight ahead. Yet it has developed the
nasal tuft to such an extent that it covers the central 30° of its visual field.
The fish (*above*) has a total visual field of 360°. A large part of this is taken up
by its own body and its tail. The hare (*near column, top and center*) and the
woodcock (*near column, bottom*), which are the prey of many others, have
evolved an extremely wide visual field amounting to some 200°. As a
consequence of the wide visual angle, the hare can see its nose and its tail
simultaneously, as can the woodcock. In all these species, some sensitive area
of the retina has been given over to perception of the animal's own body.

as the center of the optical expansion pattern consequent on forward
motion of or motion toward the observer. There are two important corol-
laries of this specification of straight ahead as the center of an expansion
pattern. If an object approaches an observer (or vice versa) along some
line that is at an angle to straight ahead (a so-called *miss path*, since it misses
the observer), there is no center of expansion *within* the object. The
absence of a focus of expansion thus serves to specify a miss path—a
direction of approach other than straight ahead. Furthermore, the form
of the displacement of the pattern specifies the angle of approach (Figure
3.20). In a similar way, given movement toward a surface that is in the
frontal-parallel plane, the rate of displacement of points will specify their
angular separation from the position that is straight ahead of the observer
(Figure 3.19.) The greater the angular separation, the greater is the rate
of change.

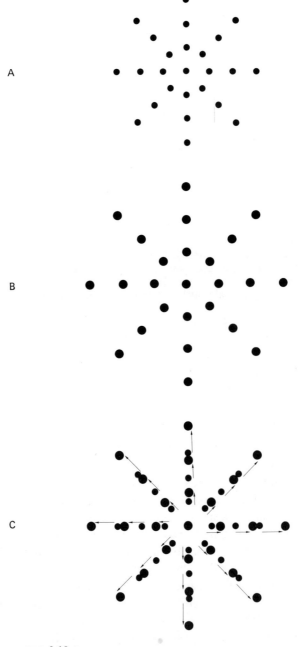

FIGURE 3.19
As the observer approaches the textured wall (A), it expands outward as shown in (B). The superimposition of B on A (C) shows how, although the center dot remains stationary, the other dots move outward, with those at the outside moving farthest. The locus of expansion is the center dot.

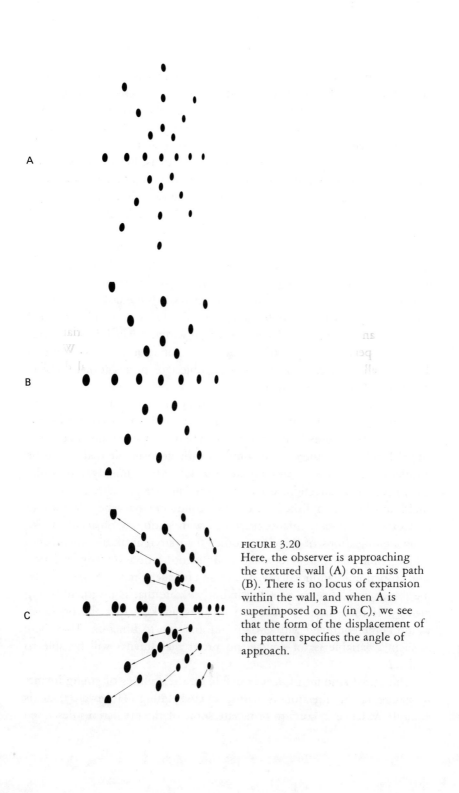

A

B

C

FIGURE 3.20
Here, the observer is approaching
the textured wall (A) on a miss path
(B). There is no locus of expansion
within the wall, and when A is
superimposed on B (in C), we see
that the form of the displacement of
the pattern specifies the angle of
approach.

Let us try to summarize the stimuli that could specify the radial position of objects. The cardinal radial direction, straight ahead, can be specified as (1) the locus of nonmotion during movement of the observer toward an object or during movement of an object toward the observer, or (2) the locus of projections onto the retinas that are symmetrical with respect to the projection of the self onto the retinas. Both of these specifying variables are invariant during growth. We might thus expect that very young infants would be sensitive to these variables. Radial position along any direction other than straight ahead can also be specified during movement of the observer or object by the locus of the center of the retinal expansion consequent to the movement. If the object is not straight ahead the center of expansion is implicit, outside the object. The further away from the straight ahead position, the greater will be the rate of minimal movement within the object. Although the utilization of this variable of stimulation would necessarily depend on complex internal circuitry, the variable is independent of growth and is valid for any size or shape of eye. We might thus expect very young infants to be able to detect the radial direction of a moving object or of a stationary object if they themselves were moving.

The stimuli that could specify stationary objects to a stationary observer pose quite different problems. Human adults can make such judgments, but the judgments must be made in terms of some kind of acquired retinal labels, since there is no stimulus variable available that would be invariant during growth. (See Figures 3.9 and 3.10.) Similarly, monocular identification of direction, even including the straight ahead direction, could only be accomplished via a set of acquired retinal labels. We would thus expect stationary infants presented with stationary objects to make poor identifications of directions other than straight ahead when functioning binocularly and to make poor identifications of any direction while functioning monocularly. The reason for such predictions is, simply, the presence or absence of a specifying variable that is invariant during growth. If there is no such invariant, it is unlikely that the organism would come equipped with enough information to function. That there is such a variable is, of course, no proof that infants will be able to utilize it.

The actual amount of data available on the abilities of young infants to gauge radial direction is hardly overwhelming. However, there is enough evidence to confirm or negate some of the predictions described above. The information contained in optical expansion patterns is invariant during growth and so could be used by young infants without requiring readjustment during growth. It has been discovered that very young infants do in fact utilize this information. Bower, Broughton, and Moore (1970a) found that very young infants display a coordinated, defensive response to an object approaching from a straight ahead direction. Ball and Tronick (1971) extended this finding and showed that the response was specific to approach from straight ahead; approach along a miss path did not produce defensive behavior at all. It would thus appear that infants in the first week of life can identify the direction of movement of objects relative to themselves.

Whether infants can identify stationary directions is a much more difficult question. Again the problem is largely one of finding appropriate response measures. An obvious measure would seem to be accuracy of eye movements. The accuracy with which an infant can move his eyes to fixate a target presented in various directions might seem to be an ideal measure of accuracy of perception. Above we predicted accurate perception of the straight ahead direction and inaccurate perception of all other directions. If one could discover that infants can turn their eyes to look at a straight ahead object more rapidly and with less undershoot or overshoot than they can turn to look at an off-straight-ahead direction, the data would lend support to the hypothesis advanced above. Unfortunately while experiments of this sort have been done, the results are ambiguous for our purposes for the simple fact that young infants are quite unwilling to look at anything that is off the straight ahead position (Tronick, 1971; Peiper, 1963). While this may indicate the sort of perceptual inability we are arguing for, it could also reflect lack of attention to peripheral areas. The required control condition would be to present an infant with an object that is, say, 15° to his right while he is looking straight ahead; one would then compare the speed and accuracy of the responses in this condition with responses to an object that is straight ahead while the infant's eyes are turned 15° to the right. To my knowledge, this has not been done systematically. The data of Tronick and Clanton (1971) could be interpreted as evidence that the accuracy of eye shifting does increase with age; however, it is not possible to say from their data whether the straight ahead position has any priority. The same lack of data prevents us from coming to any conclusion about the differences between monocular and binocular looking.

The situation then is that we know infants can identify radial direction during movement. We do not know whether they can identify radial direction while they and the objects are stationary. However, since the condition of stationary infant and stationary object is rare, and since infants can always move their heads slightly, there is no reason to believe that imprecise radial-position perception would impose a severe handicap on infants.

four/

Perception of Distance

The conventional supposition has been that it is the third dimension of space—the distance dimension—which poses the true problem of space perception. The following quote from Berkeley illustrates this view.

II. It is, I think, agreed by all, that *distance* of itself, and immediately, cannot be seen. For *distance* being a line directed end-wise to the eye, it projects only one point in the fund of the eye. Which point remains invariably the same, whether the distance be longer or shorter. [See Figure 4.1a]

III. I find it also acknowledged, that the estimate we make of the distance of *objects* considerably remote, is rather an act of judgment grounded on *experience* than of *sense*. For example, when I perceive a great number of intermediate *objects* such as houses, fields, rivers, and the like,

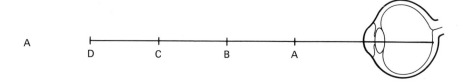

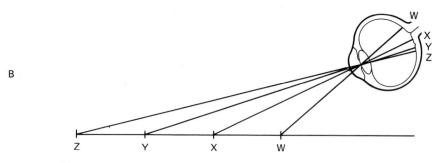

FIGURE 4.1
(A) The problem of distance perception according to Berkeley. (B) Gibson's alternative statement of the problem.

which I have experienced to take up a considerable space; I thence form a judgment or conclusion, that the *object* I see beyond them is at a great distance. Again, when an *object* appears faint and small, which, at a near distance, I have experienced to make a vigorous and large appearance; I instantly conclude it to be far off. And this, it is evident, is the result of *experience*; without which, from the faintness and littleness, I should not have inferred any thing concerning the distance of *objects*. [Berkeley, 1709]

Although this view is still encountered (see Gregory, 1966), it should not have survived the clarifying analysis of Gibson (1950). (See Figure 4.1b.) Gibson pointed out that there are many stimuli that specify distance. Once projected onto the two-dimensional retina, the stimuli are not themselves three dimensional. However, variations within these stimuli specify variations in distance to a degree of accuracy limited only by the resolving power of the optical system of the eye. We thus see distance as directly as we see color.

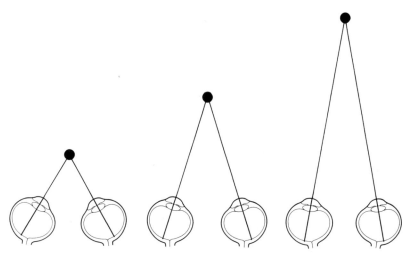

FIGURE 4.2
Convergence angle declines with distance.

There are a variety of stimuli that specify distance. One of them, *binocular parallax*, has long been supposed to be "primary" in some sense. Binocular parallax, as the name implies, is dependent on relations between the two eyes. There are two components to binocular parallax—the convergence angle for binocular fixation and binocular disparity. *Convergence angle* (Figure 4.2) changes systematically with the distance of the object being looked at (declining with the distance of the object). *Binocular disparity* arises, by contrast, whenever we have a visual field containing a nonfixated object at a distance different than the fixated object. Because our two eyes are side by side, they each get a slightly different view of the world; this means that any object that is not being fixated will be projected onto noncorresponding points in the two eyes (see Figure 4.3).

Note that there are two different forms of disparity, crossed and uncrossed. *Crossed disparity* arises when there is an object nearer than the object to be fixated. *Uncrossed disparity* arises whenever there is an object farther away than the fixated object. The nearer an object is, the greater the crossed disparity that it produces; likewise the farther away an object is, the greater the uncrossed disparity that it produces. The total range of binocular stimulation can thus specify relative position in depth with an

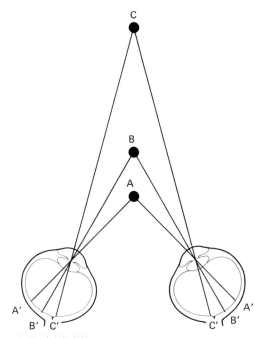

FIGURE 4.3
Crossed and uncrossed disparity. Object B is
being fixated. Object A leads to crossed disparity,
whereas uncrossed disparity arises from
Object C.

accuracy restricted only by our sensitivity to convergence angle and binocular disparity. With this set of stimuli available, we are able to gauge the
relative position in depth of objects down to a separation of 27 secs. of
arc, a truly amazing performance (Graham et al., 1965). The problems
with binocular parallax arise only when we begin to wonder whether it
can specify *absolute* distance.

Under certain circumstances, these binocular stimuli could specify
absolute as well as relative distance. Suppose we take an adult with an
interocular distance of 6 cm. For this adult a convergence angle of 60°
specifies an object 5.2 cms. away; a convergence angle of 30° specifies
an object 11.2 cms. away, and so on. So far so good; but consider this in
a developmental perspective. An adult's eyes are about 6 cms. apart, but
an infant's eyes are only half that distance apart. The specification that

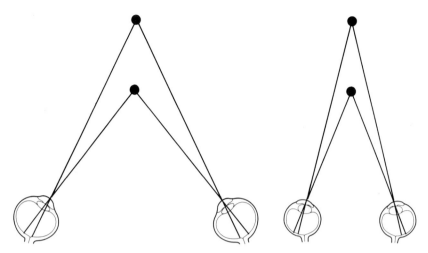

FIGURE 4.4
Convergence angle and disparity are greater for adult eyes than for infant eyes for objects the same distance away.

holds true for an adult would not be true for an infant, and vice versa. Both convergence angle and disparity are a joint function of distance and *interocular* separation (Figure 4.4). Since interocular separation changes continuously throughout development, there can be no possibility that binocular stimulation could specify absolute distance in any invariant way throughout development. If binocular stimulation does specify absolute distance at any point in development, it can only be as the result of a scaled matching or calibration process that imparts the requisite information to the binocular system.

These developmental considerations do not apply to the other major stimuli that specify distance—motion parallax and optical expansion pattern. *Motion parallax* is generated whenever an observer moves his head, as shown in Figure 4.5. If the observer's eyes are fixed on the horizon, the image of every object in the scene is displaced in the direction opposite to the movement of his head. The amount of displacement is a function of the distance of the objects; the greater the distance, the less the displacement (compare box B to box A in Figure 4.5). The situation is somewhat more complex if the fixation point is nearer than the horizon (Figure 4.6). The same relation holds for objects nearer than the fixation point; however, objects farther away than the fixation point are displaced in the

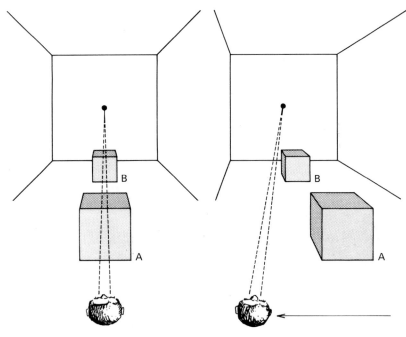

FIGURE 4.5
Motion parallax. If the head moves left and the eyes are kept fixed on the horizon, the nearer object appears to move farther and faster to the right than the more distant object does. (From T. G. R. Bower, "The Visual World of Infants." Copyright © 1966 by Scientific American, Inc. All rights reserved.)

same direction as the head movement, and the amount of displacement increases with distance beyond the fixation point.

Motion parallax, the changes in retinal projection consequent to head movement, is obviously independent of growth. Changes in the size or location of the eyeball will not affect this stimulus system. However, one must again question whether motion parallax can specify absolute distance. Consider a lateral head movement of 6 inches with the eyes fixed on a point 10 feet away. The projection of an object nearer than the fixation point, say, 2.5 feet away will be displaced through an angle of 8°. Consider the same head movement with the position of fixation 5 feet away; this time the projection of the object 2.5 feet away will be displaced through an angle of 5°. Angular shift, therefore, could only be

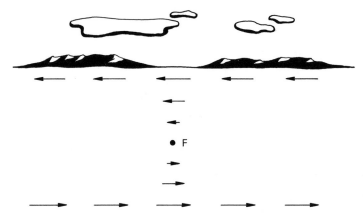

FIGURE 4.6

The effect of the distance of the fixation point on the amount of
motion parallax. Objects nearer than the fixation point (F) move
in the opposite direction when the observer looks to the left (as
in Figure 4.5, when the fixation point is the horizon). Objects
further away than the fixation point are displaced in the same
direction as the head movement. (From J. J. Gibson, *The Perception
of the Visual World*, Houghton Mifflin, 1950. Used by permission.)

mapped into absolute distance if the distance of the fixation point was
known beforehand, which would imply some means of gauging distance
other than motion parallax.

The other classical stimulus for distance is *optical expansion*. Whenever
we move toward an object (or whenever the object moves toward us), its
retinal image expands (Figure 4.7). The amount of expansion, under some
circumstances, can tell us the distance of the object. Thus, if we move 3
feet toward the object and its retinal image doubles, we know that the
object was 6 feet away when we began our movement and is now 3 feet
away at the end of our movement. If the retinal image size increases by
only 25 percent after a forward movement of 3 feet, we can deduce that
the object was 12 feet away to start with and is now 9 feet away.

We can make such judgments only if we have some nonvisual way of
calibrating our movements. Obviously, there is no requirement that such
calibration be in terms of feet and inches. An internal calibration in terms
of paces or creeps would do just as well and probably better from a functional standpoint.

FIGURE 4.7
The retinal image of an object expands as we move toward it. This optical expansion pattern can indicate the distance of the object to the observer.

The situation is somewhat different in the case of an object moving toward a stationary observer. The information contained in this sort of optical event has been extensively analyzed (Hay, 1966; Lee, 1974). The amount of expansion consequent to object movement can specify the position of the object relative to its starting point—but in relative, not absolute, terms. That is, the information can specify that the moving object is now half as far away as it was. The information cannot specify in absolute terms how far away the object is or was. Optical expansion produced by a moving object can therefore specify *proportional* but not absolute changes in distance. It follows from this, however, as Lee (1974) has shown, that an organism is supplied with information which allows it to predict when a moving object will contact it, providing the organism can make certain extrapolations from the change in stimulation on the retina. This is all of the information conveyed by the optical expansion pattern. As can be seen, it does not convey any information about absolute distance to a stationary organism.

A large amount of additional information is available to organisms which can specify the relative positions in depth of objects. Because these systems of specification do not require movement and can be picked up by a single eye, they are much used by representational artists—hence, the name commonly given them, "painter's cues." Some of these are illustrated in Figure 4.8. Gibson (1950) has presented the most complete and brilliantly lucid description of these stimulus systems. Their utility is somewhat restricted in comparison to the dynamic stimuli described above. The painter's cues can only indicate relative position, and even then they can only indicate with limited accuracy. There are many situations in which applying the painter's cues would lead the perceiver into error (Figure 4.9). Brunswik (1956) made a study of this for a number of

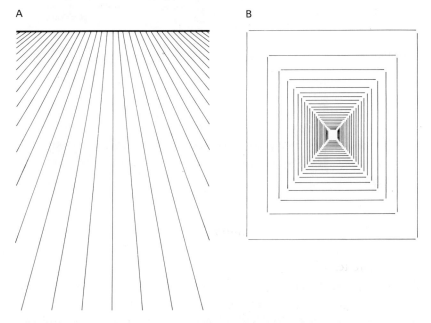

A   B

FIGURE 4.8
Painter's cues. These monocular cues do not require movement and can specify depth and distance to the observer. Other painter's cues not illustrated include interposition and relative height. (A) Linear perspective. Separation decreases with increasing distance. (B) Density gradient. Density increases with increasing distance. (From J. J. Gibson, *The Perception of the Visual World*, Houghton Mifflin, 1950. Used by permission.)

74

A

the painter's cues; the best of these was relative height. He found that, in about 50 percent of the cases, the "higher" of two objects was in fact farther away, as the cue indicated. However (excluding cases where the "higher" object was in fact at the same distance), the remaining proportion of cases where the "higher" object was in fact nearer was still very large—far too large for placing any great reliance on even this cue (Figure 4.10).

Throughout the brief review of the problem of space perception given above, we have consistently returned to the problem of how organisms gauge absolute distance as opposed to relative distance. Absolute distance is the core problem in distance perception. As we have seen, there are

B

Observer

FIGURE 4.9
(A) "Waterfall," by M. C. Escher (1961). If we trace
the various parts of this construction, we are unable
to discover any mistake in it; yet it is an impossible
whole—the two towers, for example, are the same
height and yet the one on the right is a story lower
than the one on the left. (From the collection of
C. V. S. Roosevelt, Washington, D.C.) (B) The
left portion of the further wall recedes from the
observer. The walls and windows have been
arranged to give the same retinal image as a normal
rectangular room, but the "smaller" figure is actually
almost twice as far away from the observer as the
other. (From W. H. Ittleson, The Ames
Demonstrations in Perception, OUP, Princeton,
1952).

many stimulus systems that specify relative position very reliably. They
can tell us that one object is nearer to us or farther away from us than
another with perfect reliability. But in many real life situations we need
to know how far away an object is *from us*; the expression of *how far* must
serve to control behavior taking place in the space occupied by ourselves
and the object. Take the act of reaching and grasping an object. When
this act is carried out by an adult, the hand goes to the object and grasps
it. The hand does not overshoot or undershoot; it gets to where the object is. Furthermore, the action need not be monitored by eye. We adults
can look away or even close our eyes while we perform such acts. This
means that the seen distance of the object has been translated into a set

A 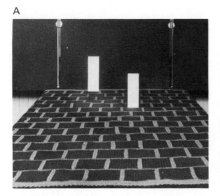 B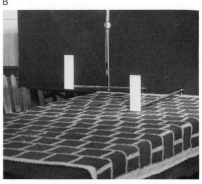

FIGURE 4.10
This illustrates how relative height can lead the perceiver into error. In picture A, the left block looks further away than the one on the right; a glance at picture B (the same array seen from a different angle) shows that this is not the case. (From J. J. Gibson, *The Perception of the Visual World*, Houghton Mifflin, 1950. Used by permission.)

of motor commands that move the hand through the appropriate distance to the object. When speaking of the problem of absolute distance, it is this translation from sensory to motor that I am referring to. If an organism displays behavior that is appropriate to the distance of objects, if it can reach objects without overshoot or undershoot, then I would say the organism is reponding to absolute distance. The term *absolute distance* serves as shorthand for "spatial variables translated into a form appropriate for the control of spatial motor movements."

This definition of absolute distance perception greatly restricts the range of experimental methods one can use to analyze the capacity. Obviously, the only acceptable indicators of this capacity are spatial behaviours—behaviors that are *necessarily* adjusted in space. I have given the example of reaching as a behavior whose successful occurrence indexes successful absolute distance perception. Reaching is a superb example of a spatial behavior. Another excellent example can be found in the classic experiment of Lashley and Russell (1934) on distance perception in rats. The subjects in this experiment were placed on a jumping stand at various distances from a target platform. The rats, who were visually naive, were forced to jump from the stand. The force of their jump to the platform was taken as an indicator of their absolute distance perception, which was extremely good.

It is difficult for a developmental psychologist not to drool with envy whenever he encounters experiments like that of Lashley and Russell. The young of nonhuman organisms have a much richer behavioral repertoire than do human infants. There is little point in testing jump responses of young infants for young infants simply do not jump. Indeed, to the casual eye, human infants seem to do little except sleep and eat. As we shall see, the casual observer misses much, but the lack of responses does limit the range of experimentation possible with young infants. Even if one does find a usable behavior, the fact that the organism is a growing one limits the conclusions that can be drawn.

The motor system grows more than does any sense organ. If we test accuracy of perception within a growing perceptual system while using as an indicator accuracy of behavior within a growing motor system, we are introducing two possible sources of error that cannot be separated. For example, it has been reported that young children—much less infants —will reach out for objects that are well beyond their reach. Does this indicate poor perception of object distance, poor awareness of arm length, or some combination of the two? This is not merely a methodological problem, it is also a severe theoretical problem. It has been argued that infants learn to see distance by watching their hands; since the motor system "knows" where the hand is, it can impart that information to the visual system and so calibrate it. It has likewise been argued that the eye educates the motor system—that infants watching their hands are learning how to interpret and control motor movements (Harris, 1965). Proponents of either position are assuming, erroneously, that either the visual system or the motor system can serve as a source of information that is invariant during growth. But neither of these systems can provide much invariant information during growth. The invariant information that the visual system can provide, as seen above, is not the sort of information that can control precise action. Action in space must be precisely oriented, not relatively oriented. The visual system can tell the infant that one object is half as far away as another, but we have not so far come across any stimulus that would say exactly how far away an object is. Without this information accurate motor behavior is impossible. The theoretical problem of how one growing system is calibrated onto another growing system is very difficult and creates the greatest single methodological problem in the study of infancy.

These problems have led many investigators, including the present writer, to take refuge in discrimination methods that rely on simple, available, easily counted responses. An elegant example of the simplicity and utility of such methods is a study of distance perception reported by Mackenzie and Day (1972). They used increase in fixation as a measure of discrimination. When an infant is repeatedly presented with the same stimulus and then the stimulus is changed, the amount of time spent looking at the new stimulus will increase if the infant can discriminate the change. Increase in fixation after a change of stimulation is thus good evidence of ability to discriminate the change. Mackenzie and Day presented an object at a given distance for ten ten-second blocks of time. On the eleventh block, the object was at a different *distance*. Fixation duly increased, indicating discrimination between the two distances.

This kind of method could be extended to test the fineness of discrimination, the range over which discriminations can be made, and so on. Obviously, these methods cannot be applied to the assessment of perception of absolute distance as it has been defined here, since that can only be indexed by spatially appropriate behavior. However, considering the growth-induced imprecision of these behaviors, one might conclude that relative-distance perception is the only capacity that could be studied anyway. Why not, then, utilize the simpler, more available discrimination methods? This would seem to be a plausible step. As we have indicated before, however, it is not a feasible step. The objections to discrimination methods that were outlined before in connection with the study of radial localization, apply here as well. Discrimination methods cannot tell us the basis of discrimination when there are alternative bases for the discrimination. Distance in perception is specified by the set of stimuli described above (binocular parallax, motion parallax, optical expansion, and painter's cues); any one of them can specify the distances of objects to some degree of precision. Distance cannot be specified unless one or another of these stimulus variables is available. Suppose our organism could display differential responses to objects at different distances. Take the Mackenzie and Day experiment as an example. If the proportion of time an infant spends looking at an object 90 cms. away is constant but increases when the distance of the object is changed, can we conclude that the looking has increased because the infant has noticed the change in distance? This is a tempting inference but entirely unwarranted. The change of distance is specified at the infant's eye by changes in the variables specifying distance. The recovery of looking indicates that the infant has detected a change, but it does *not* tell us whether the infant detected a change of distance or a change in the variables specifying distance. How can we tell from the recovery of looking that the infant detects a change in distance rather than a change in convergence angle? A change in convergence angle might be detected as such without being translated into perceived change in distance. The same goes for all of the other stimulus variables specifying distance. Motion parallax changes might be seen as changes in movement across the retina. The approach of an object might be seen as expansion with no approach.

To some extent, human adults can "see" the variables that specify distance rather than distance itself, although they are not very good at it. Perhaps this is because it takes a long time to develop the ability to see these variables, or because the habit of perceiving in terms of distance overcomes the initial tendency to perceive the variables rather than what they specify. Both theories have been put forward. Infants are the only organisms who can decide between the theories. Unfortunately, the discrimination methods cannot make the decision; no simple discrimination experiment can tell us whether an organism is responding to distance as specified by some variable, or responding to the variable itself. The key word here is *simple*. It is theoretically possible to devise discrimination experiments that would index distance perception, although such experiments would be rather complex.

Suppose that we presented an infant with an event in space specified by only one of the possible variables that could specify such an event. For example, an infant could be presented with an object moving toward and away from him, the approach and withdrawal being specified by the optical expansion pattern. In time, we might suppose, attention to the event will decline. Suppose one then presented the same event, this time specified by binocular parallax changes only. Would the attention to the event continue to decline? If it did, we could conclude that the infant was responding to the spatial event and not to the variables that specify it. The spatial event is constant, and there is no reason to expect recovery of attention when the same event is presented, even though specified by different variables. If on the other hand the infant were responding to the variables, we would expect an upsurge in attention after the transition from one variable to the other. I have attempted experiments of this sort but have continually been defeated by methodological problems, such as selection of an attention measure, methods of ensuring smooth transition from one variable to the other, selection of an appropriate event, and the like. Faced with problems of this sort, one feels that the natural response methods are a refuge. If an infant reaches out for an object intentionally, no matter how inaccurately, there can be no doubt that the infant sees the object in the third-dimension.* This kind of simple certainty we just cannot get from discrimination experiments.

To sum up, there are three main problem areas that concern us when we study the perception of distance in infants. The first is: do infants perceive distance at all, or do they simply perceive the variables that specify distance? When presented with an approaching object, do they see the object approach (perception of distance), or do they simply see it expand (perception of the specifying variables)? The second problem area is: when and how do infants succeed in correlating perception and action to produce accurate behavior in space? Thirdly, once these two are correlated, how does the organism adjust to growth within the components?

The first of these questions has provoked a great deal of theoretical argument but little research. As indicated, the problem really requires spatial behavior as an indicator measure, and the repertoire of the infant is not rich in spatial behavior. In the classic studies of Gibson and Walk (1960) on behavior on the visual cliff, crawling was used as an indicator behavior. The *visual cliff* is illustrated in Figure 4.11. The researchers found that infants who could crawl would not crawl over the deep side of the visual cliff under any circumstances, showing clearly that infants of that age do perceive distance. Unfortunately infants who are old enough to be able to crawl have a long history of experience behind them and so can hardly tell us anything about the origins of space perception.

A number of authors have thought that response to approaching objects might allow us to assess the perceptual abilities of younger infants. White (1963) did a very carefully controlled study of the development of one response to approaching objects—the blink. The infants in the experiment were laid on their backs. Immediately over their faces was an optical tunnel containing an object that could be dropped toward the baby from various heights. (See Figure 4.12.) A window of transparent plastic at the bottom of the tunnel prevented the object from actually hitting the baby. The window also prevented any air from being blown in the baby's face as the object dropped. This made sure that the response was a response

---

*An attempt to demonstrate the role of intention in infant reaching has been made by Bower, Broughton, and Moore (1970b).

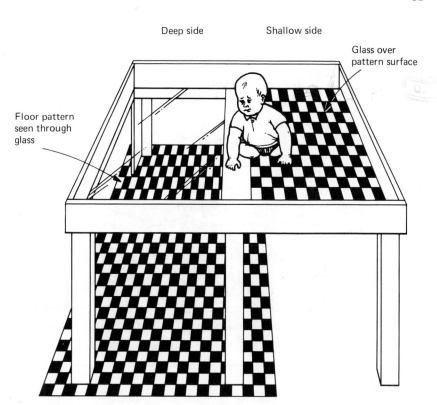

Deep side   Shallow side

Glass over
pattern surface

Floor pattern
seen through
glass

FIGURE 4.11
The visual cliff. The infant crawled across a heavy sheet of glass towards his
mother. Under the glass was a textured piece of checkered linoleum. For half
the distance, the linoleum was just beneath the glass; for the second half of
the distance, it was 3½ feet below the surface of the glass. At the midpoint,
the infant was faced with a visual cliff. (Drawing from John C. Wright and
Jerome Kagan, "Basic Cognitive Processes in Children," 1963. The Society
for Research in Child Development, Inc.)

to the visual event, not the air movement. The blink reponses were picked
up by electrodes attached to the baby's temples and recorded on the
moving paper tape of a polygraph. It was found that the first blink in
response to the dropping object occurred around the age of eight weeks.
The blink at that time was specific to the dropping object; withdrawal of
the object produced no blink response at all. Prior to eight weeks of age
no blinking could be elicited.

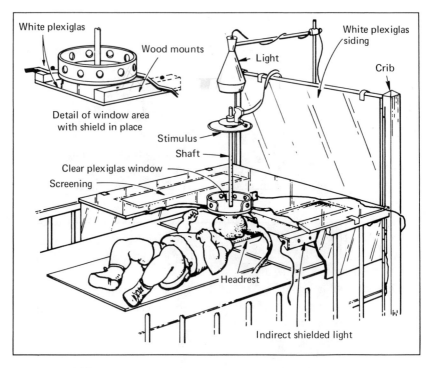

FIGURE 4.12
The blink-eliciting apparatus used by White (1963). (From B. L. White, *Human Infants: Experience and Psychological Development.* Copyright 1971. Reproduced by permission of Prentice-Hall, Inc., Englewood Cliffs, N.J.)

It would thus appear from this study that distance perception can be demonstrated around the age of eight weeks. But can we therefore conclude that it is absent prior to this time? Blinking is in the infant's behavioral repertoire and can be elicited by air movement alone well before eight weeks. If we accept blinking as a fair indicator of distance perception, it seems that we must also accept the conclusion that distance perception is absent prior to eight weeks in the conditions of this experiment. There are two qualifications that must be entered at this point. Can we accept blinking as a fair indicator of distance perception, and can we accept the conditions of this experiment as representative of the conditions under which perception normally occurs? Let us first consider blinking. In a functional context, does it make any sense for an organism to close its eyes as an object approaches its face? It would surely make more sense to take some kind of avoiding action, with eyes open on the object. It would also make more sense for experimenters to look for functional responses, rather than what appears to be a maladaptive response to the approach of an object. After all there is no evidence that human adults close their eyes when an object approaches their face, save as a desperate last resort. Why should infants? The second problem concerns the conditions of the experiment. The range of object movements used by White was very short. The longest drop was 12 inches. Since the object dropped under the force of gravity, accelerating at 32 feet per second, the entire event was over, drop and stop, in a few milliseconds, very possibly too quickly for any response to be organized. Before the infant could respond to approach, the event would be over. If a response were simply triggered by the event, this would not matter, but there is no reason to believe that human behavior is triggered and will then continue in the absence of the stimulation that caused it.

One last point about the conditions of stimulation must be made. White used a transparent plastic shield to prevent displaced air from reaching the infant's face, thereby ensuring that the response was elicited by the visual stimulus alone. This might seem like a very necessary control measure; however, it makes the stimulation presented very unrepresentative of the stimuli that occur in the real world. Whenever an object approaches an observer outside a laboratory, it simultaneously produces a complex of visual changes and a gradient in time of air pressure against the skin. Either change alone is abnormal. It may be that both together are necessary to produce a response very early in infancy. Since this kind of compounding is quite probable, the presentation conditions should allow one to discover whether or not it is important. Vision plus air movement may be quite different from vision alone or air movement alone. We cannot assume from a vision alone presentation that vision is not important; we must test for its role in conjunction with stimuli that normally covary with it.

Bower, Broughton, and Moore (1970a) have carried out a study that attempted to meet these criteria. They presented infants with real object movements which produced air displacement as well as visual changes. The objects were moved in slowly, and all of the behavior produced by the infants was recorded, not just the behavior of their eyelids. The results, unfortunately, were exiguous until one further modification was introduced—that was to present the stimuli only when the infants were in an upright or semi-upright position. This modification was necessary

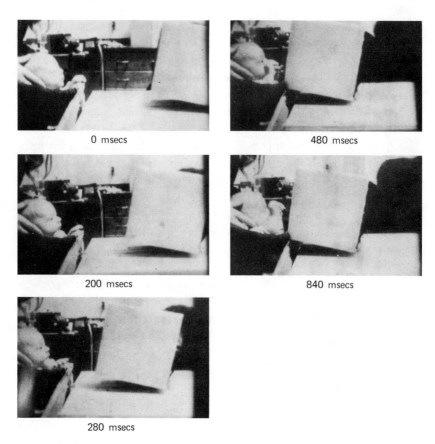

0 msecs

480 msecs

200 msecs

840 msecs

280 msecs

FIGURE 4.13
Defensive behavior of a ten-day-old infant elicited by an approaching object.

since it appears that very young infants never become fully awake as long as they are lying on their backs. (Prechtl, 1965). Since one can hardly expect coordinated behavior from an organism that is half asleep, at least a semi-upright posture seemed necessary. Once the latter modification was introduced, an obvious defensive behavior was elicited from the infants, who were in their second week of life. This is illustrated in Figure 4.13. The defensive behavior had three clear components: (1) eye widening, (2) head retraction, and (3) interposition of hands between face and object. Blinking was not observed. The behavior was clearly functional. It would have produced the best possible defense against the object, had

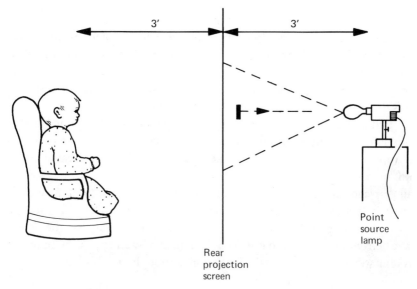

FIGURE 4.14
Shadow caster. As the object is moved farther and farther away from the screen and toward the point-source lamp, the shadow of the object increases in size. As there are no distance cues from binocular or motion parallax, the optical expansion pattern is the only distance-specifying variable present.

the object been allowed to strike the infant. The response of course was a response to real object movement with associated air displacement.

The next stage of the experiment was to discover the response to air displacement alone and to the visual changes alone. Air displacement produced a marked response that was totally different from the response produced by the approaching objects. The air movement alone produced very rapid eye closure followed by slight rotary head movements; there was no head retraction and no hand raising. Air displacement alone cannot, therefore, be responsible for the defensive movements elicited by an approaching object. The next thing that should have been studied was the response to visual stimulation alone, but unfortunately this was not done. Instead of testing response to the whole complex of visual changes, the investigators studied response to one component of the visual changes —the optical expansion pattern—using the device shown in Figure 4.14. This device excluded changes in binocular parallax and changes in motion parallax. The only specifying variable presented was the optical expansion pattern. Infants in the second week of life did show defensive behavior when presented with an approaching object defined solely by an optical expansion pattern. However, the intensity of the response was less than that elicited in the natural situation. Since the other variables were not presented, we cannot say whether the diminished intensity of response was due to lack of visual stimuli or to lack of air movement.

Ball and Tronick (1971) repeated the experiment, adding the variable of relative movement within the moving object by rotating the object as it approached. They found that the addition of this visual variable did not increase the intensity of response. This might seem to argue that the air displacement is required for a total response; however, until the experiment is repeated using the full battery of visual variables, the question must remain open. It seems safe to conclude nonetheless that the defensive behavior elicited from one-week-old infants by an approaching object is primarily elicited by visual stimulation, although possibly supported by air displacement stimulation.

Bower et al. (1970a) performed two further modifications in a series of experiments. One modification was carried out to ensure that the infants were in fact responding to changes in the distance of the object. It could be argued that the infants were responding not to the approach of an object, but rather to its apparent expansion. It is not clear why an organism would defend itself against an expanding object; however the argument can be made. To control against this complication, the experimenters presented the infants with a pair of objects, first one then the other. One object was small (a foam-rubber cube with 20 cm. sides) and approached to 8 cm. from the infants; the other object was large (a 50 cm. cube) and approached only to 20 cms. from the infants. At a 20-cms. distance, the large object projected an image on to the infants' retinas that was identical in size to the image projected by the small object only 8 cms. away. The geometry of the situation is shown in Figure 4.15. If the infants were responding simply to magnification of the retinal image seen as such, they should not differentiate between the two presentations which would be seen as equally threatening. If, on the other hand, they are responding to change in distance, we would expect a much greater response to the small, near object, since it comes closer and is that much more dangerous. There was indeed full-scale response to the small, near object and no response at all to the large, distant object. This indicates that it was in fact perceived change in distance that was being responded to.

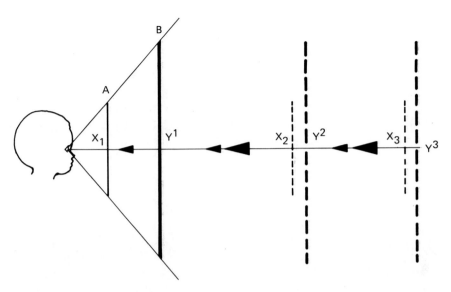

FIGURE 4.15

Different sized objects approaching to the points where they project the same size of retinal image for the infant. Object A is a 20 cm. cube and approaches to a point 8 cms. (X_1) from the infant. Object B is a 50-cm. cube and approaches to a point 20 cm. (Y_1) from the infant. At these points, the large and small objects project retinal images which are identical in size, since the angle of convergence is the same in both cases.

The last variation of this presentation was varying the speed of the approaching object. It was found that as object speed increased, probability of response declined. At the highest speed used, the event still took 2.7 seconds, so the decline in response was not due to lack of time to complete a response. Instead, it seems likely that the information specifying the event was presented too fast for the infant's visual system to register it. Object movement above a rate of 32° per second cannot be seen as movement by adults (Graham et al., 1965). It seems quite likely that the infant visual system has a much lower cut-off point.

This set of experiments would thus seem to indicate that one-week-old infants do perceive distance and change of distance as specified by, at least, the optical expansion pattern. Since the ability is present at one week, it seems likely that it is an unlearned ability. Without emulating the heroic experiments of Wertheimer (1961), one cannot be certain on this point. However, an argument for learning would seem to be most

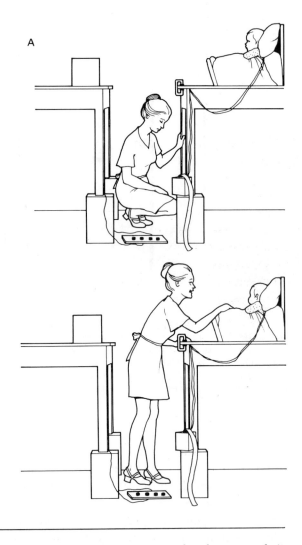

implausible. How many times has a one-week-old infant been struck in the face by an approaching object? Almost certainly, this has never happened, and unless it did there is no possible basis for learning.

A demonstration that infants perceive the third dimension allows us to make a strong interpretation of the results of discrimination experiments. Since infants perceive distance in one situation, it would seem overly cautious to deny that they can perceive it in other situations. It seems most likely that distance is the basis for the discriminations demonstrated, for example, in experiments by Bower (1965a). See Figure 4.16.

FIGURE 4.16
Bower investigated size constancy by using cubes of different sizes placed at
different distances from the infants. The conditioned stimulus was a 30-cm.
cube at 1 meter, and the test stimuli were 30- or 90-cm. cubes at a distance of
1 or 3 meters away. (A) The experimental set-up. The experimental procedure
began with conditioning, and the response was reinforced by a "peekaboo"
(see lower picture). The conditioned response, head turning, closed a micro-
switch which operated a recorder. After training, a screen was placed between
the infant and the stimulus area each time the stimulus object was changed.
(From photographs by Sol Mednick.) (B) This portion of the figure shows
how the test stimuli were related to the conditioned stimulus in various respects
and the results obtained. From these results, it would seem reasonable to
conclude that distance perception contributes to the discriminations shown.
(From T. G. R. Bower, "The Visual World of Infants." Copyright © 1966 by
Scientific American, Inc. All rights reserved.)

Conditioned stimulus	Test stimuli		
	1	2	3
True size			
True distance 1	3	1	3
Retinal size			
Retinal distance cues	Different	Same	Different
Average number of responses elicited 98	58	54	22

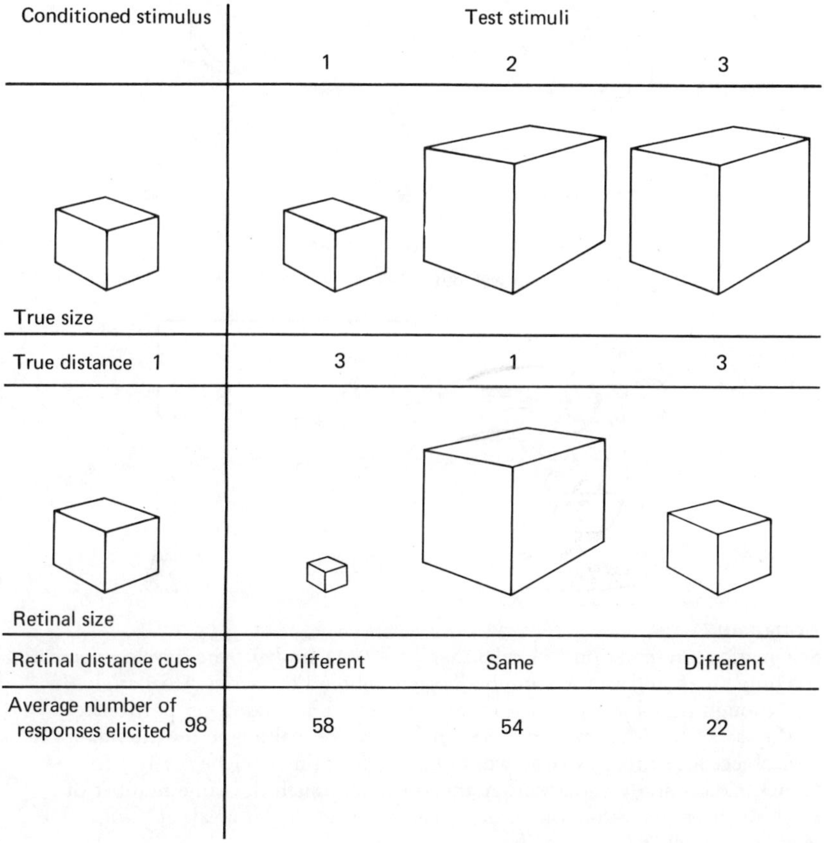

A   Small object within reach

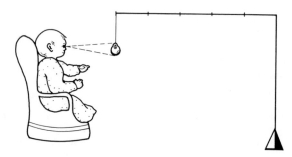

B   Large object well out of reach

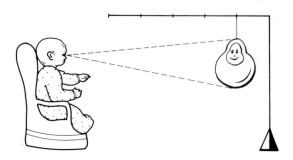

C   Small object well out of reach

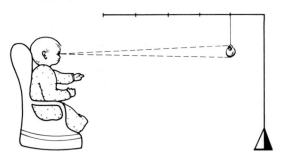

FIGURE 4.17

Schematic representation of Cruickshank's (1941) study of the development of reaching: In A and B, the stimulus objects subtend the same visual angle. In B, although the object is much longer, it is set at a distance proportionately further away so that it projects the same size of retinal image for the infant. (An object four times as large would be put four times further away.) In Cruickshank's study, situations A and B elicited much the same number of reaching attempts. Situation C, the small object at the far away position, elicited somewhat fewer reaches.

Bower's experiments would imply that motion parallax is important in early visual perception and that painter's cues are simply not registered as stimuli. Very young infants, then, perceive distance and differences in distance.

How soon do they become able to perceive distance in ways precise enough to control precise action? A number of investigators have studied the development of reaching. The results seem to indicate that this behavior (subject to growth within its perceptual control system and its effector system) does not become precise until quite late in infancy. The classic study is that of Cruikshank (1941). Her experiment is shown schematically in Figure 4.17. In essence she presented infants with two objects of different size at two distances and counted the number of arm extensions that occurred toward the objects. She found that the infants, five to six months of age, would extend their arms toward the far away objects, even though these objects were very well out of reach. Since the infants tried to reach these objects, either their perception of object distance, their perception of their own arm length, or both must have been in error.

Cruikshank (1941) and Brunswik (1956), her main interpreter, had no doubt that it was object perception that was defective. Indeed, neither of these researchers mentioned the possibility that faulty arm perception might be responsible—a surprising omission since the growth problems of the arm are much greater than those of the eye. Before getting into the nasty problem of trying to separate out the relative contributions of arm perception and object perception to the erroneous behavior of the infants, it might be well to ascertain that the behavior was indeed as erroneous as it initially seemed to be. The observed arm extensions might not indicate anything erroneous at all. The infant might extend his arm for a number of reasons other than to grasp an object lying within his field of view. How can we be sure that the extensions observed in this kind of experiment are really attempts to grasp the object? How in fact can we be sure that arm extensions in any kind of experiment are really attempts to reach and grasp an object that happens to be in the visual field at the time? An adult who points at the moon is not reaching for it. Pointing and reaching both involve arm extension; one must therefore be certain that the *intent* of an extension is reaching, and not pointing or some other activity. The point is that different functional behaviors use the same behavioral components. It is risky to infer one particular functional behavior from the occurrence of a behavioral component that is used in a variety of situations.

How can we be sure that the infants in Cruikshank's experiments were really trying to reach the distant objects? One way is to look for other behavior components that are characteristic of reaching. In the normal reaching of infants of the age studied by Cruikshank, one can observe finger adjustments prior to contact with the object and hand closure simultaneous with arrival at the object. One could thus inspect the behavior of the infants for the presence of these other components that occur in the course of reaching for objects that are attainable. If they do not occur, one could not conclude that the infants were trying to reach the objects. On balance, it would seem more reasonable to conclude that the arm extension indexed some other behavior. One could also observe the behavior of the infants after the arm extension. If the infants were trying to reach the distant object, the arm extension would necessarily fail. One might then expect to see some signs of disappointment or upset at the failure. Lack of upset along with lack of grasping components would seem to indicate that the behavior is not reaching. Unfortunately these measures were not taken in Cruikshank's study, nor do they seem to have been taken in any follow up study. However, informal observations by a number of individuals would suggest that the arm extensions toward out-of-reach objects by five-month-old infants are not true reaching. These arm extensions are not accompanied by hand shaping; their termination with no grasping does not produce upset; the infant tends to keep his arm extended toward the object; and the attempts are usually accompanied by "pleading" vocalizations. One could interpret these arm movements as indicator gestures intended to affect the behavior of nearby adults, rather than as attempts to obtain the object without help. This interpretation could be tested quite easily. If correct, the behavior should disappear in the absence of adults, and appear again whenever attentive adults are around. If the infant can reach the object, the behaviors associated with the arm extensions should be quite different. Samples of the two behaviors are shown in Figure 4.18.

If this interpretation is correct, the Cruikshank experiment does not show that five-month-old infants lack precise perceptual-motor maps. In addition, other investigators have found that reaching within reaching range is accurate around this age (White et al., 1964; Alt, Trevarthen, & Ingersoll, 1973). Thus we can tentatively conclude that perceptual-motor mapping is complete by this age. This does not tell us how the map has been constructed, of course, but simply that we should study infants younger than five months if we wish to get a handle on the process of construction.

A

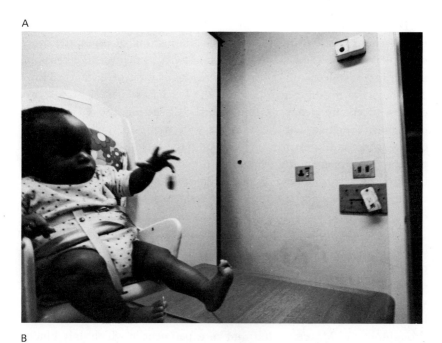

B

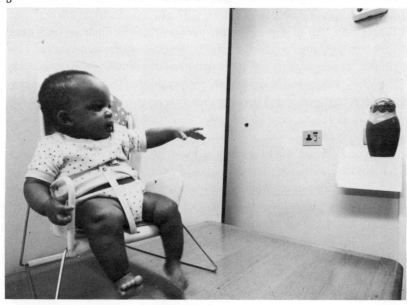

FIGURE 4.18
(A) Infant reaching for object within reach. (B) Infant "reaching" for object well out of reach.

Bower (1972) studied reaching in infants in the second week of life. He presented infants with two objects—one just out of reach, the other twice as far away. The near object elicited twice as many arm extensions as the distant object, indicating some discrimination of distance. However there was no difference between the behaviors elicited by the two objects, except frequency. In line with the discussion above, we apparently must conclude that these infants were trying to reach the distant object, which indicates that at this young age there is as yet no precise perceptual-motor mapping. The interim period between two weeks and five months is bare of data. We simply do not know when the behavior becomes precise, since the relevant experiments have simply not been done.

Some points are to be made in connection with this experiment. First of all, the infants did reach out for the objects. Since neither infants nor objects were moving, so that there was therefore no possibility of optical expansion information, some or all of the other space-specifying variables were being responded to and were specifying position in depth. The most likely variables would be motion parallax and binocular parallax. Bower, Broughton, and Moore (1970b) did an experiment in which only binocular parallax was available to the infants. The experimental set-up is shown in Figure 4.19. All of the infants in the study (all in their second week of life) reached out for the intangible, binocularly created object. This demonstrates that, by this age, binocular parallax specifies objects in depth. To be sure, it does not specify with perfect accuracy, but at least extension in depth is specified. There are thus at least two variables that specify position in depth to very young infants—binocular parallax and optical expansion pattern.

A second feature of the binocular experiment may suggest a way in which absolute distance perception could be attained. All of the infants were surprised and upset when their hand reached the location of the intangible object and failed, of course, to make contact with it. The upset was much greater than the upset observed in the Bower experiment (1972) where the infants failed to contact the object because the object was out of reach. Also, whereas the rate of reaching dropped off in the out-of-reach case, it stayed high in the binocular object case. This might be taken as an indication that the infants know why they failed in the out-of-reach case; they know that their hand had not reached the position where the object was. In the binocular object case, the infants know that their hand had reached the object location; therefore, they could not comprehend their error. If infants are able to detect the conjunction of hand and object,

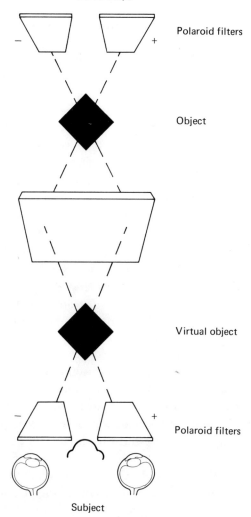

Point source lamps

Polaroid filters

Object

Virtual object

Polaroid filters

Subject

FIGURE 4.19
A schematic diagram of a device to produce
virtual objects. An intangible object is
produced by a shadow caster, in which two
oppositely polarized beams of light cast a
double shadow of an object on a rear projection
screen. An infant views the double shadows
through polarizing goggles that make a
different shadow visible to each eye. The
innate processes of stereopsis fuse the two
images to make the infant think he is seeing a
solid object in front of the screen. (From
Bower, Broughton, and Moore, *Nature*,
228: 679–681, 1970).

they can obviously detect errors and, therefore, possibly correct them. This sort of error correction could produce perfectly accurate behavior *with no calibration of the perceptual system or the motor system*. Each of these systems could remain erroneous without detracting from the accuracy of performance at all, provided an error-detecting and correcting mechanism is built in, as these two experiments would suggest.

An hypothesis very similar to this has been advanced by Held, who has performed a number of ingenious experiments designed to demonstrate its validity (Held and Hein, 1963; Held and Bauer, 1966). If a correcting mechanism is truly operative in infants, then the problem of absolute space perception is no problem at all. The mechanisms sensitive to binocular parallax, motion parallax, and the optical expansion pattern can specify the relative positions of objects very precisely in very young infants. The processes of adjustment would ensure that accurate relative-position perception could be converted into accurate spatial behavior, provided the effector in use (the hand, say) could be seen in the same visual field as the object it was directed against. Held has performed numerous experiments to show that sight of the effector organs is necessary for accurate spatial behavior (absolute space perception) in cats and monkeys.*Although the experiments Held has performed would not be possible with human infants, there is no reason to doubt that similar results would be obtained if the experiments were performed. The factor that makes a correcting mechanism necessary is growth, and humans grow more than either cats or monkeys; thus they have an even greater need of a calibration mechanism to allow them to discount the changes caused by growth.

A mechanism of this sort could also be used to adjust perception of radial position. A stationary infant, uncertain of the precise position off the straight ahead of an object, could nonetheless get his hand to the object if he could use sight of hand and object together as an error-correcting signal. There is evidence that infants can and do make such adjustments. However, the process is developmentally complex, as we shall see in Chapter 6.

---

*R. D. Walk has reported results suggesting that sight of the hand is not necessary for perception of absolute distance in the context of reaching in monkeys—at least if one considers only initial reaches. This raises the possibility that the process of adjustment to growth is initially genetically preprogrammed. However, this seems unlikely for most postnatal growth, since this is subject to environmental vicissitudes.

five /

Object Perception

The problem of things and the spaces between them • The Gestalt laws • The validity of these laws • Their utility in infancy • Limitations of Gestalt laws • Descriptions of objects • Phenomenal reality • Tangibility • Graspability • Visual specification of tangible properties • Theories of the development of such specification • Infant behavior related to visual specification of tactile properties • Differentiation of the senses in the development of object perception • Discrimination between real objects and representation of objects • Auditory specification of objects • Auditory-visual and auditory-tactual coordination • Differentiation of audition from vision and touch-size as an intermodal variable • Size constancy • Perception of distance and slant • Information handling in infancy

---

Thus far we have been discussing objects only as things in space. We have considered how the infant comes to locate objects in space, but we have not considered how the infant comes to see objects as objects. This is not a meaningless question. There is a profound problem to be worked out in relation to why we see *things* rather than the spaces between them. Illustrations like those shown in Figure 5.1 indicate the nature of the problem. As we look at those figures we see segments of them now as things and now as spaces between things. Why is it that in our normal environment we do not make such errors? How do we predict as well as we do that things are things and the empty spaces between them are in fact empty? The Gestalt psychologist worked out a set of rules which human adults seem to use to define objects in an array.

A

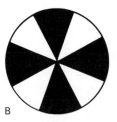

B

FIGURE 5.1

Figures such as these alternate spontaneously. (A) "Sun and Moon" by M. C. Esher (1961). In this figure we sometimes see the white birds as birds, whereas at other times they become spaces between the grey birds. They alternate between being object and background. (From the collection of C. V. S. Roosevelt, Washington, D.C.) (B) Similarly, this figure alternates between being a white cross on a black background and a black cross on a white background.

There were very many of such rules (well over 100 in one count) formulated in the heydey of Gestalt psychology (Helson, 1933), but most of these are of no great importance.

Three major rules include many of the others as special cases. They are called common fate, good continuation, and proximity. The rule of *common fate* states that, in any array, those contours that move together along a common path of movement will be seen as the external edges of a single moving object (Figure 5.2A). Common fate is a rule that can be applied not only to an array that contains moving objects but also to a stationary array seen by an organism that is moving itself. (See Figure 5.2B.) This rule is of no use to a stationary observer looking at a stationary array. The rules of good continuation and proximity, by contrast, are specific to a stationary array and a stationary observer. *Good continuation* states that the contours within a visual array, which can be described by the same equation in a coordinate system, will be seen as contours of a single object. In fact, the rule requires some more complex factors to be taken into account. As Figure 5.3 shows, location in the third dimension is a necessary prerequisite to applying the rule of good continuation. The same constraint does not apply to the rule of *proximity*, which states that, in any array containing more than two contours, the contours which are closer than average will be seen as contours of a single unit. Some examples of this are shown in Figure 5.4.

These rules are extremely effective in predicting which units adults will see in an array. They are psychophysical rules which predict what will be seen from the characteristics of the stimulation at the eye. One might expect that the rules would be valid and useful in predicting the true units in an array. Brunswik (1956) tested the utility of these laws in an ingenious experiment. He took a large number of photographs of everyday objects in normal surroundings and then measured the separations between contours. He used the rule of proximity to predict where the objects actually were in the photographs. The rule was useful, but not *very* useful since its application led to a number of errors. (See Figure 5.5.) A similar analysis was carried out for good continuation which turned out to be slightly more useful. Common fate has not been analyzed in this way. It seems unlikely that it could ever lead to errors, except in very special cases. Although its utility has not been analyzed it seems likely that it is the most useful of the three rules.

The Gestalt psychologists argued vigorously that these three rules could not be learned—that they must be built into the structure of the

A

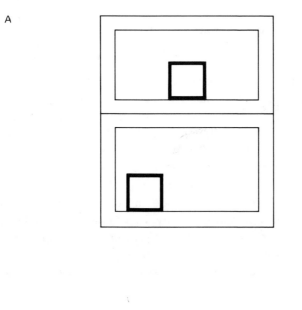

B

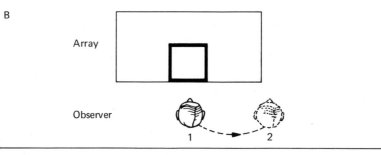

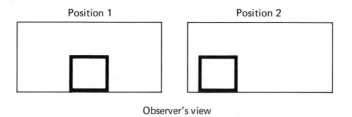

Observer's view

FIGURE 5.2
The rule of common fate. (A) When the thick lines move together along a common path of movement to their new position, they will be seen as the external edges of a single object which has moved to the left. (B) When the observer moves, his view of the contours changes. As he moves to the right, the contours move to the left. The rule of common fate holds in this situation also, and the contours are seen as a single object.

FIGURE 5.3
This figure is not seen as a triangle by human adults unless a pencil or similar object is placed in front of the gaps. The pencil occludes information that the triangle is not complete, allowing good continuation to operate.

This is seen as four vertical columns.

This is seen as four horizontal rows.

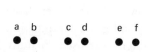

This is seen as three pairs, ab, cd, and ef; bc and de are never seen as pairs.

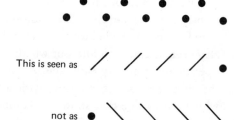

This is seen as

not as

FIGURE 5.4
Rule of proximity.

infant's nervous system. Their reasons for this were complex and relied heavily on inferences from physics and physiology. They did not rely on direct observation of infants. Despite this, their arguments were almost universally accepted (see Hebb, 1949). The only person who offered an alternative explanation was Brunswik (1956) who argued that these rules could be learned by trial and error in infancy.

	Contours closer than average	Contours farther apart than average
N (units)	219	115
N (not units)	57	113

FIGURE 5.5
The shaded boxes indicate the number of times application of the rule of proximity led to incorrect predictions in Brunswik's experiment.

Recently, a few experiments have been carried out to discover whether infants perceive units and whether the rules they use are in accord with the Gestalt rules. The evidence that infants do segregate their environment into units is clear. A large number of studies on the eye-fixation behavior of infants has shown that infants will fix on the external contours of objects in their visual field. If the objects are moved, the infants will track them. If after moving together, the contours of an object break up (Figure 5.6) and begin to move independently, very young infants will display massive surprise. This indicates that the common motion (common fate) had specified for them a single unit (Bower, 1965b). There have also been attempts to find out whether proximity and good continuation operate at a similarly early age. A surprise paradigm was used to study the effectiveness of these rules with infants. The infants were presented with an array like that shown in Figure 5.7. Adults seeing such an array tend to see it as two units—*ab* and *c*. After some time one of the dots, either *a* or *c*, was made to move while the other two stayed stationary. It was argued that if the infants see *a* and *b* as a unit, the movement of *a* should surprise the infants more than the movement of *c*, since it results in the breakup of unit *ab*. Surprise was measured by cessation of sucking. It was argued that the more surprising event should lead to a longer cessation of sucking. To the experimenter's own surprise, there was no effect of proximity until very nearly one year of age (Bower, 1965b). These results thus do not at all support the Gestaltist claims, but rather are in accord with Brunswik.

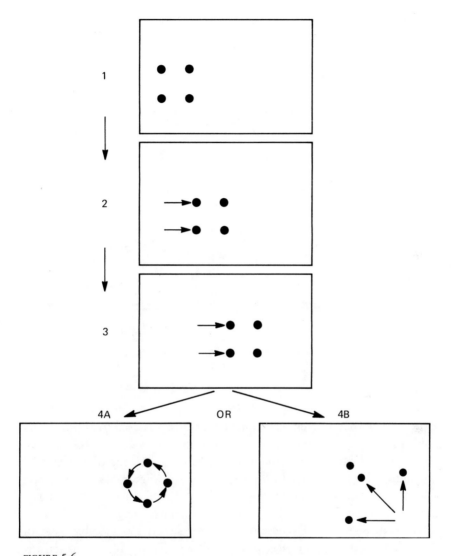

FIGURE 5.6
The event on the left (4A) is *consonant* with the information given in the first three frames. The dots still move on a common path. The event on the right (4B) *contradicts* the information given before, since the dots now move independently after having moved together. When three-week-old infants are shown the first sequence and then one of the other two events, the infants shown the *contradictory* event are more surprised than those shown the *consonant* event.

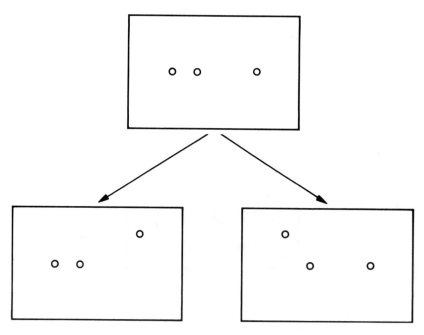

FIGURE 5.7
Application of the rule of proximity to the first picture makes the picture on the right surprising, whereas the picture on the left is not surprising. Infants do not see things in this way until near the end of the first year.

A somewhat different experimental method was used to assess the validity of the rule of good continuation (Bower, 1967a). Infants of around six weeks of age were presented with a display consisting of a black-wire triangle with a bar over it, like that shown in Figure 5.8A. They were trained to emit a conditioned response in the presence of this display. After a brief training period, the infants were shown one of the four stimuli shown in Figure 5.8B. These figures were selected as possible ways of seeing the display they were originally trained with. If the infants perceived in accord with the rule of good continuation, they would perceive the training display, as adults do, as a triangle with a bar over it. If they do not perceive in accord with the rule of good continuation, then they might think there was nothing where the bar had been. In this case, they might have seen the training display in any of the other three ways shown in Figure 5.8B. The number of responses elicited by each display was

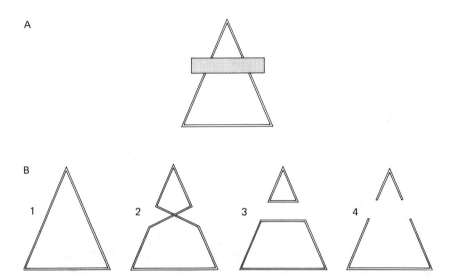

FIGURE 5.8
The completion experiment was conducted with these objects. (A) The conditioned stimulus was a triangle with a bar attached to it, thus interrupting its shape. (B) Of the test stimuli, 3 and 4 are more like the conditioned stimulus than 1 and 2 are. Actually infants seem to complete objects as adults do, as shown by the fact that 1 was the most effective stimulus. (From T. G. R. Bower, "The Visual World of Infants." Copyright © 1966 by Scientific American, Inc. All rights reserved.)

tallied. The more responses a display elicited, then the more that figure resembled the training display. The results unambiguously favored the complete triangle, indicating that the infants had seen the training figure as a triangle with a bar over it. This shows that even six-week-old infants can use the rule of good continuation.

It thus seems that the Gestalt rules are not all innate; at least one of them, proximity, develops very slowly, while common fate has been shown to be effective at very early ages. It seems quite likely that a mechanism for using the more valid common-fate information could be built in, while the less useful rules for stationary displays could be learned later on. An alternative possibility to which we shall return is that the infants *could* respond to the rules for stationary displays but do not, attending exclusively to the dynamic movement information. As we shall see later, there is more support for such an hypothesis than might at first appear.

Perhaps at this point the reader is beginning to feel restive about the experiments mentioned thus far. The experiments used to assess object perception were discrimination experiments. But surely *object* means something more than a discriminable unit in the visual field. To an adult, an object is not merely a discriminable unit akin to the discernable units in a drawing or photograph. An object is something solid and tangible; it can be grasped; it has a definite size; it can be hard or soft; and if dropped it will make a particular sort of noise. None of these properties are described by the Gestalt rules. Whereas the Gestalt rules may suffice to account for perception of units, there is nothing in them to account for the perception of the other, more distinctive properties of objects.

The Gestalt rules apply very well to marks on paper. They do not, however, tell us how we differentiate marks on paper from objects in the world—surely an important capacity. Tangibility, graspability, hardness, acoustic qualities, and specific size are all properties that differentiate real objects from representations. They sum up the quality that Michotte called "phenomenal reality" (Michotte, 1962). None of these properties is purely visual. Adults can predict the hardness of an object by eye, but hardness is a property that is more usually associated with the sense of touch, as are graspability and even size, as will be shown later in this chapter. Similarly, on the basis of visual information, adults can predict the sort of noise an object will make if dropped or struck; but noise is a property associated with the sense of hearing. The complex of object properties that define phenomenal reality is thus an intermodal complex involving several senses. Information is fed in through one sense—vision—specifying the information that would be fed in through other senses if they were utilized in the situation. When reality is detected by eye, it involves a prediction about information that is *potentially* available to other senses.

How does the eye predict properties such as hardness or tangibility? The psychophysics of visual tangibility have been worked out; Katz (1911) found that subjects will see surfaces of objects—tangible, contactable areas—whenever there is texture or microstructure within the area. If there is no texture or no variations in brightness within an area, the area is seen as empty and penetrable—the sort of area one could reach through or walk through without meeting any resistance (Figure 5.9). If a texture or microstructure remains the same as long as the observer remains stationary, but changes when the observer changes position, the area

FIGURE 5.9
Film color. The white area has neither texture nor variations in brightness; it is seen as empty and penetrable.

FIGURE 5.10
Surface color. Unlike the white area in Figure 5.9, this area seems hard and unyielding.

will tend to be seen as hard or unyielding (Figure 5.10). If, by contrast, the texture and highlighting change spontaneously, while the observer is stationary, it will tend to be seen as liquid or foggy, yielding on contact, but different from the nothingness of an empty untextured area. This is known as volume color and can be seen by looking, for example, at a puff of smoke. It is quite easy to produce and control perception of tangibility in adults. Although the information is presented visually, adult subjects perceive the situation so as to predict the intermodal consequences of the stimulus source.

Tangibility is not the most important of the properties listed above. Far more important for perception of the reality of an object is the dimension of graspability. Michotte showed adults pictures of objects and asked them either to grasp the object or insert another small object within the pictured object. All of his subjects, according to his own report, looked at him as if he were mad. A pictured object can be seen, and indeed usually is seen, as tangible; but it is never seen as graspable. What variables determine perception of graspability then? Other phenomenal properties such as size are related to graspability but do not determine it. The most relevant correlate of graspability would seem to be three dimensionality. A graspable object has a top and a bottom, a left and a right, and a front and a back. The critical dimension is obviously the front-back dimension.

A real, graspable object has a front surface that is all its own, unlike the front surface of a pictured object which is the same as that of the paper, canvas, or whatever the object is drawn on. A real object also has a perceptually distinct, if invisible, rear boundary that is just as important as the front boundary in the context of action. When grasping an object, we curl our hands round *behind* the object, to contact the rear boundary of the object. It is a matter of common observation that adults can do this accurately; adults can predict where the rear boundary of an object is and also what shape it will have (Michotte, 1962; Johansen, 1957). (See Figure 5.11.)

What stimulus variables allow us to do this? Since it is a matter of tridimensionality, we can draw on the information discussed in the last chapter. Specification of a front surface standing free of adjacent surfaces can be accomplished by motion parallax and binocular parallax. As we saw in the previous chapter, these variables can specify with very high accuracy the relative position of planes in depth, which is all that is needed

FIGURE 5.11
Adults can predict with a good degree of accuracy where the rear boundary of an object is and what shape it will have, even if the object is as unfamiliar as the one shown here. (From M. Johansen, "The Experienced Continuations." *Acta Psychologica*, 1957).

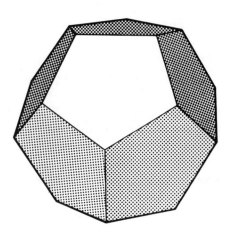

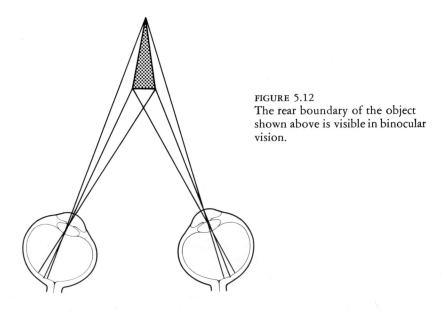

FIGURE 5.12
The rear boundary of the object
shown above is visible in binocular
vision.

to specify the separation of the front surface of an object. The back surface is more difficult. In the case of some objects, the location of the rear
boundary of an object may be visible to binocular vision (Figure 5.12) or
to a single eye that is moved to pick up motion parallax. However, there
are cases in which neither of these variables is present and yet subjects
still distinctly perceive the invisible side of an object.

Michotte had a nice example of this with perception of a sphere. Subjects presented with a whole sphere report seeing a sphere. If the invisible
side of the sphere is progressively sliced away (Figure 5.13A), there comes
a point where subjects report seeing a section of a sphere. According to
Michotte, that point comes when the top-bottom-right-left boundary of
the sphere cuts the surface of the sphere so that the subject can see the
surface does not continue on the same three-dimensional path (Figure
5.13B). In the absence of this information, subjects apparently assume
that the surface of an object will continue on the same path. Michotte
explicitly links this kind of rule with the rule of good continuation. Subjects seem to operate the rule in three dimensions as well as in two dimensions. From the available information, it would seem that parallax information plus a rule of good continuation could account for perception of
the rear boundary of objects, and thus for perception of graspability.

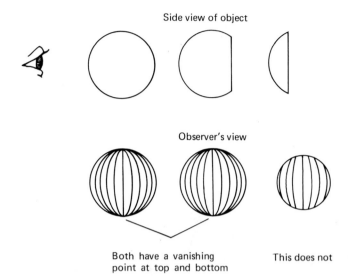

Side view of object

Observer's view

Both have a vanishing   This does not
point at top and bottom

FIGURE 5.13
If an observer is presented with a sphere that is progressively
cut away from behind, as shown, there comes a point at
which the subject can *see* that it is not a sphere, and that
its rear surface is not the same as its front surface.

An intimate connection exists between perception of tangibility and perception of graspability. Presence of parallax variables at the edges of a bounded contour does not ensure perception of graspability, if the information specifying tangibility within the contour is not simultaneously present. This can be demonstrated by using a binocular shadow caster to project a shadow of an object (Figure 5.14). If one cuts a hole in the center of a screen and projects the shadow of the screen binocularly onto another screen, the subject will only be able to see two discs of light, one going to each eye. The edges of these discs are binocularly disparate; this does not result in perception of a disc in depth, however, but rather perception of a hole in a black surface—something that no adult will try to grasp. If texture is put in the hole, by contrast, it immediately takes on the appearance of a textured *object*. Thus parallax and texture variations are both required for perception of an *object*.

Texture and parallax variables are visual stimuli that specify the tactual properties of an object. At first sight, size might seem to be a purely visual

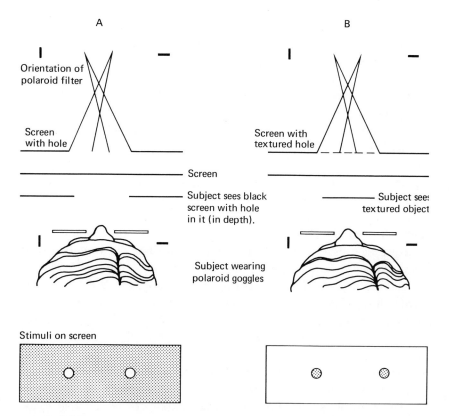

FIGURE 5.14
If one sets up a binocular shadow caster (see Figure 4.19) and projects two luminous discs on to a screen (one going to one eye, the other going to the other), a subject will see a black screen with a hole in it, in depth (A). If texture is put in the hole, the subject will see a textured object (B).

variable, giving no apparent intermodal predictions. There certainly is a purely visual sense in which we can judge the size of objects relative to other objects. However, size in the context of an action is judged relative to the size of our own bodies or body parts. The size of an object functionally means its size relative to our hands or mouths. Adult subjects are able to make judgments of the size of an object relative to their hands without having to look at hand and object simultaneously. Visual information is thus once again used to predict tactual information.

It has classically been argued that these intermodal predictions are learned. The sense of sight and sense of touch are different senses, so the argument goes, and the only way one sense can come to predict the information potentially available to another sense is by associative learning. Chance tactile contact simultaneous with visual input will teach the developing child what visual inputs specify what tactual inputs—touch teaches vision. This argument was derived from discussion between adults. There was no inspection of infants or developing children involved in the theorizing. Recently, the theory has come under attack because it apparently fails to predict the results of experiments done on adults (Rock and Harris, 1967). It has been found that when vision and touch are put into conflict, vision invariably dominates. Thus, if an adult subject looks through a minifying lens that makes objects look smaller and simultaneously grasps an object, he feels the object to be the same size as he sees it to be. The subject grasps the object through a cloth, so that he has no clues to the size of the object from the sight of his minified hand. He is not aware of any conflict between vision and touch, and vision seems to dominate (Figure 5.15). If touch were the teacher of vision, presumably the reverse would happen and the object seen would "grow" as soon as it was grasped. Rock and Harris report a number of other ingenious studies all pointing to the conclusion that, in adults, vision dominates touch and is, if anything, the teacher of touch.

The available studies on infants also contradict the idea that touch teaches vision. We have already described some studies that point in this direction. In the last chapter, we saw how visual information could specify the approach of an object so as to elicit a defensive reaction from very young babies (Bower, Broughton, and Moore, 1970a). The defensive reaction would imply that the infants expected a tactile input and were taking measures to protect themselves against it. The defensive reaction occurred, you will remember, when the input was purely visual, a shadow on a screen. On the other hand, when the input was purely tactual (a blast of air) and could have specified the approach of an object, no defensive reaction occurred at all. This result certainly is not in accord with traditional ideas. It suggests that vision can pick up hardness quite directly from the beginning.

In our culture, it is unlikely that an infant less than two weeks old could have been exposed to situations where he learned to fear an approaching object and expect it to have tactile qualities. The only conclu-

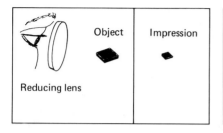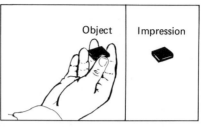

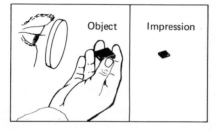

FIGURE 5.15

Vision dominates touch. Subject's impressions in various experiments involving the reducing lens are indicated. In some cases (*left*) he merely saw an object through the lens; in some (*center*) he only felt the object, and in others (*right*) he simultaneously saw an object and felt it, although he could not see his hand. (From Rock and Harris, "Vision and Touch." Copyright © 1967 by Scientific American, Inc. All rights reserved.)

sion is that in man there is a primitive unity of the senses, with visual variables specifying tactile consequences; further, this primitive unity is built into the structure of the human nervous system.

In an effort to test this hypothesis further, the original virtual-object experiment was repeated with a group of newborn infants (Bower, Broughton, and Moore, 1970b). It was not easy to do this, since the infants had to wear the polarizing goggles without fussing. Newborn infants do not reach for objects in the same way that older infants do; newborn infants will, however, reach out and grasp objects if they are supported so that their hands and arms are free to move to the objects in front of them.

It was found that all the newborn infants touched and grasped real objects without any sign of being disturbed. They also grasped at empty air without upset when no visible object was present. The virtual object (a visible object that is empty air to the sense of touch), however, produced a howl as soon as the infant's hand went to the location of the intangible object. Here too, then, we have evidence of a primitive unity of the senses. (Tactile input was absent in a situation where it was expected.) This unity is unlikely to have been learned, given the early age and the history of the infants studied.

These results do not support the notion that visual information can come to specify tactual properties only after a long period of apprenticeship. The youngest infant in these experiments was only four days old. Once again, in a Western culture at least, it is most improbable that infants of this age have experienced the tactual consequences of an approaching object. If they have, there is no particular reason why they should associate the tactual consequences with the visual input rather than with the concurrent air movement. Such arguments cannot *prove* that the coordination is not learned; one-trial learning is, after all, possible. But the subsequent history of the development of visual-tactual coordination would seem to argue against a learning-theory explanation.

Consider the virtual-object experiment (Figure 4.19). The young infants showed some considerable degree of upset when their hands arrived at the location of the seen object but contacted nothing. This upset must reflect the violation of an expectancy that seen objects will be tangible. If the expectancy were learned through chance contacts with objects, one would assume that its strength would increase as the infants grow older and have more contacts with objects. This apparently does not happen, however.

If one studies the reactions of older infants to the virtual object, it is hard to see any change in behavior up to the age of approximately six months (Bower, Broughton, and Moore, 1970c). There is the same degree of upset and continued persistent attempts to grasp the ungraspable object. However, around six months of age the quality of the upset and the behavior changes. The infants are still startled by the virtual object; however, their grasping behavior is quite different. Younger infants close their hands on the virtual object and, indeed, usually end up with their hands clenched at the object locus. The older infants stop the grasp action with their hands still open. One may also observe in older infants a variety of behaviors such as prolonged hand regard, rubbing the hands together, and banging the hand on a surface—all interspersed with further single attempts to grasp the virtual object. One could say that the infants were trying to verify that their hands were really working and had not

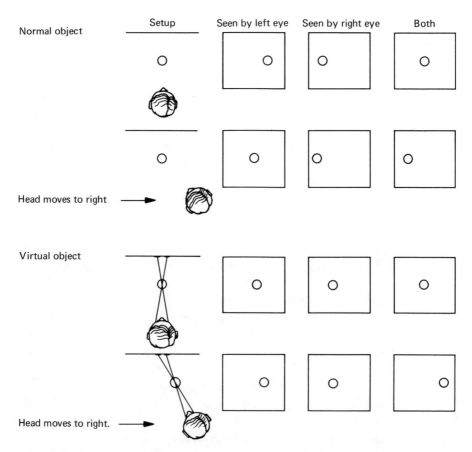

FIGURE 5.16
The motion parallax obtained with a binocular virtual object is extremely peculiar. The direction of shift consequent to a head movement is the opposite of that normally seen.

suffered a loss of sensitivity. If one persists in observing the infant in this situation, one can usually then observe a range of exploratory *visual* behaviors. For example, the infant may sway his head from side to side through an extreme arc, thereby picking up the maximum amount of motion parallax. The motion parallax thus generated is the opposite of normal motion parallax (Figure 5.16) and is highly abnormal visually. The infant will usually then stop reaching for the virtual object. If presented with new objects in that situation, infants will not reach out until they have tested the parallax properties of the objects; then they will only reach for those objects that have normal parallax properties.

Apparently, infants faced with this abnormal situation first of all check out their hand and then check out the visual properties of the object. If the object is visually abnormal, they stop trying to reach for it. All of this is in marked contrast to the responses of younger infants who persist in their attempts to grasp the object—upset but seemingly unable to localize their upset. The older infants know something is wrong with the visual-tactual coordination and systematically check the tactual and then the visual halves of it. The responses of older infants are differentiated; they seem to be aware of vision and touch as separate modalities, unlike the younger infants who apparently have a wholistic, unanalyzed awareness of the situation. The younger infants have at their disposal all of the behaviors used by the older infants. They can show hand regard; they can generate motion parallax; but they do not do so in this situation. One must conclude that they have not yet differentiated the visible qualities of an object from its tangible qualities.

If one pursues development further yet, one can clearly observe the establishment of vision as the dominant sense. Infants between four and five months old will try to grasp a seen object and will continue to grasp an object which they cannot see. This indicates that both visual input and tactual input can specify the presence of an object to be grasped. Around six months of age this is no longer true, however. An infant will drop an object that he is grasping if he can no longer see it. One only has to cover the infant's hand with a cloth for him to drop a grasped object. Indeed, if one places a tiny object in the palm of an infant's hand and the infant closes his hand over it, he will drop the object as soon as it is out of sight! It thus seems that one consequence of the differentiation of vision from touch is that touch loses its ability to specify the presence of an object and regains this ability only after a prolonged period. The process of recovery from differentiation is discussed more fully in the next chapter.

Thus far we have pointed out that a real object or a virtual object with all of the visual attributes of a real object will be seen as real (graspable) by infants—even very young infants. Some further analysis of this has been undertaken and can be reviewed here. Adults clearly distinguish between objects and representations of objects. Infants do too (Fantz, 1961) and will only attempt to grasp an object which is defined by parallax variables. A representation of an object, a photograph or a drawing, will not be grasped at all. The infant will look at it but will make no attempt

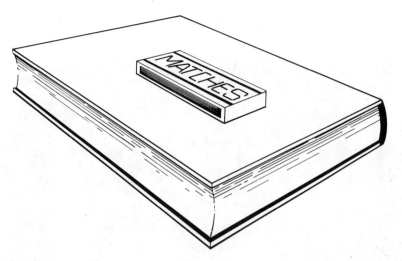

FIGURE 5.17
Until the age of nine to ten months, an infant will not reach out to pick
up the matchbox from the book. If the infant is reaching for the box
before it is placed on the book, he will withdraw his hand and commonly
grasp the book instead, making no attempt to remove the box. It would
seem that he is unable to dissociate the two objects, especially if the
support (in this case, the book) is not much larger than the object it is
supporting.

to grasp it. Thus, parallax variables are necessary for perception of graspability in infants. They are necessary, but they are not sufficient. If infants are presented with a luminous disc in depth with no texture or microstructure, like adults, they will make no attempt to grasp the disc (Bower,
Broughton, and Moore, 1970c). Furthermore, if infants are presented
with an object that lacks a boundary of its own—whether top, bottom,
front, or back—they will not attempt to grasp the object until they are
nine or ten months of age (Piaget, 1937). One can make an object seemingly "disappear" by placing it in such a way that one of its boundaries
becomes invisible (Figure 5.17).

For infants, then, it seems that an object is a volume with its own
bounds, defined by parallax and texture variables. The object thus defined
is *seen* to be tangible; developmentally, visual tangibility precedes tactual
tangibility, whereas undifferentiated visual-tactual concordance precedes
both.

Thus far, we have discussed the ways in which the visual and tactual
modalities can specify objects. We have not considered *audition* as a modality that can specify the nature of objects. In the previous chapter, we

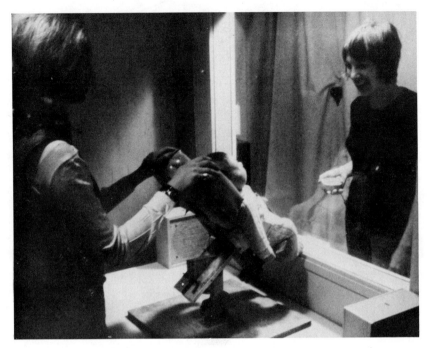

FIGURE 5.18
Mother-voice apparatus. (Courtesy of Eric Aronson.)

mentioned some experiments which indicated that sounds can specify objects in very young infants. Wertheimer (1961) showed that a newborn baby would *look at* a sound source, indicating that the infant expected to see something. Similarly, infants will reach out to touch a sound source presented in darkness, indicating that they expect to grasp the thing specified by auditory stimulation (Bower and Wishart, 1973). Aronson and Rosenbloom (1971) have been able to demonstrate an even more complex degree of auditory-visual coordination. Their apparatus is shown in Figure 5.18. The mother sits facing the baby who can see her through the sound-proof screen. The baby can hear his mother only through the loud speakers. When the loud speakers are equally loud, the voice is heard as coming from its seen location. If the volumes of the speakers are made unequal, the location of the voice shifts toward the louder speaker and away from the seen location of the mouth. This latter condition was very disturbing to a three-week-old infant, indicating that by the age of three weeks an infant expects a voice to proceed from a mouth. The infant could tell when the voice (a sound source) came from a different location than its mouth (a visible source).*

The question remains: are these auditory-visual and auditory-tactual responses built in or acquired? In the case of the coordination studied by Wertheimer (1961), there is no question that acquisition was possible since the infant was newborn. This does not hold for the other results, however, since the babies were older. Nevertheless, the pattern of development does not fit an acquisition hypothesis—but rather a differentiation hypothesis.

Using the mother-voice apparatus, Aronson and Dunkeld (1972) found that older infants are distressed by the display, just as are young babies. However, the older babies show a clear double orientation in the situation, looking at the visual source while turning their heads to center the auditory source. The younger infants do not show this simultaneous double orientation but rather orient ears and eyes to a position midway between sound location and mouth location. Their responses are thus less differentiated than those of the older babies. Similar differentiation effects were found in the case of auditory-manual coordination (Bower and Wishart, 1973). Infants up to five months of age are quite willing and able to reach out and grasp an audible object presented in darkness. Older infants are increasingly less likely to do this; by the age of seven months, the behavior simply cannot be elicited at all. The behavior does come back, of course, but it is not until the age of nearly one year that the infant is as good again at reaching as he was at five months.

These various results suggest that we restate the problem of integration and its development. According to the view presented in Figure 5.19, sensory integration does not develop. Rather, it is sensory differentiation that develops. It would be fair to ask why this should be the particular developmental path followed in the relations among the senses. Why should an infant be born with a high level of sensory integration that will be taken apart in sensory differentiation? This question implies that integration is the real problem rather than differentiation, but I would argue that this view is completely wrong. In the course of evolution, it is differentiation—rather than integration—that has been the sign of advance.

---

*This experiment has been criticized with the argument that the infants are trying to orient in two directions at the same time. It is this conflict rather than the dissociation which produces distress. This is a very important issue which should be resolved; as yet, the necessary experiments have not been done.

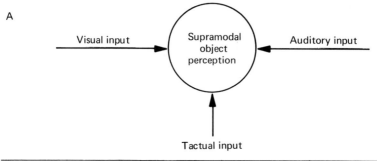

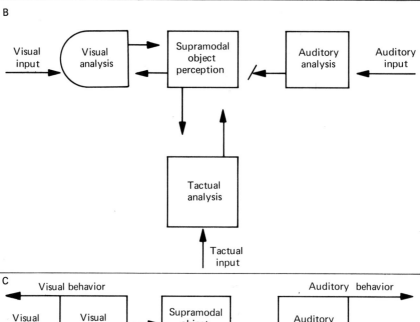

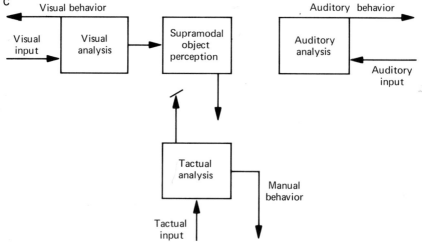

FIGURE 5.19
Three stages in sensory differentiation: (A) birth—4.5 months; (B) 4.5 months—6.5 months; (C) 6.5 months on.

Lower organisms show no differentiation whatsoever between modalities (Bower, 1974a). It is apparently easier for an organism to grow with an undifferentiated perceptual system than with differentiated sensory modalities.

Indeed, if we consider the evolutionary context of perceptual development, this is hardly surprising. The simplest organisms have perceptual systems that respond to the important dimensions of objects in their environments and then control behavior toward the objects. Even a deepwater fish with no visual system and no auditory system can detect the location of objects via pressure changes on its skin. It is most probable that perceptual systems evolved eyes, ears, and noses to pick up the different energy spectra that can specify objects. It is highly improbable that any organism evolved a visual system or an auditory system that was not an outgrowth of the supramodal perceptual system—the system that responds to those properties of objects that can be specified via any sensory modality. If this is the case, one can reasonably ask why differentiation then occurs. This is a question at two levels. One can speculate that differentiation increases adaptation by increasing the range of possible different responses. One must ask what processes generate differentiation in development. Is it some inevitable growth process, or is it that function and experience in the world play a role in the development? The relevant experiments simply have not been done. The single piece of relevant evidence I have been able to discover indicates that babies born blind (and therefore more dependent on audition than normal infants) still lose intersensory coordinations at about the same age as sighted infants (Freedman, 1964). They stop turning their eyes to a sound source and stop looking at their hands, even though they have never had a visual input as a result of exercising one of these coordinations. This would suggest that function cannot affect the process of differentiation, which would therefore seem to be endogenously generated. Further research will be required to establish or reject this conclusion.

One intermodal dimension we have not yet discussed in a developmental context is *object size*. Size poses a double problem to psychologists. The seen size of objects depends on the size of the image projected on the retina. Image size varies with the distance of an object from the eye (Figure 5.20); despite this, adults at least see objects as maintaining a constant size at any distance. However, image size also varies with eye size, which changes in development (Figure 5.21). Nevertheless, infants as well as adults can successfully adjust their hands to grasp objects at

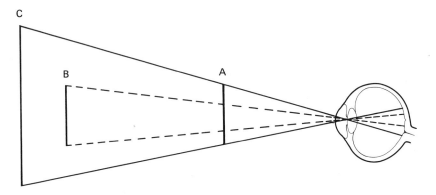

FIGURE 5.20
Size constancy. An adult will see A = B and smaller than C, even though the retinal image of A is the same size as that of C, and larger than that of B.

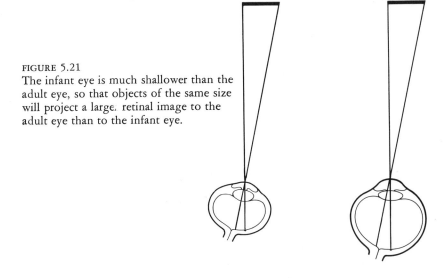

FIGURE 5.21
The infant eye is much shallower than the adult eye, so that objects of the same size will project a large. retinal image to the adult eye than to the infant eye.

various distances. It is this motor adjustment of hand to object that poses the theoretical problem. In the act of grasping, it is not necessary for an adult to match up his hand separation to the size of an object he is attempting to grasp. He can reach out, open and close his hand on an object without waiting for visual feedback of any sort, which implies that the seen size of an object can be matched to a finger-thumb separation. Visual information can be matched to manual information. Even very young infants are capable of this sort of matching (Figure 5.22); despite this, it seems a priori very unlikely that this degree of organization could be built into the structure of the human brain.

In addition to the developmental problems posed by the growth of the eye, there are massive developmental problems posed by the growth

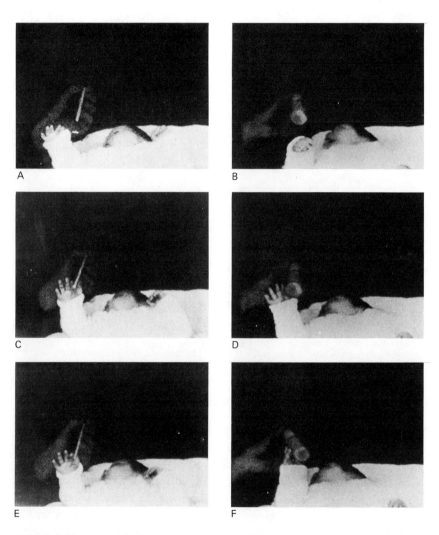

A

B

C

D

E

F

FIGURE 5.22
Neonate matching seen size of object to finger-thumb separation. (From Bower, 1972.)

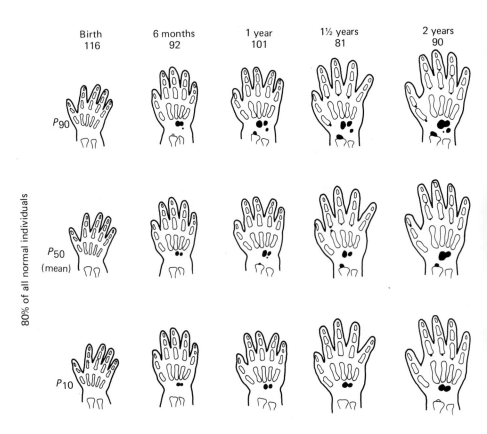

FIGURE 5.23
Diagram of boys' hands at various ages showing change of size and change of size of components. P = percentile. (From Documenta Geigy Scientific Tables, K. Diem and C. Lentner, Eds. CIBA-Geigy, 1940.)

of the hand (Figure 5.23), which has a growth curve quite different from that of the eye. Held (1965) has argued that the matching of visual and proprioceptive extents is done visually. Infants look at their hands in the visual field; they can thus see their hand and the object simultaneously. By watching his finger-thumb separation, the baby comes to calibrate its seen extent with its felt extent, so that, in time, when presented with a seen object, the baby can match his finger-thumb separation to the extent of the object, without having to look at both simultaneously. This theory is highly plausible, and Held has been able to back it up with a number of highly ingenious animal experiments (Held, 1965). It is certainly true that in the context of reaching for objects neonate humans will look at their hands in a way that is rarely observed in older infants (Figure 5.24). It may well be that in this kind of situation infants are calibrating a seen extent with a felt extent. It may be that this kind of behavior is necessary for the accurate grasping behavior that is seen in very young infants. It would take an heroic effort after the fashion of Wertheimer's study of auditory localization to prove the point, and that effort has not so far been made. Although Held's theory seems very plausible, it might be worth while to make an effort to put this issue in a position beyond doubt.

The problem of size constancy is less complicated than that of size perception itself. It is generally agreed that any organism that has distance perception should be capable of size constancy. As we have seen, young infants do perceive distance, and they do seem to be able to use distance information to attain size constancy (Bower, 1966a; Bower et al., 1970a). It is usually assumed that size constancy can be attained by combining retinal-image size information with distance information to yield a true size for any object. Something like this must indeed go on. However, it has also been assumed that at an early stage of development the infant might be *aware* of retinal image size, distance, and then true size and that it is only with practice that the infant can go directly to true size without the other variables entering consciousness. This does not seem to be the case. Infants are apparently quite unaware of retinal image variables and, indeed, of distance variables in situations where they show an ability to appreciate "true" size. In an experiment on shape constancy (a special form of size constancy), it was found that infants could identify a shape even after it had been rotated into the third dimension, altering its projected retinal image as well as its orientation (the relative distance of its edges). (See Figure 5.25.) Despite being quite able to identify true shape, the infants were unable to discriminate or identify on the basis of retinal image shape or orientation alone. The infants were quite unable to respond differentially to a square in its fronto-parallel plane and to a square that had been rotated 45° away from the fronto-parallel plane. These two presentations were very different in retinal image shape and orientation. The only thing they had in common was their true shape, and the infants' responses to the shape were so forceful that the other variables were simply ignored.

A

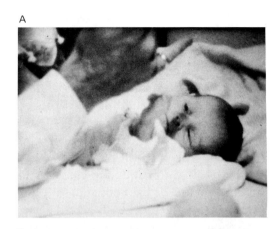

B

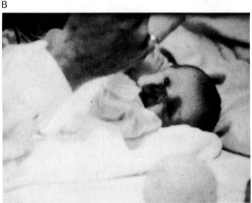

C

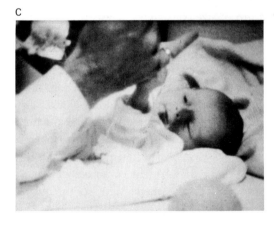

FIGURE 5.24
Hand regard in a 12-day-old
infant. This neonate, when
given a finger to reach for,
looks at her hand when it
comes into the visual field (A).
She looks at the finger as she
raises her hand to it (B), but
the reach stops as she catches
sight of her own hand again
(C). (From Bower, 1972).

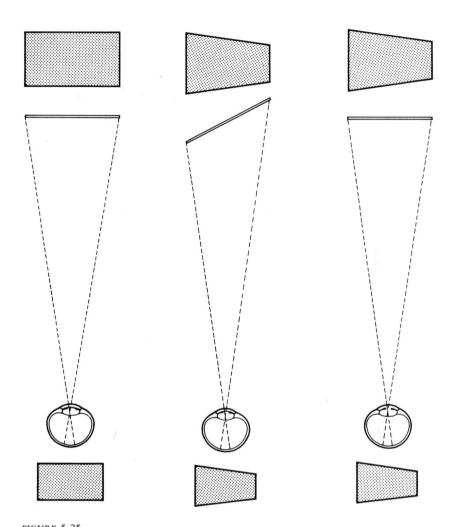

FIGURE 5.25
Shape constancy is illustrated by shapes in different orientations. A rectangle
presented in the parallel plane (*left*) projects a rectangular image on the retina
(*bottom*) and is seen as a rectangle. Presented at a slant, it projects a
trapezoidal image (*center*), yet is usually seen as a rectangle. A trapezoid in the
parallel plane projects the same shape (*right*). (From T. G. R. Bower, "The
Visual World of Infants." Copyright © 1966 by Scientific American, Inc.
All rights reserved.)

A study by Henderson (1969) attempted to discover at what age the discrimination between the same shape in two orientations becomes possible. She found that it was not until the age of at least two years that the discrimination could be made, and not until seven years of age that children could see that two objects of different shape in the same orientation had anything in common. A variety of studies seem to indicate that it is not until adulthood that one is able to identify objects of the same retinal image shape but different true shapes; even with practice, this ability is rarely perfected (Piaget, 1961; Rock and McDermott, 1964). It thus seems that utilization of information is not the same as awareness. Infants and children must be able to utilize orientation information and retinal shape information to identify true shape. However, they seem quite unaware of this information—so unaware that they cannot use it in its own right, unconverted to true shape information.

Inability to handle all of the information presented in an array is a characteristic of young infants. It has been found, for example, that young infants around six weeks of age are as likely to smile at two dots as at a real face with two eyes, implying that all of the other information in a real face is not registered by the baby (Ahrens, 1954). Gradually over the next three months, the overall contour of a face, the presence of a mouth, eyebrows, and so forth becomes important. However, up to the age of three months and even beyond that age, a single feature such as eyes or face contour can be just as effective as the whole face; it is not until five or six months of age that a whole face is essential for smiling. At that age a mutilated face elicits withdrawal, showing that the whole of the information in a face is being picked up and absent features are being detected (Ahrens, 1954).

It might be thought that the human face, a particularly significant stimulus for infants, is a peculiar case. However, Bower (1966b) found similar results with an abstract display, as shown in Figure 5.26. Infants who were trained to respond to the whole pattern would respond to any of its components presented in isolation. They would respond to *any* of the components in isolation, showing that they had detected that component. However, the fact that the components were aggregated in the CS (conditioned stimulus) was not detected until the age of 16 weeks; not until that age or later did the whole pattern become essential for response.

These results suggest that young infants simply cannot take in at one moment all of the information they can take in over time. If given a com-

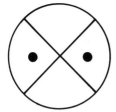

Abstract display used as CS

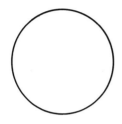

Test stimuli
(Each is a component of the original CS.)

FIGURE 5.26
Stimuli used in Bower's 1966 experiment (see text).

plex object to look at, they are likely to be aware of only one of the dimensions that distinguish the object. Salapatek (1966) has found that infants under ten weeks of age will attend to the external detail of a pattern and will not look at internal detail; as long as the internal detail remains internal, it is functionally invisible. Bower and Dunkeld (1973) suggested that results like these show that infants have a low rate of information handling. Infants can attend to only one feature of an object at a time, and the time spent on that feature may be very lengthy in comparison to that spent by older infants and children.

There are other indications that the rate of information handling is low in infants. Response to moving displays drops off very rapidly as the speed of movement increases, indicating that the change stimulation is coming in too rapidly to be processed. The same limitation might account for the apparent inability of infants to use the information in pictures. Hershenson (1965) and Lewis (1965) found that infants could barely discriminate between quite different pictures. More recently, Dunkeld (1972) in an unpublished study has found that infants are quite unable to use the information in a picture to make a discrimination between two objects. If shown a picture of two cups, one slightly tilted to reveal a piece of candy underneath it, and then shown the actual two cups, the infants are unable to get above chance in obtaining the candy. The information in the picture is simply not usable by infants. It could be that response to a picture as an object precludes response to the objects in a picture; this kind of double awareness must require more information handling than does a single response to the picture as object.

How could information-handling capacity increase in development? One possibility is that physical growth of the brain and its circuits could allow for more information to be processed simultaneously. The alternative, of course, is that experience plays a role in the development. Lee and Bower (1969) were able to find evidence in favor of both hypotheses. They studied the ability of infants to detect changes in arrays which were made up of a large number (over 200) of randomly placed dots. The infants were shown a first array for varying periods of time and then shown a second array identical to the first, except that 40 of the dots in the shape of a rectangle had been displaced from one side of the array to the other. The place where these displaced dots had been was filled with a new set of randomly arranged dots; the dots which had originally been on the other side of the array were deleted (See Figure 5.27).

The response indicator used was an eye movement in the direction of displacement. If the infants' eyes moved to follow the rectangle, it was argued that the infants must have detected the position of all of the dots that made up the rectangle. The variable in the experiment was the exposure time of the first array. The longer it is exposed, the more time there is to detect the dots. The longer the time taken to register the details, the longer it should take to detect the dots. Figure 5.28 shows the minimum time necessary to elicit eye movements from infants of various ages and from adults in this experiment. The infants develop very rapidly to

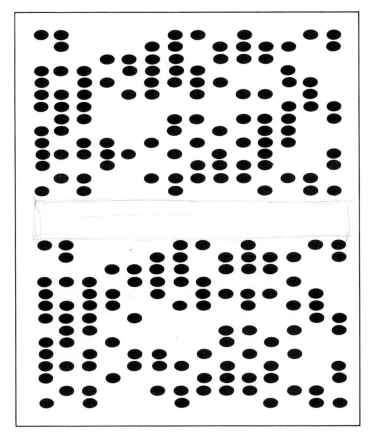

FIGURE 5.27
In the center of these arrays, there is a rectangular array of dots. In the static view of a single array, the rectangular part is invisible. However, when it is displaced, it can be detected by adults and infants. This implies that some memory trace of the position of all the dots in an array is retained and used as a basis for comparison when the next array appears.

a level that does not differ greatly from adults. A group of two-month premature infants (see Chapter 6) were also run on this experiment. At the age of five months, these infants were like normal three-month-old infants, which indicates that extra experience gives no advantage. In a simpler experiment where proximity and good continuation (Figure 5.29)

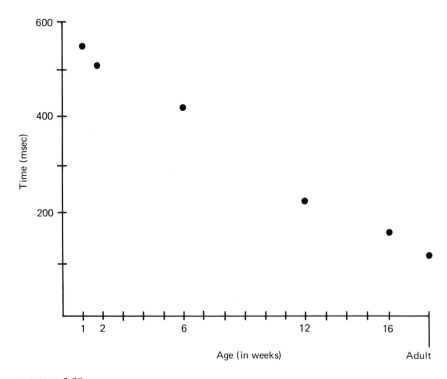

FIGURE 5.28
Minimum exposure time required for a change of position of the components of a pattern to be detected at various ages.

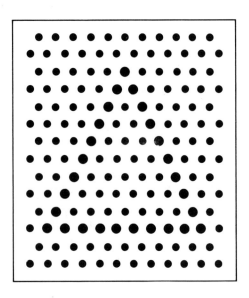

FIGURE 5.29
The triangle that can be detected here was displaced, adding motion to the other variables that define it. Proximity and good continuation were also operating since the displaced dots were larger and closer together than the surrounding dots.

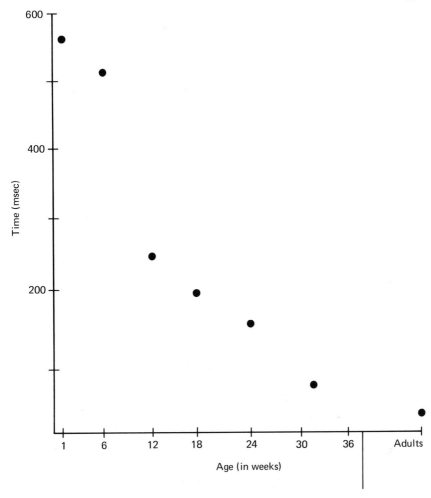

FIGURE 5.30
Minimum exposure time necessary to detect change of position of triangle shown in Figure 5.29 and similar figures.

were added to the initial array to help define the displaced figure, premature infants did as well at a chronological age of six months as did full-term infants of the same age; both did not do nearly as well as adults, however (Figure 5.30). It thus seems that selective attention, where selection is possible, can be trained and improved, regardless of maturational stage.

There have been no specific studies on how best to improve the selective attention of infants. Most likely, a common-sensical addition such as diversity of objects would allow the infant to devote his limited information-handling capacity to the most informative aspects of the environment. This kind of optimal environment would be a fascinating area for research and probably highly rewarding in practical terms. From what we have seen in this chapter, it would seem that in the area of selective attention—minimizing of attention to irrelevant features of objects—are the greatest opportunities for improving perception.*

---

*This is an enormously busy area of research in itself. At this time there is little basic agreement on the stimulus variables that control attention. Indeed, whether attention is in fact controlled by stimulus variables at all is questioned by some: certainly there is no agreed metric for such studies. The best type of response measure to use is also a matter of some controversy. For these reasons, it is very difficult to obtain any comprehensive picture of the pattern of development from the studies that have been done (Gibson, 1969).

The Development of Motor Behavior

Motor behavior presents a much more satisfactory area of study than perception. In the study of perception, one is always forced to make inferences from indicator behaviors. In studying motor behavior, the subject of study is at least clearly visible, even though the mechanisms controlling it are not. Perhaps because of this, there have been many studies of the development of motor behaviors during infancy. Most texts include a schedule of development like that shown in Figure 6.1. Investigators have been concerned both with the details of development and with the general principles that a particular behavior can elucidate.

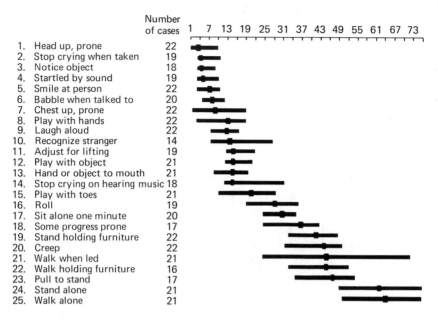

	Number of cases	1 7 13 19 25 31 37 43 49 55 61 67 73
1. Head up, prone	22	
2. Stop crying when taken	19	
3. Notice object	18	
4. Startled by sound	19	
5. Smile at person	22	
6. Babble when talked to	20	
7. Chest up, prone	22	
8. Play with hands	22	
9. Laugh aloud	22	
10. Recognize stranger	14	
11. Adjust for lifting	19	
12. Play with object	21	
13. Hand or object to mouth	21	
14. Stop crying on hearing music	18	
15. Play with toes	21	
16. Roll	19	
17. Sit alone one minute	20	
18. Some progress prone	17	
19. Stand holding furniture	22	
20. Creep	22	
21. Walk when led	21	
22. Walk holding furniture	16	
23. Pull to stand	17	
24. Stand alone	21	
25. Walk alone	21	

FIGURE 6.1

A schedule of motor development. (From M. M. Shirley, *The First Two Years, Vol. 1: Postural and Locomotor Developments.* University of Minnesota Press, © 1931, 1959 University of Minnesota.)

Studies of motor behaviors have contributed much to our understanding of the process of maturation, the role of learning in constructing behavior, and the nature of nonspecific environmental effects in the growth of specific motor skills.

Despite the general importance of learning theory in psychology, there have been few attempts to account for motor development in terms of learning theory. This must be partially due to the fact that whereas learning theories can account for changes in the frequency of a behavior or for establishment of a sequence of behaviors, learning theory has nothing to say about the genesis of *new* behaviors. The behaviors that appear in development are or seem to be new behaviors, so that learning theory is not really applicable.

A number of ingenious studies have been carried out to support the general hypothesis that motor behavior develops as a result of maturational processes—simple growth of nerve circuits, apparently unfolding inevitably, and requiring no specific intervention. One of the simplest ways of testing this hypothesis is to compare the behavior of premature infants with that of full-term or post-term babies. The normal infant is born forty weeks after conception; thus when his chronological age is zero, his conceptual age is forty weeks. Premature infants may survive when born at a conceptual age of twenty-eight weeks. Thus when a premature infant has a chronological age of zero, his conceptual age may be only twenty-eight weeks. At the other extreme, some infants remain in the womb as long as four weeks past term; thus when a post-term infant has a chronological age of zero, his conceptual age may be forty-four weeks. Now, if behavior development is determined entirely by experience outside the womb, then chronological age should be our best predictor of the onset of any particular behavior. Further, we should find no differences between premature, term, and post-term infants of the same chronological age. On the other hand, if behavior simply "grows" from conception onward and is unaffected by events in the environment, then conceptual age should be our best predictor of the onset of a particular behavior, and we should find no differences between premature, term, and post-term babies of the same conceptual age. The logic of such studies is very clear. It allows us to decide between two extreme theories of the development of motor behavior.

Smiling is one behavior that has been studied in this way. Normal infants will smile in response to a visual stimulus such as that described in Chapter 5 at a chronological age of 6 weeks, at which time their conceptual age is 46 weeks. The question is: will premature and post-term babies also smile at a chronological age of 6 weeks, or will their response begin at a conceptual age of 46 weeks, regardless of chronological age. The results for smiling are quite unambiguous. Infants smile at a conceptual age of 46 weeks, regardless of their chronological age. The extra time outside the womb does not accelerate the development of the premature infants, nor does the extra time inside the womb retard development of post-term infants. Is it therefore fair to conclude that smiling is primarily determined by processes of maturation? The answer must be a negative. The study shows that the environmental differences of premature, term, and post-term infants do not affect the conceptual age at which smiling begins. It is possible that stimulation from the environment is critical; but, if so, it is only effective after a conceptual age of 44 weeks has been reached. Thus the study could indicate that a given level of maturation is required before environmental events could have any effect. Further research is needed to show that no environmental event is critical for the development of the behavior, however.

Investigators have also used intercultural differences in rearing patterns to assess the effects of environment on behavior development. Different cultures treat infants in different ways. If these differences produce no differences in the onset of behavior, it is argued that the behavior is the result of maturation rather than the result of environmentally induced processes. A classic example of this kind of study is Dennis's (1940) investigation of the development of walking in the Hopi Indian culture. Some groups of traditionally minded Hopi Indians still bind their infants to cradle boards during the early months of life (Figure 6.2). An infant tied to a cradle board cannot raise his body, roll over, or move his hands. Infants on the cradle board are unwrapped only once or twice a day to have their clothes changed. Even feeding and nursing is carried out on the cradle board. These traditionally reared infants were compared with other Hopi infants whose parents, affected by European practices, did not restrict their infants at all. The results, perhaps surprisingly, indicated no difference at all between the two groups of infants. Both groups walked unaided around the age of 15 months. The seemingly severe restrictions on the traditionally reared infants did not slow down their development in comparison to the unrestricted infants. This finding would therefore tend to support the argument for the primacy of maturation over experience in producing behavior.

One argument that could be made against experiments like these is that, even though the numbers of infants in the experiments were quite large, there was still no control over the individual rates of maturation. The age of onset of any behavior is variable in any population of infants. Some children simply develop faster than others. Whenever we compare two groups of infants, it is possible that one group of infants contains a greater number of fast developers than does the other group. There are various ways of controlling against this—the simplest being the use of large numbers of infants. The most satisfactory guard is to use matched pairs of genetically identical infants, so that the genetically determined rate of development will be the same. Identical twins satisfy this requirement, since it is argued that differences between identical twins can only result from environmental differences. Similarly, if different environments fail to produce differences in behavior between identical twins, then the behavior in question must be genetically or maturationally determined.

Quite a number of studies have been carried out on this somewhat suspect logical base. One of the most interesting, certainly from a practical point of view, is McGraw's (1940) study of toilet training. McGraw

FIGURE 6.2
An infant secured to a cradle board.

introduced one twin to toilet training at a rather young age. When the behavior had reached a very high level of success, the other twin was introduced to toilet training. The level of success of the previously untrained twin was no different from that of the trained twin (Figure 6.3). In other words, 23 months of toilet training had produced no higher level of proficiency than did no training at all—a fascinating result which is completely contrary to the folklore on the subject.

Gesell and Thompson (1929) found similar results in their study of the development of two motor skills in a pair of identical twins. One of the skills studied was stair climbing. The trained twin (T) was introduced

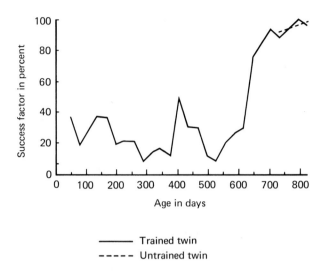

FIGURE 6.3
Success rates of response to toilet training in a trained and untrained twin. (From M. B. McGraw, "Neural maturation as exemplified in achievement of bladder control," *J. of Paediatrics*, 16:580–590, 1940.)

to stair climbing at the age of 46 weeks and was given daily practice in climbing until the age of 52 weeks; at this time she had been climbing the stairs alone for 2 weeks and could get from bottom to top in 26 seconds. The other twin, the control (C), was introduced to climbing at 53 weeks of age. At this point, without practice, she could climb the stairs alone in 46 seconds. After only two weeks of practice, the control twin could climb the stairs in 10 seconds. In other words, the study showed that climbing ability developed without benefit of practice and that speed of climbing was only minimally affected by practice. The same twins were used in a subsequent study of cube stacking. After 6 weeks of training, T did no better in terms of speed or numbers stacked than did C who had no practice whatsoever. The training experience produced no acceleration of development at all. The conclusion of both studies is that maturation is what produces development of new behaviors; practice at best merely serves to produce a fine tuning of behaviors already established by maturation; at worst practice has no effect at all.

Any straightforward interpretation of these studies leads to problems. None of the studies mentioned thus far has provided precise definitions of the behavior, its antecedents, the practice, or the environment. The studies show that certain selective manipulations of a baby's environment do not accelerate or retard the appearance of certain behaviors in some form. There are no criteria as yet for assuming that the manipulations involved are likely to be relevant to the behavior under study. When twin T in Gesell's study was undergoing practice in stair climbing, she was simply moved up and down the stairs for the first four weeks: she was quite passive, and her limbs were moved for her. The question is: why on earth should we assume that passive limb movements are in any sense an antecedent to active stair climbing? In fact, this seems to be rather unlikely. It seems much more likely that active crawling on a flat floor would be the antecedent of stair climbing behavior, but crawling of that sort was not observed or controlled in Gesell's study. The point is that we do not know whether or not crawling on a flat surface is the true antecedent of climbing; and, unless we do know, we are in no position to talk about the effects of special experience on the development of climbing. If the special experience is not applied to the relevant behavior, then it is hardly surprising that it produces no effects.

The problem of defining the antecedents of a behavior is a considerable one. Indeed, the magnitude of the problem sets behavioral embryology apart from any other branch of embryology. In embryology one can stain a cell in such a way that all of the descendants of the cell show traces of the stain. It is thus relatively easy to identify the antecedents of any organ as far back as one wishes. In the case of a mosaic egg, one can destroy a cell or set of cells; the normal descendants of the destroyed cell will be missing in the experimental animal, again allowing one to infer the antecedents of the structures in question (Figure 6.4). Obviously, one cannot stain behaviors, nor can one destroy them. This makes it difficult to say with certainty that any particular behavior is the ancestor or antecedent of any subsequent behavior. If a behavior appears de novo in fully fledged fashion, it is difficult to argue that it was formed by any other process than the maturation of independent circuits within the brain. However, even when a late appearing behavior is very much like an earlier behavior, one cannot say for sure that the earlier behavior is the causal ancestor of the later one. Temporal succession simply does not imply a causal relation.

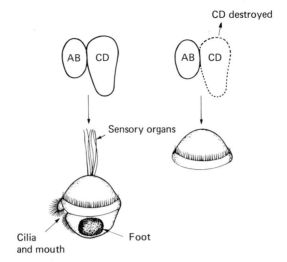

CD destroyed

Sensory organs

Cilia
and mouth

Foot

FIGURE 6.4
In studying structural development, it is possible
to trace the ancestry of body parts by destroying
cells at an early stage of development and
then observing what part of the developed
organism is missing. A normal *trochophore larva*
is shown on the left above. If the CD cell is
destroyed at the two-cell stage, one obtains
the part organism shown on the right, indicating
that all of the missing parts develop from the
destroyed CD cell, and all of the existing parts
develop from the AB cell.

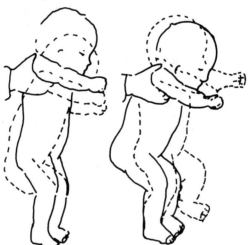

FIGURE 6.5
Neonate walking. (From M. B. McGraw, *The
Neuromuscular Maturation of the Human Infant.*
Columbia University Press, 1943).

The development of walking exemplifies one such problem. Newborn infants will "walk" after a fashion if supported (Figure 6.5). This behavior normally disappears, and true walking begins many months later. Is the early walking an ancestor of later walking? The two behaviors are separated by many months; yet they are commonly referred to as primary walking and secondary walking. It is argued that primary walking disappears because of an active inhibition that is necessary for secondary walking to appear. Such theorizing is purely speculative, however, since it is quite possible that the two behaviors are independent of one another. We could ask what evidence would convince us that the two behaviors are connected? If the earlier behavior is an ancestor of the later behavior, surely environmental modifications that affect the first would also affect the later behavior; this could be compared to introducing a stain into a primordial cell which can later be discovered in its descendants. An experiment of this sort was done by André-Thomas and St. A. Dargassies (1952). They exercised the primary walking of a group of infants on a daily basis, rather than ignoring the behavior as is commonly done.* When it came to secondary walking, this group of infants was greatly accelerated. Since the early training produced effects on the later behavior, the study demonstrated that primary walking is indeed the ancestor of secondary walking. If the early training had produced no effects, we would have been forced to conclude that the two behaviors were unrelated. If one accepts this criterion for the connection between earlier and later behaviors, then one must assume that studies where early practice has no effect on later behavior are in fact showing that the practiced behavior is unrelated to the criterion behavior—a conclusion quite different from the desired one.

If there are severe problems in connecting an early behavior with a later behavior, then there are far more difficult problems involved in establishing the relation between an environmental event and some subsequent behavior. The studies cited thus far have all tried to prove that *no* environmental event is involved in the development of a particular behavior. But it would seem to me that this kind of experimental conclusion simply cannot be sustained—except under severely abnormal conditions. Just how abnormal these conditions must be is shown by one study which can claim to show some development as the result of pure maturation with no possibility of the influence of environmental events.

---

*The duration of primary walking was much longer in these infants than in normal infants, which rules out the inhibition hypothesis mentioned above.

Wolff (1969) studied an infant with congenital arrhinencephaly (failure of separation of the hemispheres of the brain) along with other neural disorders. A consequence of this condition was that the infant experienced continuous random seizures—a condition which prevents the registration of external events in human adults. If this infant was similarly disturbed by the seizures then she too would have had no awareness or registration of the events in her environment. Despite this, some development did occur. The infant developed the ability to raise her head in a prone position, to support herself on her elbows, and to make coordinated "creep" movements. This is no great catalog of development, and yet it apparently occurred with no external support at all.

Studies of infants with less severe sensory handicaps have provided models for the ways in which environmental events seem to interact with maturational processes in generating behavior. The study of vocal behavior in deaf infants is a case in point. Normal infants begin to babble around the age of five months. This initial phase of babbling continues for about one month, with the infants producing a wide variety of sounds. Indeed, some have claimed that infants produce all possible sounds of all possible human languages. Deaf infants also go through this babbling phase, even though they have never heard a spoken word. They continue babbling as long as normal infants do, despite the fact they cannot hear themselves babble. This evidence would seem to show conclusively that audition is not necessary for the establishment of this phase of babbling and that auditory feedback is not necessary for its maintenance. After the first phase of babbling is over toward the end of the first year, normal infants begin to change their babbling; this babbling turns gradually into the spoken language of the child's environment. This second phase does not occur in deaf infants. It would seem then that the second phase of babbling which leads on to proper speech does require auditory input for its initiation and maintenance. Evidence also shows that maintaining speech depends on auditory input for some time after this; the utterances of children who are deafened during childhood regress in extreme cases to the level of congenitally deaf children. The later the deafening occurs, the less likely this is, however. Eventually, around the age of six or so, deafening has no effect on the vocal behavior of children. At this point, the behavior has become independent of auditory support. Further evidence is provided by studies on the speech of children who are born deaf and provided with hearing aids at some point during development. The earlier this is done, the more rapid is the acquisition of language. If it is postponed long enough, language may never be acquired (Lenneberg, 1967).

Data like these force one to reconsider the relationship between environmental events and development. Learning-theory approaches argue that development will not occur without specific environmental intervention; if the specific environmental event does not occur, development does not occur, and *neither does anything else*. The organism simply stays stationary until the event comes along. The maturational theorists—Gesell, McGraw, and Dennis—argue that development proceeds successfully in the absence of any particular environmental event. They emphasize the attainment of successful behavior through maturational processes. We must agree that the learning theorists are wrong in asserting that behavior will remain stationary in the absence of environmental stimulation. Behavior, as we have seen, will change regardless; but the change need not be successful. In the absence of relevant input from the environment, behavior may take a completely aberrant direction, and that direction may become so firmly established that no environmental intervention will suffice to redirect the behavior back to its proper course.

Waddington (1957) has proposed a model of development that encompasses the features of interaction between the organism and environment which have so far been mentioned. Suppose we imagine a landscape like that shown in Figure 6.6. The ball rolling down the valley on the right represents the path of development of vocal behavior. The hillock to be seen there represents the environmental intervention—the effect of hearing spoken language. It serves to tip the path of development down the route leading to language. If the hillock were not present, the ball would continue down the path leading to nonlinguistic vocal behavior. The later the hillock is introduced, the more difficult it must be to redirect development. The path of normal development is at a higher level than the other path, so that if linguistic support is removed, the ball will roll back to the nonlinguistic behavioral path, at least initially. This *epigenetic landscape* is a convenient model for many aspects of development, particularly organogenesis. It serves to describe some aspects of behavioral development as well, as we have seen. It must be emphasized that the epigenetic landscape is primarily a *model* of development. It is not intended to serve as a theory which makes predictions; it is rather an after-the-fact, descriptive model.

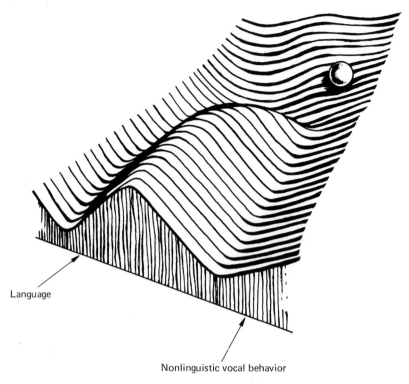

Language

Nonlinguistic vocal behavior

FIGURE 6.6
Part of an epigenetic landscape. (After Waddington, *The Strategy of Genes.*
George Allen & Unwin Ltd., 1957.)

Piaget (1954) has presented an account of the development of some motor behaviors which is primarily descriptive but still does justice to the complexities of behavior development, while introducing concepts that could be predictive. In Piaget's model, the initial creation of behaviors is still accomplished through maturational processes. What happens thereafter is determined by interaction with the environment; the interaction itself is determined by two fundamental processes—assimilation and accommodation. *Assimilation* is the process that determines the range of things or events to which the behavior will be applied. In more conventional terminology, we might say that an object elicits a behavior; a seen object might elicit reaching. In Piaget's terminology, the seen object is assimilated to the behavior of reaching. Piaget argues that, if a behavior is given nothing to assimilate, it will simply die away. As we have seen, language development fits such a description. *Accommodation* is the process whereby behavior is adjusted to the requirements of the object or event assimilated to it. In the case of reaching and grasping, the behavior must be adjusted to the size, weight, and shape of the object grasped. In Piaget's theory, development is accomplished by the interaction of assimilation and accommodation which continues until a state of equilibrium is reached. The processes leading up to equilibrium are called *equilibration*. Equilibrium is reached when a behavior assimilates only those objects to which it can accommodate. In the case of reaching and grasping, the infant will only attempt to grasp those objects whose size and weight are within his capacities when equilibration is over. Larger or heavier objects are excluded, as are objects that are too fragile or insubstantial.

In the last chapter, we talked about hand adjustments made prior to contacting objects. These are examples of the processes Piaget is talking about. Infants will only reach for objects which they can grasp. That is, assimilation is restricted to objects that are within the range of accommodation. The hand adjustments—accommodation—are anticipatory, and they result in successful assimilation. Assimilation and accommodation are thus in equilibrium.

Indeed, there are some subtleties in this statement of equilibrium and equilibration. A behavior is only in equilibrium if the infant can anticipate its consequences. In order to inhibit grasping, for example, the infant must know that an object is too heavy *before* he tries to grasp it; he must know how heavy an object is *before* he can grasp it without dropping or crushing it. Thus equilibrium requires anticipation; in addition, since the theory provides no mechanism for the establishment of the anticipation of consequences, some anticipation must be built in and must develop along with the behavior. Perhaps this characteristic more than any other sets Piaget's theory apart from the other theories into which it could be translated.

One other feature of the equilibration model of development must be mentioned. Equilibration may terminate when equilibrium is reached with a specific set of environmental inputs; it may then start anew when the set is enlarged to include new objects or events. In the case of reaching and grasping, one can imagine an infant in perfect equilibrium with a single object. As long as that one object is presented, behavior will remain equilibrated, and *there will be no further development of that behavior*. When a new object is presented (an object beyond the accommodatory range of the behavior), the behavior will assimilate it, compelling a new process of equilibration, and with it, development. Eventually such specific adjustments must cease, and accommodation must become predictive over the entire range of assimilation, including all objects that could be met as well as those that already have been met. In other words, a very special kind of *generalization* is required. In behavior theory, generalization refers to the process whereby different objects come to elicit the same response. What is required for equilibration is a process whereby objects that differ along some particular dimension will elicit appropriate, differentially graded responses. Thus, in grasping, the heavier an object is, the greater is the force that must be applied to grasp it securely.

Piaget would insist that these rules exist in some form within the nervous system of the child, interposed between perceptual input and the responses to it. Although these rules are formed in the course of equilibration, Piaget (1967) has argued very forcefully that all behaviors, from the very beginning, occur under the control of rules, however crude or general they may be. For Piaget, behavior is never the result of simple stimuli eliciting simple reponses in a one to one fashion; behavior is always a matter of the assimilation of objects, graded in some fashion, to a class of behaviors, graded appropriately, through a mediating rule that links input to output.

Piaget is relatively open on the precise processes that go on during equilibration. One problem that he preserves his options on is whether development is best described as a process of *differentiation* or *integration*, or whether both terms are required. Some theorists (Gesell and Amatruda, 1941) have argued that development is differentiation; in development, behavior becomes more selective and more precise, and its components became segregated from one another. An example of the studies supporting this view is shown in Figure 6.7. Other researchers have argued that behavior begins as a set of segmental reponses and that these are organized together during development. Although Piaget's theory tends to reflect the differentiation view, he has not committed himself on this point. He appears to argue that both processes may be necessary at some stages in development.

Reaching and grasping is a convenient behavior for the analysis of these various models. It is a behavior of tremendous importance in human life. Our whole tool-using society depends on the refined manual skills

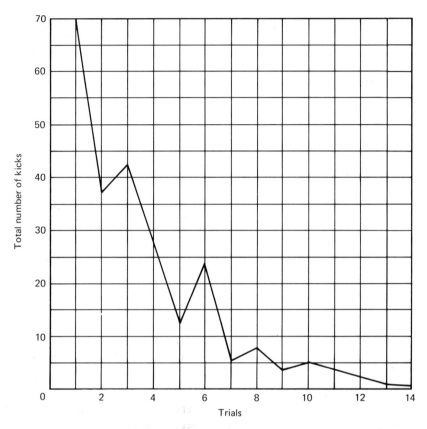

FIGURE 6.7
Differentiation as illustrated in the development of grasping. The curve shows the decrease in diffuse (kicking) activity involved in attempts to grasp a rattle held before the baby. (From M. W. Curti, 1930.)

which man shares with no other primate. This superior skill is largely due to man's superior skeletal equipment (Figure 6.8). The question is: does the ability to use this superior skeletal equipment grow with it, or is interaction with the environment necessary for the formation of the skills that capitalize on this endowment?

Like walking, reaching begins well before birth. All of the components for reaching and grasping can be elicited in fetuses at a conceptual age of

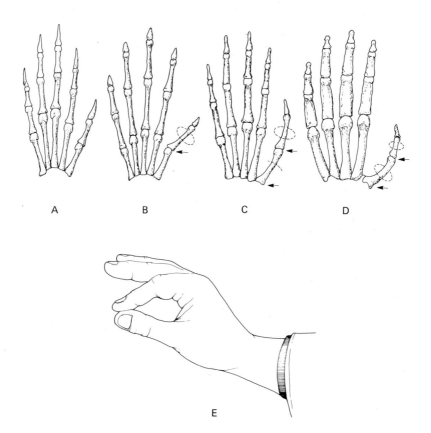

FIGURE 6.8
The superior skeletal equipment of man allows perfect opposability of the thumb. While convergent fingers and an opposable thumb are present in many primates (A–D), only man (E) has perfected thumb and index finger opposition.

14 to 16 weeks. As mentioned previously, visually initiated reaching can be elicited in newborn human infants. In the average infant, this precocious behavior vanishes, and reaching reappears somewhere between 4 and 5 months of age. Humphrey (1969) has argued that this, as in walking, is the takeover of reaching by cortical centers; the inhibitory connections grow in first, so that the behavior *necessarily* disappears during the period when inhibitory connections are the only ones that have been formed. The behavior will reappear as soon as excitatory connections are formed. Humphrey is quite explicit in pointing out that it is the same behaviors that reappear. The corticalization enhances coordination between behaviors, but the behaviors remain the same. Humphrey is quite em-

phatic that the observed sequences are caused by maturation, by the growth of circuits within the nervous system.

White (White, 1963; White, Castle, and Held, 1964; White and Held, 1966) has reported research which shares some affinities with Humphrey's interpretations, even though the work seems diametrically opposed. White has emphasized the role of environmental factors in the development of reaching. He sees environmental influences as coordinating forces, generating integration between disparate behaviors. White's model is explicitly Piagetian, although it is also different from Piaget's. White sees mature reaching and grasping as the result of the integration of diverse sets of initial coordinations, including touch-grasp, eye-object, eye-hand, and eye-arm.

According to White, the development of reaching takes the following path. In the beginning, infants have a primitive visual-attentional behavior, that involves them in looking at and following seen objects. This behavior is limited in range initially. Infants also have a touch-grasp behavior that leads them to grasp objects which touch their hands. In White's view, these behaviors are initially isolated from one another. However, as visual attention improves and as the baby latches on to moving objects or attends to nearer or farther objects, the infant catches sight of his hand—an interesting object in its own right. This generates a new behavior—eye-hand coordination—which is evidenced by the fact that infants spend a good deal of their time looking at their hands. Soon after this occurs, the hand is brought to an object in a fast swipe, with no opening of the hand prior to contact. The next step in the development occurs when the infant looks back and forth from an object to his hand, while holding his hand in the visual field. At this point, according to White, the infant is putting together his eye-hand and eye-object behaviors.

Another behavior that emerges at this point is mutual hand clasping with visual attention to the hands. This results in awareness that the seen hand is also the grasping hand. After this point, the various behaviors become coordinated, and one can see the hand go out and grasp an object. With practice, this crude grasp becomes what White calls a top-level reach; it is anticipatory, with the hand opening before contacting the object and with initiation of the act from outside the visual field.

White's model of development represents a considerable advance over Humphrey's model in that clear patterns of behavior are supposed to change and to coordinate with one another to yield new behaviors. Humphrey and other maturationists have left reaching a relatively unanalyzed behavior. Clearly, White has an environmentalist position. His theory postulates several essential environmental occurrences in the development of visually guided reaching.

First, the infant must catch sight of his hand. The sight of the hand then generates eye-hand coordination, without which no further development would be possible. It follows that any procedure which speeds eye-hand coordination should also speed the development of mature reaching. Anything that retards it should necessarily retard the development of mature reaching. After eye-hand coordination is attained, the infant must still integrate arm movements with his hand movements. White argues that, when targets for swiping are touched, grasping is produced; in time, the object-eye-hand-touch-grasp sequence will be short-circuited to produce direct reaching with grasping anticipated. Thus, on White's model, once swiping is established, presenting further objects for the baby to swipe at should accelerate the development of mature reaching and grasping. However, as Piaget cogently points out, withdrawal of objects at this stage will not retard the development of reaching and grasping for long; as soon as the infant can bring both hands into the visual field, one hand may serve as a target for reaching and grasping by the other. One hand can serve as a surrogate object, ensuring that the mature behavior will not be indefinitely retarded in the absence of objects.

Nevertheless, if White is correct about the growth of mature reaching and grasping, the presentation of objects immediately after the establishment of swiping should accelerate the development of mature reaching and grasping—particularly in comparison with infants who must utilize their own hand as an object. White's theory therefore can be reduced to a sequence of behaviors that must be invariant, along with a list of environmental events that trigger the steps from one behavior to another. The hypothetical sequence is:

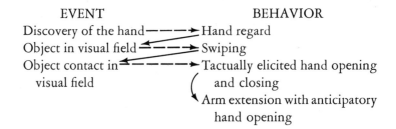

EVENT   BEHAVIOR
Discovery of the hand———► Hand regard
Object in visual field ◄———► Swiping
Object contact in ◄— — — ► Tactually elicited hand opening
    visual field   and closing
                  Arm extension with anticipatory
                  hand opening

White constructed his theory upon observations of development in 34 infants. The infants were in an institution which provided a somewhat odd environment. The infants lay in a supine position on mattresses which, hollowed out with use, served to restrict their movements. The visual surroundings were a homogeneous white, with few contours. The environment thus contained few of the features we would deem normal. To test his theory, White modified the environment of two other groups of infants. Two different modifications were introduced. One group—the massively enriched group—had a very elaborate multicolored stabile hung above their cots from age 37 days to 124 days. Multicolored sheets and cot sides were also substituted for the standard white ones. The intention was that these changes would heighten visual interest and increase viewing of hand movements, since infants tend to swipe at visible objects nearby. With the other group—the slightly enriched group—there was only one modification to the standard institutional situation from age 37 days to age 68 days. Two pacifiers which stood out visually against a red and white polka-dot disc were attached to the sides of the cot, in a position designed to elicit maximum attention, 6 to 7 inches away from the infants' eyes. At 68 days, until 124 days of age, this second group of infants was given the stabile used in the massively-enriched situation.

If White's theory is correct, what changes would one expect from these modifications? The first significant environmental effect is discovery of the hands. White has argued that the more things there are for the infant to look at, the less likely he is to notice his hands. We should thus expect hand regard to be delayed, and with it, swiping. However, once swiping begins, there will always be an object for the hand to contact which should nurture tactually elicited grasping; this would then speed the conversion to anticipatory grasping.

By trying to produce two effects working in opposite directions, White has elegantly solved the problem of how to ensure that an accelerated group of infants are not simply fast developers (see p. 138 above). If both effects occur in opposite directions, there could be no argument that White had simply hit on a group of faster developers. Unfortunately, though both effects did occur, they occurred in a way that destroyed the theory used to predict them. Hand regard was delayed in the massive enrichment group. In fact, it was delayed until after the onset of swiping; hand regard did not begin until the hand was seen in contact with an object. This clearly contradicts the theory, since it was claimed that hand regard is a necessary precursor of swiping. Similarly, top-level reaching with anticipatory grasping was accelerated in both groups. It was accelerated so much that it appeared *before* tactually elicited grasping. This also clearly contradicts the theory since it asserts that top-level reaching grows out of tactually elicited grasping. Thus, while White has clearly demonstrated environmental effects, his results also destroyed his theory of development.

How should one interpret these results? One argument is that White's control group did not show normal development, but rather the disintegration of a behavior given nothing to assimilate. In this view, the components which White thought led up to mature reaching and grasping would have appeared individually as the integrated behavior fell apart. Further, the group which was given objects to assimilate would not show the same disintegration. This is a plausible argument, since we know that matured behaviors will disintegrate through lack of use. (See p. 144 above.) However, this account does not explain the occurrence of behaviors (such as tactually elicited grasping) that did appear in *all* groups, albeit in no consistent order with anticipatory grasping. If the control group displayed this behavior as a result of the degeneration of anticipatory grasping, why then did the group with objects to assimilate and therefore no reason for degeneration show the same behavior? Certainly, no maturational theory could give a coherent account of why this occurred after the attainment of anticipatory grasping—supposedly the end point of development.

It is possible that the behaviors are quite unrelated. However, before multiplying the behaviors to be explained, it would be as well to re-examine the whole sequence of development. White began his study when his subjects were four weeks of age and ended it when they were about five months—at which point he assumed reaching had attained an adult form. There were two errors in this selection of a segment for study: the segment begins too late and ends too early.

As we have noted in earlier chapters, reaching can be elicited in the immediate postnatal period. Also the reaching of the average five-month-old has some way to go before it becomes the same as that of an adult. If one begins at the beginning of postnatal life, one can observe behavior that looks like reaching and grasping. Newborn humans will reach out and grasp objects under certain specific conditions. The infants must be wide awake if the behavior is to occur—a state not always easily obtained. They must also be in a specific posture that allows then free use of their

A

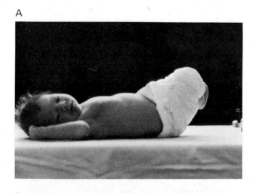

B

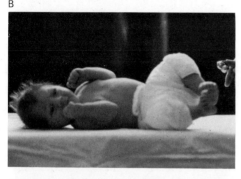

C

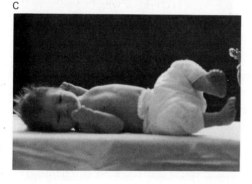

FIGURE 6.9
Neonate lying unsupported on tabletop. Note the support role of head and arms (A). If the baby moves his arms, he is unable to maintain posture (B), save by propping himself on his arm (C). This precludes any attempt to reach.

arms and free head movement. This too is a condition not always readily obtained. Newborn infants tend to use their head and arms as supports while lying or reclining (Figure 6.9). Obviously, if arms are being used as supports, they cannot move freely. Conditions where the head and arms are free to move occur naturally while the infant is being held or carried.

FIGURE 6.10
Infant carriers such as the one shown above allow the infant
free arm and head movement—this is essential if precocious
reaching is to occur.

Some infant carriers seem ideal for this purpose (Figure 6.10). In laboratory situations, a certain amount of propping is required to ensure free
movement. When these conditions are met, newborn infants will reach
out and grasp visually presented objects. Their reaching has a hit rate of
about 40 percent, more than half of their misses landing within a hands-
width of the target object. Reaching is primarily one handed (Figure 6.11).
Two-handed reaches are only observed when an object is in the midline
position. Some of the reaches clearly anticipate grasping. The hand opens
before contact and closes on contact, but too quickly for the contact to
have released the hand closure.

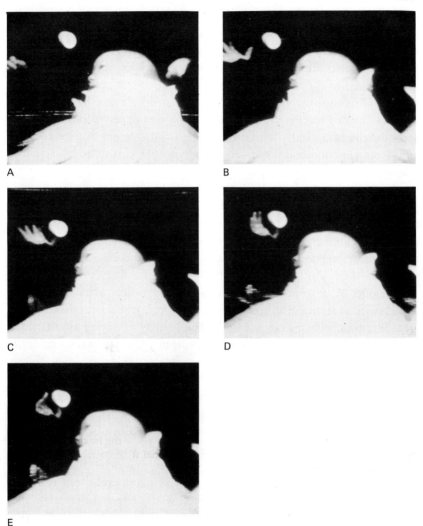

A

B

C

D

E

FIGURE 6.11
A neonate infant reaching. Note that the hand is closing before it gets to the object.

The infants do anticipate the tactile consequences of reaching since they seem to expect tactile input when their hand reaches the place where the object is seen to be. Virtual objects produce considerable upset, as we have previously discussed. Also, reaching at this stage is at least partly accommodated to the size and distance of objects.

In British and American babies studied cross-sectionally, reaching behavior is very hard to elicit after the age of 4 weeks. The behavior recurs around 20 weeks, at which time it is less posture specific and more accurate; hit rates of 80 percent are common. Reaching is still primarily one handed, although the proportion of two-handed reaches has increased, and two-handed reaches are made toward objects in any position. Again some reaches are clearly anticipatory, the hand opening before contact and closing as contact is made—too rapidly for the closure to be tactually released.

At 20 weeks, the behavior is still adjusted to the size of objects and still anticipates tactile consequences when the hand reaches object locations. In other words, there seems to be little to choose between the neonate reaching and 20-week-old reaching, save for changes in the quantitative parameters of the performance. There are three main quantitative changes.

For one, behavior can be elicited in a wider variety of postures. It is about twice as accurate, although still not perfect. It seems to show somewhat less anticipation as measured by hand behavior during approach to an object. This last measure is the most surprising. It can hardly reflect a loss of knowledge that seen objects are tangible, since the virtual object presentation still produces just as much, if not more, upset. Nonetheless on at least one measure of anticipation, anticipation declines. This particular measure involved timing the interval when the hand closed on an object after it had reached a position where it could do so. In practice, this measure is easily obtained, since the hand and arm are always stationary for some time at the end of a reach. One can thus determine when the hand as a whole stops moving. Taking that as a zero point, one can find when the fingers close down on the object. With perfect anticipation, the offset time should be zero. The hand should close just as it reaches the object, no earlier and no later. Figure 6.12 shows the distribution of offsets in neonates and 20-week-old infants. As can be seen there, offset increases steadily, until by 20 weeks of age, the reaching component and grasping component are temporally quite separate. The mean offset time in newborns is, in fact, zero. In 20-week-old infants, the mean offset time is greater than zero—about 450 msec. on average.

How is one to interpret these quantitative changes? At first sight, they would seem to support the sort of theory proposed by Humphrey. The behaviors seem identical, and the quantitative differences could be ac-

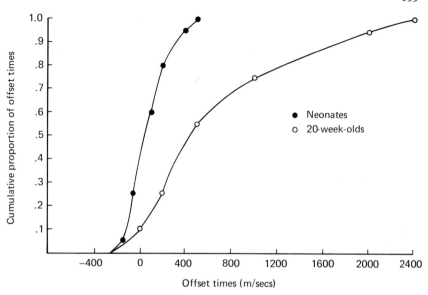

FIGURE 6.12
Distribution of offset times in neonates and 20-week-old infants. Note the increased offset time in the older group.

counted for by certain assumptions. It would be plausible to assume, for example, that cortical function is more precise than subcortical function and that, until growth is complete, we must expect some desynchronization. However, examination of the performance of older infants around 26 weeks of age suggests a completely different interpretation. These older infants, as noted in Chapter 5, are much less upset by the virtual object than are younger infants. Their reaching is 100 percent accurate, and two-handed reaches to all positions are common. Lastly, and most significant, in the virtual-object situation these infants do not grasp at all. Visual control of grasping has disappeared, and reaching can occur without grasping. In other words, it seems that the process of development—rather than coalescing reaching and grasping—has differentiated them, converting a single act (reach-to-grasp) into two acts (reach then grasp). (See also Bruner, 1973.)

Why this differentiation? This question can be answered in several different ways. First, we can look at what it implies for future development. Once the infant can reach and then grasp, it should be possible for him to grasp and then reach; since grasping followed by reaching is characteristic of tool use, the importance of this possibility cannot be overestimated. As long as reaching and grasping are coalesced into a single act, tool use is not possible.

Another obvious and important payoff of differentiation is that it permits more *successful* reaching and grasping. If the offset time is intended to be zero, the coordination of the reach and grasp components must be perfect; otherwise the fingers will close too soon, and the object will be lost. With a long offset time, this cannot happen. Reaching and grasping will thus become more successful.

If this is the case, does the dissociation alone produce the greater accuracy seen in older infants? Are they more accurate simply because they have grasping in a more functional relationship with reaching, or is something else involved? There is evidence that something else is involved. If one checks to see what happens when a newborn or a 20-week-old infant misses a target object, one observes retraction of the hand, often completely out of the visual field, followed by a second reach. In older infants, by contrast, the hand may start off on a miss path, but it is brought onto a hit path as soon as it enters the visual field. The hand is not withdrawn to begin again but rather alters its trajectory in flight. There is correction within the act, rather than correction between acts. This was clearly brought out in an experiment by Aronson and Dunkeld (1973), who presented infants with a situation that produced mislocalization of objects.

If a visual field contains one large object on one side, an object presented in the center of the field will be seen as displaced away from the large object (Figure 6.13). Adults are susceptible to this illusion. When asked to judge where the center of such a field is, they consistently mislocalize it. When asked to reach for an object in the center of such a field, however, adults are wholly successful. Infants below 20 weeks are wholly unsuccessful. They reach for the object where they erroneously see it to be. When they miss, they cannot correct their error and will sit with their hand extended in the wrong place (Figure 6.14). Older infants, by contrast, make the same mistake initially but correct it during the action (Figure 6.15).

Reaching thus develops from a unitary reach-grasp pattern that is visually initiated into two separate, recombinable acts—reaching and grasping—that are visually initiated and visually guided. How are we to

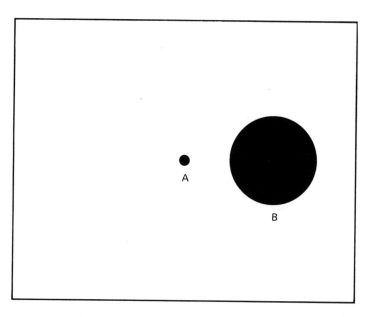

FIGURE 6.13
Position illusion. Although the small object is in the center of the field, it is perceived as being displaced to the left, because of the large object.

FIGURE 6.14
The infant, having mislocalized the object as a result of the illusion shown in Figure 6.13 makes no attempt to correct his error.

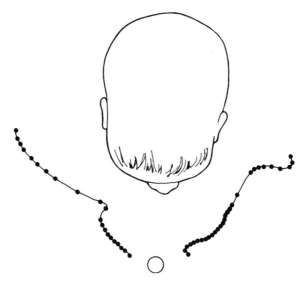

FIGURE 6.15
This tracing from a film record shows clearly that the infant is correcting his hand position as he attempts to grasp the object. Each dot represents the position of the hand at one instant in time.

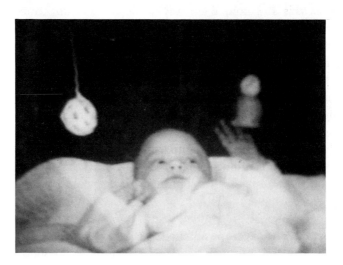

FIGURE 16.6
A nine-week-old infant reaching to touch an object without attempting to grasp it.

explain this pattern of development? Is this simply the result of neural growth, or are there critical environmental inputs that produce and channel the growth? One critical period for the neural growth theory is the "silent" period when no reaching occurs. Neural growth theory offers an account of this period in terms of the growth of inhibitory connections. A Piagetian position might argue that the silent period results from lack of use. This controversy is easily resolved. One simply gives newborn infants objects to reach for every day and observes what happens. This has been done in two studies (Bower, 1973), and the results were quite clear. Infants who had an object to reach for every day from birth demonstrated no decline in reaching at all. The decline in reaching that is normally observed must therefore result from lack of use of the behavior, rather than from inevitable neural growth processes.

How then does the behavior change as described above? If one observes infants longitudinally, one can observe the behavior changing. Reaching without grasping becomes more common. The infants begin to touch objects without grasping them (Figure 6.16). This process is accelerated, if the infants are given an object that is not rigidly fastened down. It is difficult for the infant to grasp such an object with his unitary reach-grasp action. Apparently, the grasp component, which is rarely successful in this situation, dies away while the reaching component, which produces interesting object movement at least, predominates. Infants given rigidly tethered objects to reach for do not show the dissociation so early (Figure 6.17). Meantime, of course, both groups are engaging in tactually elicited grasping—at their clothes, their cribs, their mothers, or anything that touches their hands.

During this period, visually initiated reaching is reinforced; visually initiated grasping is not always reinforced, but tactually initiated grasping is. On any simple learning-theory model, we would thus expect visually initiated reaching to continue, whereas visually initiated grasping should decline and be replaced by tactually initiated grasping. This, in fact, is what happens. In the virtual-object situation, the younger infants grasp at the virtual object; the older infants bring their hands to the object but do not close their hands in the absence of tactile input. In normal reaching, younger infants close their hands on a seen object as soon as their hand reaches it; older infants touch an object before grasping it. This can be seen with the naked eye. It is revealed more precisely by comparing the pressure pattern applied to an object in the visually initiated grasping

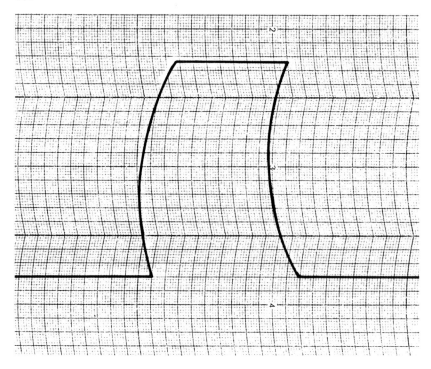

FIGURE 6.17
Polygraph tracing of pressure applied by an infant given only rigidly tethered objects to reach for; note the unitary touch and grasp.

of younger and older infants. Younger infants apply a full-force grasp straight away; older infants touch the object and then grasp it. During all of this, the anticipatory hand shaping that occurs under visual control is not lost; the hand remains adjusted to size and shape prior to contact. However the visual expectation of graspability no longer controls grasping; that has become the province of tactile input.

None of this says anything about the shift from visual initiation to visual control of reaching. There is a strong temptation to interpret hand regard as a precursor to visual control. If hand regard is a precursor to visual control, then it is another maturationally determined precursor. All infants go through a stage of looking at their hand as they move it to and fro. Blind infants have even been observed to track their hands to and fro, in and out, keeping their unseeing eyes firmly fixed on the place where their hand was (Freedman, 1964; Urwin, 1973). This behavior degenerated and disappeared in time, but its very occurrence is enough to rule out many interpretations of the function of the behavior. Since the behavior occurred without visual input, it could hardly serve to produce coordination between the seen and the felt hand. Indeed, that coordination must be built in for the behavior to have occurred at all in a blind baby. Does the behavior serve to dissociate the seen hand from the felt hand? It is hard to see why this would necessarily be the case. Does the behavior help to produce visual dominance over the joint information that specifies hand location? It might, but there is no evidence that it does.

One could continue indefinitely with such speculations. It is more profitable to look at what happens when reaching has become visually controlled. When that state is reached, the infant can correct his reaching movements as they occur. In the Aronson and Dunkeld experiment where an illusion is created, one can clearly see the hand movement change direction to home in on the object. This is what we mean by visual control. Younger infants, by contrast, continue after once starting on a miss path, making their corrections between reaches rather than within reaches. This is what we refer to as visually initiated reaching. Developmentally, visually initiated reaching precedes visually guided reaching. Does this mean, then, that visually initiated reaching is replaced by visually guided reaching? Does the infant lose the ability to launch his hand toward an object without continuous visual guidance? Is continuous visual monitoring *necessary* for successful reaching in older infants, or is it merely *available* when required? There is evidence that it is not necessary.

If infants of around 26 weeks of age are shown an object and the lights are then extinguished, the infants can reach out in total darkness and grasp the object with very high accuracy. If reaching at this stage required visual control, this would not be possible (Bower and Wishart, 1972). Thus, visual control is available but not necessary. How then would hand regard serve to make visual control available? I do not think hand regard could serve this function. Visual control requires the infant to attend simultaneously to the object and to his hand. Attention to two objects must be more difficult than attention to one. The change that is needed to attain double attention is precisely the kind of change produced by the maturation of processing capacity. (See Chapter 5.) The only function hand regard might have is to familiarize the infant with his "visual" hand; this would minimize the attentional capacities needed to register the hand. Certainly, the sight of the hand during reaching is initially disruptive.

The eyes shift away from the object to the hand; this interrupts the reach, which is then stopped while the infant looks at his hand. Presumably, when the hand has been looked at for a while, it becomes boring; the object is then reengaged and reaching begins again.

According to this view, hand regard could result from growing attentional capacity which allows the infant to notice his hand as it goes toward an object. Hand regard disappears as growing attentional capacity allows for simultaneous registration of hand and object. Thus, in this view, hand regard is an epiphenomenon—an accidental consequence of other processes—rather than a direct precursor of later behavior. One could presumably obliterate hand regard by presenting objects that preclude attention to the hand, without retarding the development of later visually guided reaching.

Thus far, the following model of the development of reaching has been presented: the development of the behavior relies on a maturational process producing growth in attention span, plus simple learning effects of the sort known to occur in infants. Growth in attention span, extinction of visually elicited grasping, and reinforcement of tactually elicited grasping are enough to account for the development thus far—given the perceptual tuning we have considered in other chapters.

One thing that has been left in the air, however, is the hand regard observed in a blind infant. If hand regard is an epiphenomenon, why did it occur in the blind baby at all? This topic cannot be considered apart from the whole problem of the development of reaching in blind infants. This segment of development has been described in a series of papers (Fraiberg, 1968; Fraiberg and Freedman, 1964; Fraiberg, Siegel, and Gibson, 1966) that show a rare combination of clinical sympathy with systematic experimentation. The development of reaching in the blind is not a problem of mere academic interest. Many blind children apparently fail to develop reaching ability at all. As Fraiberg and Freedman say:

> The child may be two years old, five years, nine, or even thirteen years old and the picture is almost unvarying. Typically the deviant child spends hours in bed or in a chair or lying on the floor, absently mouthing an object. There is no interest in toys or any objects that are not in themselves satisfying or stimulating to the mouth. Contact with human objects is often initiated by biting and even more often by a primitive clutching and clawing with the hands. For all these children the mouth remains the primary organ of perception. New objects are brought to the mouth and are rarely explored manually.

The behavior of the hand is striking. While many of the children can use the hand for self-feeding and can even use spoons and forks, the hand appears to have no autonomy of its own. It can serve the mouth; it can bring objects to the mouth; but it is not employed for examination or manipulation of objects. Discrimination of objects remains centered in the mouth; however, as already seen, objects are important not for their own characteristics but for their qualities in stimulating the mouth. [1964]

Blind children as old as 12 or 13 years will hold their hands in a stereotyped shoulder-high position, while they engage in stereotyped finger and hand movements quite unrelated to events in the external world. Reaching and grasping simply have not developed in these children—a tragically restricting consequence of their loss of sight. A careful analysis of how one blind child developed reaching and grasping can be found in the papers of Fraiberg et al. (1966). When tested between 23 and 28 weeks of age, the infant made no attempt to reach out after an object that had been removed from his hands. When a noise-making toy was presented, no attempt was made to reach out for it. Indeed, the infant did not even turn toward it. During the next stage, 27 to 36 weeks, some hand movements were made after an object was withdrawn from the hand. These hand movements were not particularly oriented at this stage, but they did occur. Presentation of a noise-making toy still produced no reaching, although some head orientation occurred.

During the next stage, 37 to 48 weeks, the baby was able to reach after a removed object in a way that showed he had registered its direction of movement. The baby could also find objects left in a familiar place. Sound alone still produced no attempt to reach the object; however, toward the end of this period, sound did produce finger movements without reaching —a behavior that could index some awareness that sound can signify something to be grasped. Finally, at 49 weeks, the baby searched for objects that had been taken away, and he also attempted to reach and grasp a sound-making object.

This brief summary has done little justice to the detail of Fraiberg's extremely careful and systematic report. Nevertheless, as much as I admire the study, I must quarrel with its theoretical interpretation. The authors state that the absence of vision is the reason why the coordination of hearing and prehension takes so long. They imply that the coordination should develop much earlier in sighted infants. One study on auditory-manual coordination in sighted infants has been done up to this time; in this study, the sighted infants seemed to have no advantage over the blind infants studied by Fraiberg and her associates. In that study (Bower and Wishart, 1973), sighted infants were placed in darkness where they could see no objects nor any part of their own body. In this respect then, the sighted infants were in the same state as were the blind infants in their normal testing situation. A sound-making object (a bell) was then introduced. The behavior of the infants was recorded on videotape, using an infrared sensitive camera. If we look at the results of the sighted babies over 28 weeks of age, we find that on average they too did not look nor reach out for a sound-making object presented in darkness. They did not reach or look until the age of 44 weeks—no better than the blind babies studied by Fraiberg (1968). (See Figure 6.18.) It thus seems that vision does not link audition and prehension in the sighted infant either.

The picture changes somewhat if we look at the behavior of sighted infants of less than 28 weeks. These younger infants (up to 20 weeks of age) have a far greater ability to reach out and grasp audible objects than

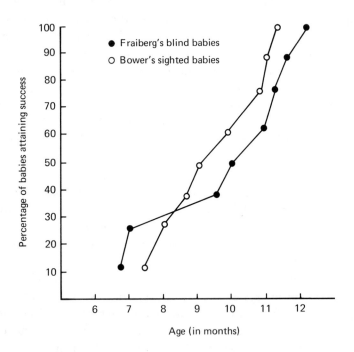

FIGURE 6.18
Comparison of success in obtaining an object specified by sound alone in sighted and blind infants.

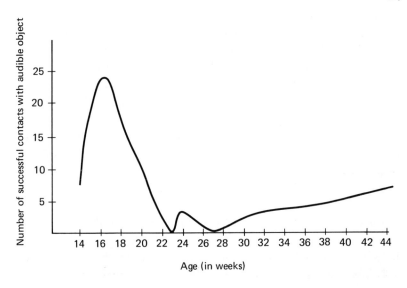

FIGURE 6.19
Success of infants in obtaining an audible object presented in darkness.

do infants between 20 and 40 weeks of age. Looking at the frequency with which sighted infants can grasp an audible object presented in darkness, we see that the success rate begins quite high, increases up to the age of 16 weeks, and then declines precipitously until 28 weeks; after 28 weeks, it gradually recovers (Figure 6.19). There are two sets of observations on blind babies, however, that can perhaps be taken as indicative of general development. The observation that a blind baby girl seemed to "look" at her hands has already been mentioned. Another observation was made when the baby was 16 weeks old; at that age she would turn her eyes to "look" at a source of sound (Freedman, 1964). The author emphasizes that the eyes turned. This was not mere aural centering; rather the unseeing eyes turned to look at the sound source. Shortly after 16 weeks, this behavior disappeared. By the age of six months this baby would no longer turn her eyes toward a sound source. Urwin (1973) has made more striking observations on an infant born with no eyeballs. This infant, at 16 weeks, would reach out to grasp noise-making objects. The behavior disappeared by the age of six months, despite considerable reinforcement and practice, and had not reappeared by the age of ten months.

Although these changes were only seen in two blind babies, they are strikingly similar to the behavior change seen in sighted babies tested in darkness. Because of this, I would argue that both blind and sighted babies begin life with some degree of auditory-manual coordination; this initial auditory-manual coordination is then lost during the early months of development. We have already argued that auditory-visual coordination is present at birth. Wertheimer (1961) showed that a newborn baby will turn to look at a source of sound. Aronson and Rosenbloom (1971) have shown that very young infants know when a sound source and a seen object are in the same place. This coordination is not acquired through experience. Indeed, experience in the environment seems to degrade the coordination. We have argued that visual-manual coordination is built in and declines with age, rather than improving. The experiment cited above showed that sighted infants would reach out to an audible object presented in darkness. Taken together, these observations suggest that the object-specifying properties of audition decline after birth, to be reconstructed toward the end of the first year.

We do not know why audition loses its ability to elicit reaching. Since the phenomenon occurs in both blind and sighted infants, it is not possible that vision takes over the functions of audition. It must be that audition loses its properties by itself. The pattern of disappearance followed by reappearance is familiar to us; and, as we know, there is a well-articulated theory of neural growth to explain such patterns. However, in the cases of walking and reaching, we have found reasons to substitute functional explanations for the growth theory. This might suggest that we attempt a functional explanation here as well.

One explanation stems from the nature of the information provided by auditory stimulation. As we saw before, audition can only specify the radial direction of objects. During locomotion there is a kind of "auditory expansion pattern" that could specify distance, but it is not available to immobile infants. The only way audition can specify distance, as long as we talk about sound-emitting objects, is through familiarity with the characteristic loudness of an object at specified distances. Such familiarity is certainly not built in; young infants reaching on sound cue alone must misreach in depth most of the time. Such continuous failure could well explain the decline in reaching toward sound sources. Acquired familiarity with the characteristic loudness of sound-making objects might also explain the recovery of reaching toward sound sources. An alternative possi-

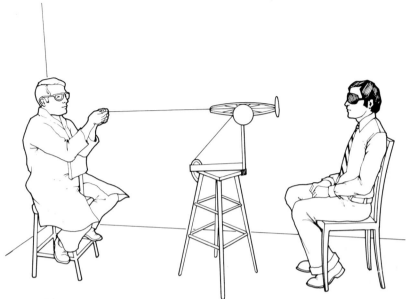

FIGURE 6.20

Apparatus used to demonstrate that echo can specify size as well as distance. The standard and comparison discs were mounted on a wheel which could be silently rotated by the experimenter. The discs were made of one-fourth inch fir plywood and painted with sand-textured paint to give a hard, diffuse reflecting surface. Later experiments by Rice and Feinstein showed that objects with area ratios as low as 1.07/1 could be discriminated by blind subjects. (From Kellogg, W. N., "Sonar System of the Blind," *Science*, 137:399–404, 1962. Copyright © 1962 by the American Association for the Advancement of Science.)

bility that has never been explored is that infants learn to use echoes. The sound reflected back from an object can specify not only its distance but also its size (Figure 6.20). Human adults at least can use the echoes from their own voice. Perhaps infants can do this as well. Human adults do much better if given artificial aids such as clickers (Rice and Feinstein, 1965), and perhaps infants would too.

Thus far we have seen that the development of reaching can be described as the result of maturational processes with sharpening due to simple learning effects. These processes could be fitted into the Piagetian model of development. The simple learning effects could be described as changes in accommodation; the greater success resulting from these changes could be described as a greater degree of equilibration.

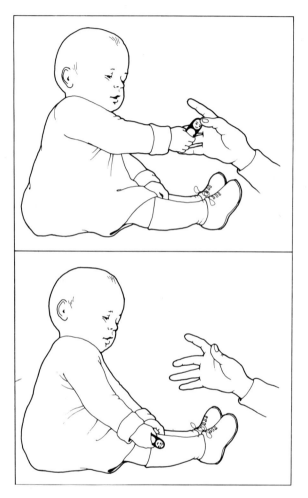

FIGURE 6.21
This picture shows two arm positions: (*top*) the
position on taking the object, and (*bottom*) the position
of the arm at the end of its first excursion. It clearly
shows how the baby's arm falls as he takes the
object. (Drawn from video records.)

The development of reaching is far from over at this point. The infants we have been concerned with (up to about 6 months of age) can reach out and grasp objects in any direction from any posture. This is a considerable advance, as we have seen, but the behavior is still far from the adult level of competence. The behavior is equilibrated as far as the size and shape of objects are concerned. It is not yet equilibrated with respect to the weight of objects (Mounoud and Bower, 1974). That is to say, prior to actual contact with the objects, infants do not yet adjust the force of their grip or the tension of their arms in accordance with the weight of objects.

This can be shown by analyzing the grasping patterns consequent to contacting an object. A six- or seven-month-old infant grips an object as tightly as possible, regardless of the weight of the object. The grasping force varies between babies; the point is that, in an individual baby, it is constant and independent of the weight of the object being grasped. At this age, there is some accommodation of arm tension to object weight, although it is not yet anticipatory. Infants of this age can bring objects to their mouths; they do so with a tremor at the beginning which indicates changes in the tension exerted. When infants of this age are handed an object, invariably their arm initially drops under the weight of the object (Figure 6.21). Tension is adjusted very quickly, and the object is pulled back up to the desired position. The initial hand drop indicates lack of anticipation of the weight of the object. Even on repeated presentations, the hand drop continues, indicating that anticipatory behavior cannot be built in at this stage.

Around nine months of age behavior begins to change. The force of grasp is adjusted to the weight of the object presented, although this still does not happen until after the object has been grasped (Figure 6.22). The hand continues to drop on presentation of an object, even after repeated trials. At this point both grasping and arm tension have differentiated to produce accommodation to different weights of objects. However, the accommodation is still after the fact; there is no anticipation of weight, even after the same object has been presented several times.

Around the age of one year, a significant advance toward equilibration occurs. On repeated presentations of an object, the errors in force of grasp and arm tension decline to zero. Indeed, shortly after this pattern appears, the errors will disappear on the second presentation of any given object. The force needed to hold an object is discovered on the first presentation. The same force is applied instantaneously on the second trial.

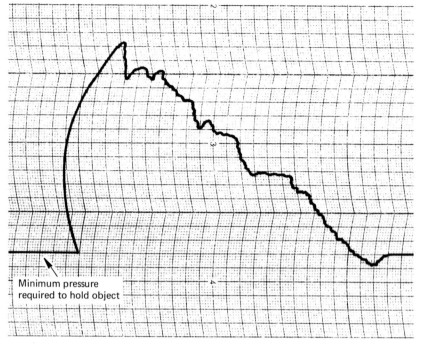

Minimum pressure
required to hold object

FIGURE 6.22
This polygraph tracing shows that the baby adjusts his grasp to the weight
of the object, but this adjustment is still not made until *after* the object has
been grasped.

Likewise, the required arm tension is discovered during the first trial, and
it is applied straight away on the second trial. (See Figure 6.23.)

This amount of anticipation represents a considerable advance, but
the behavior is still very restricted. Suppose that a child can reach out,
grasp, and transport an object with just the right force for successful
holding, and just the right arm tension for smooth transport. If that child
is then given another object, say twice as long and twice as heavy as the
first, his response to that object is just as erroneous as it would have been
if he had had no prior information about the weight of the new object.
In this stage, therefore, equilibration can be attained—but only for single
objects. The responses are sufficiently differentiated to permit adjustment;
however, there is as yet no predictive rule that permits anticipatory adjustments for new objects. The only predictive rule we could infer from the

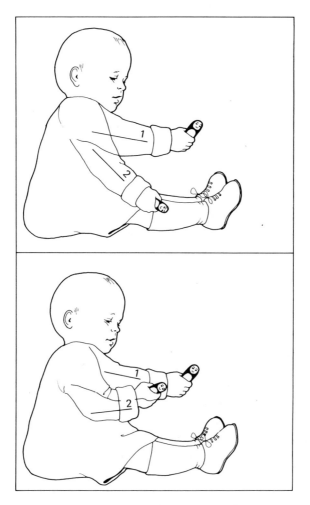

FIGURE 6.23
Each picture shows two arm positions superimposed:
the position on taking the object, and the position
of the arm at the end of its first excursion. On
comparing the top and bottom picture, we can see
that the information about the weight of the object
gained in the first presentation is applied
immediately on the second presentation of the same
object. Note the greatly diminished arm excursion.
(Drawn from video records.)

behavior would be something like: "The same objects weigh the same every time they are picked up." Some such rule must be in use to produce the instantaneous adjustments seen on repeated presentations of the same object.

Toward 18 months of age, the behavior changes once again; at this age there is anticipation of the weight of objects that have not yet been grasped. If one presents a child with a series of objects, graded according to length and weight, the child is seemingly able to predict the weight from the perceived length. Suppose we have a series of lengths—say, 1, 2, 3, 4, and 5. Each constant increase in length is correlated with a constant increase in weight. If the infant is given object number 1, his initial grasp force and arm tension will probably be wrong. The second presentation of 1 will elicit no error. There is nothing new in this. However, the *first* presentation of object number 2 likewise elicits no error; nor does the first presentation of objects 3, 4, and 5. The infant now seems able to *predict* the weight of objects, prior to actual interaction with them. The rule controlling the infant's behavior now seems to be: "The longer an object is, the heavier it will be when picked up." Paradoxically, this rule can lead infants to make mistakes that younger infants would never make. Suppose we add to our series a trick object, of length 6 and weight 3. The infants will overestimate the weight of the object, gripping it too hard and applying too much arm tension. The result is that the infant's arm will fly up as shown in Figure 6.24. The opposite will happen if an object of length 2 and weight 5 is presented. The object will probably be dropped. The existence of these errors shows that accommodation is now anticipatory for all objects that can be serially ordered in some visible dimension which covaries with weight.

The stages in the development can now by summarized into four stages:

Stage I. No differential response to objects of different weight.

Stage II. Differential response to objects of different weight after grasping.

Stage III. Differential response after grasping with anticipation that the same object will weigh the same on repeated presentations.

Stage IV. Differential response after grasping with anticipation that the same object will weigh the same on repeated presentations, and anticipation that objects graded in length will be correspondingly graded in weight.

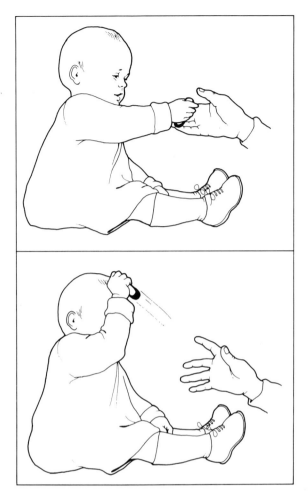

FIGURE 6.24
Here the baby has overestimated the weight of the
object, and her arm flies up. (Drawn from video
records.)

The critical steps in the development so far are the differentiation of
responses and the emergence of anticipation. We can only speculate about
the mechanisms that produce differentiation. It is possible, indeed plausible, that experience with different objects is required to produce the
differentiation of behavior. In the absence of relevant experiments, no
conclusions can be drawn. If such experience is necessary, then one should
be able to demonstrate acceleration effects by introducing an assortment

of weights to the infant. Infants given different objects should display differentiated behavior earlier, if the behavioral differentiation is environmentally mediated. If it is not so mediated, then the environmental modification should produce no effect.

One must also wonder about the nature of the sequence leading from differentiated behavior to anticipation. Is it simply a sequence, or must differentiation precede anticipation? What is it that produces anticipation? We have at the moment no answers to questions like these. It is difficult to say why this development should occur on a learning-theory model of development. In terms of successful manipulation of objects, the younger infants do as well as the older infants. Their exceedingly tight grip is a safety-first procedure. It ensures that they do not make the errors characteristic of the older infants. Why then should there be development? In principle one could give a Piagetian explanation in terms of tendencies toward equilibrium. At the beginning of this segment of development, assimilation and accommodation are both undifferentiated, perhaps even from one another. There is no prediction of weight and no adjustment to weight. There is thus a kind of equilibrium. Once there are differentiated responses to different weights, however, this fragile equilibrium is lost. The range of accommodation—the number of differentiated responses—exceeds the range of differentiated instructions that can be sent out by the mechanism of assimilation. This state of disequilibrium should produce development until the range of assimilation and accommodation covary. The Piagetian model thus predicts development of anticipation after response differentiation has taken place. It says nothing about how the development will take place. Although perhaps strained, this model, unlike other models, at least predicts that development will take place.

The development at this point is still far from complete. We have followed the infant up to a point where he can make two different kinds of anticipation. He anticipates that an object will be the same weight on repeated presentations. He also anticipates that the longer an object is, the heavier it will be. What will happen if we put the two kinds of anticipation in conflict? Suppose we present an infant with a pliable object, so that the infant can ascertain the force required to grasp it. On the second presentation the infant should apply the same force. Suppose, though, that we elongate the object before giving it to the infant again (Figure 6.25). What should the infant do? Since it is the same object, should he apply the same force? But it is also longer; should he therefore apply more

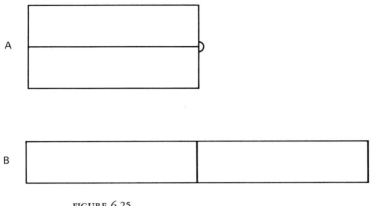

FIGURE 6.25
Object B is produced by unfolding Object A.

force? How should the infant resolve the conflict? At this point it is surely
obvious that we are no longer talking about motor behavior at all—but
rather about the rules that control the behavior. The conflict between these
rules can be resolved, as we shall see. The processes of resolution will not
change the behavior, however, but the way in which the behavior is
applied. With increasing age *behavior* changes less and less, while the
complexity of its *control* processes increases more and more. The study
of these control processes is the subject of our next chapter.

seven /

Cognitive Development

Development of the object concept • Startle experiments • Eye movement experiments • Is out of sight out of mind? • The problem of object identity • Place and movement as criteria for identity • The coordination of place and movement • Motor skill and object permanence • The concept of décalage • Behind versus under as spatial relations • Processes in the development of the object concept • s-r theory • Piagetian theory • Stages in development • The role of conflict in development • Development of quantitative concepts • Size and weight • The continuity of cognitive development • The multiplicity of paths in cognitive development

---

In preceding chapters, we have already given an indication of the subject matter of this chapter. In Chapter 4, it was pointed out that there comes a stage in development when the infant ignores perceptual information and relies on other kinds of information, such as that supplied by memory, consistency, or other nonperceptual processes. In Chapter 6, we discussed how a behavior may develop to a peak of perfection without development necessarily being over; the rules for the application of the behavior must still be elaborated. In development, there is thus a progression away from dependence on immediate stimulus input toward dependence on rules that combine perceptual information with information from memory. This progression—cognitive development—is the subject of this chapter.

Piaget has described the processes and details of infant cognitive development in his famous trilogy, *The Origins of Intelligence in Children* (1936), *The Construction of Reality in the Child* (1937), and *Play, Dreams and Imitation in Childhood* (1946). The breadth and originality of these works dwarfs all of the other essays in this field. It would be impossible to summarize these books within the compass of the present work. Indeed they depend on an interplay between observation and theory that defies summarization. Instead of attempting a summary of the whole trilogy, I shall select one or two topics to describe in full; hopefully, a detailed analysis of selected topics will illuminate the processes at work in cognitive development.

The choice of a topic is not an easy one for the whole range of topics is fascinating and important. There is one topic that stands out, however, and that is the development of the *object concept*. Piaget refers to this segment of development as the prototype of cognitive development; he describes the attainment of the object concept as the most precocious expression of processes that will eventually generate mathematical reasoning and logical thinking in adults. Other authors are equally convinced of the importance of the object concept. Elkind and Sameroff (1970) refer to it as Piaget's most significant discovery—no mean attribution when one considers how many revolutionary discoveries Piaget has made.

What then is the object concept and how does it develop? According to Piaget, the main landmarks of the development are best seen by studying the infants' reactions to objects that have vanished or been hidden. Initially, as Piaget describes it, there is no special behavior toward vanished objects. This description, as we shall see, must be qualified. In terms of gross searching behavior, there is nothing to be seen at this early stage. The infants do not reach out nor crawl after objects that have left their field of view; this, perhaps, is not a surprising result since the infants we are discussing are under four months of age. Infants in the second half of this period (two to four months) will look after objects that have moved out of their field of view. Infants in the first half (zero to two months— referred to as stage I) do not even do this. During stage II, head and eye tracking and looking after objects that have moved out of view does occur. By stage III, infants can reach out to pick up objects that they see. If presented with a partially covered object, they can reach out and take it. (See Figure 7.1.) If the object is completely covered with a cloth or a cup, the stage-III infants make no attempt whatsoever to get the object. They pull back from the object and its cover and make no attempt at all to

182

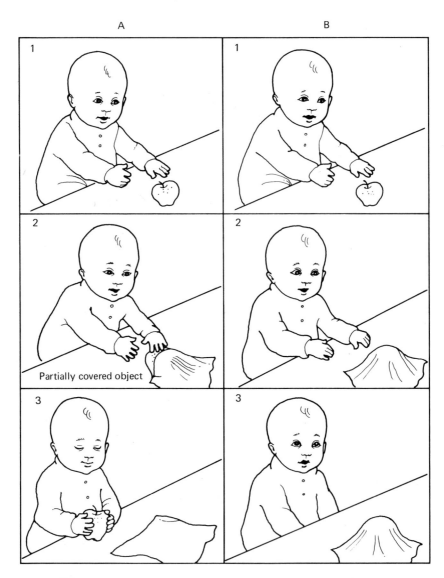

FIGURE 7.1
Stage III. A stage-III infant (A) will reach out and take a partially covered object, but he is unable to obtain an object that has been completely covered by a cloth (B).

remove the cover. Indeed, they act as if the object no longer exists. Many authors have interpreted this behavior as evidence that infants of this age (4 to 6 months) in fact believe that an object no longer exists when it is out of sight.

When the infant can recover an object that has been hidden under a cloth this third stage ends. The stage-IV infant, though, still seems to have a peculiar concept of objects. The infant will look for an object if the object is hidden under a cloth. If however the infant is allowed to find an object under the same cloth two or more times and then the object is hidden within the infant's view but under a different cloth in a different place, the infant will look for the object in its original place under the first cloth—totally ignoring the actual location of the object. This happens even if the hidden object is quite large; the infant will still pick up the flat cloth that had previously covered the object. (See Figure 7.2.) This error implies that the infant does not yet really understand that an object which has been covered by a cloth is under that cloth. The infants seem to think that an object that has been hidden will always be found in the same place. This place error is characteristic of the stage-IV baby. It is usually overcome around the age of 10 to 12 months.

By the age of 10 months, we might think that the object concept was fully developed. However, infants of this age can still be confused by some methods of hiding objects. Suppose we place two cloths on a table; we put an object under one of them and then transpose the position of the cloths, as shown in Figure 7.3A. The stage-V infant will pick up the cloth on the side where the object was first placed, ignoring the cloth that is actually concealing the object. At this point, infants seem to believe that an object will be found where it was hidden; they do not take into account invisible displacements of the object even when the displacements of the thing covering the object are fully visible. Figure 7.3B illustrates a similar failure in a related task. Eventually infants succeed in even these tasks; this normally occurs somewhere around 18 months of age. For future reference these stages are summarized in Table 7.1.

These then are the main behavioral landmarks in the development of the object concept. But a summary of this sort tells us little about the meaning of the infant's failures and successes. Our interpretation of the behavior is critical, and many different interpretations have been made. Consider the behavior that is characteristic of the infant in stage III; if an infant is presented with a desirable toy that is then covered with the infant watching, the infant will make no attempt to remove the cover.

A

B

FIGURE 7.2
Stage IV place error. The infant thinks that an object which has
been hidden will always be found in the same place. Even
when the hidden object is quite large, the infant will still go
to the place where the object was previously hidden.

TABLE 7.1
Stages of Development

Stage	Age (in Months)*	Success	Fail
I	0–2	No particular behavior shown in response to hiding event.	
II	2–4	Infant will track a moving object that goes behind a screen. Infant can learn to track an object from place to place.	Infant continues to track a moving object after it has stopped. Infant will look for an object in its familar place even when sees object moving to new place.
III	4–6	Infant no longer makes tracking errors of Stage II. Infant recovers an object which has been partially covered by a cloth.	Infant cannot recover an object which has been fully covered by a cloth.
IV	6–12	Infant can now recover an object which has been completely hidden under a cloth.	Infant searches for an object in place where previously found, ignoring the place where seen hidden.
V	12–15	Infant no longer makes place error of Stage IV.	Infant cannot cope with invisible displacements of an object.
VI	15–18	Complete success—infant can find object no matter where or how hidden.	

These ages are approximate; there may be considerable individual differences.

One interpretation—the standard one—is that the infant thinks that the object no longer exists when it is under the cover. According to this interpretation, once the object is out of sight, the infant thinks it is no longer to be found anywhere and, therefore, makes no attempt to search for it.

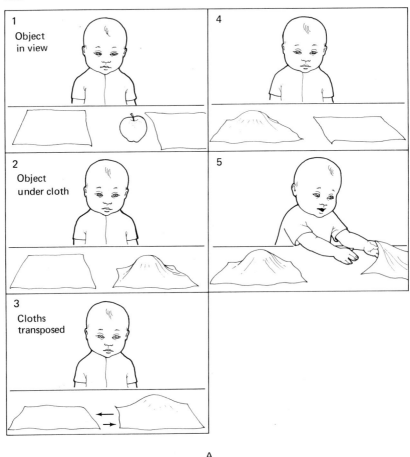

A

FIGURE 7.3
Stage V switching error. (A) The infant cannot yet cope with invisible displacements of the object. (B) The child is unable to infer that if the object is not in the experimenter's hand, it must be under the cloth.

This explanation certainly accounts for the observed behavior. If the infant thinks the object no longer exists, we could hardly expect him to pick up the cover. However, there are other possible alternative explanations. Suppose the infant doesn't pick up the cloth because he simply doesn't have the motor skill to pick up cloths? It is surely possible that the infant knows that the object is under the cloth but doesn't know how to remove the cloth; in this case, of course, the same lack of behavior

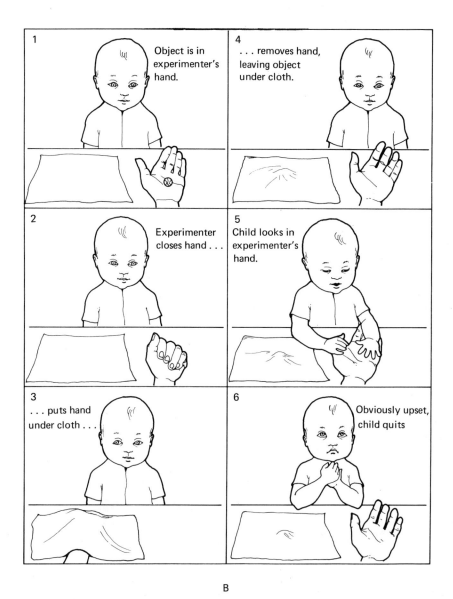

1 Object is in experimenter's hand.

2 Experimenter closes hand . . .

3 . . . puts hand under cloth . . .

4 . . . removes hand, leaving object under cloth.

5 Child looks in experimenter's hand.

6 Obviously upset, child quits

B

would ensue. These two explanations are obviously quite different ways of accounting for the same behavior. Nothing we have said so far allows us to decide between these explanations; however, the relevant sorts of experiments are not too hard to do. What we need is some measure— other than search behavior—to indicate whether an infant thinks that an out-of-sight object still exists. Startle measures could obviously be useful in this account.

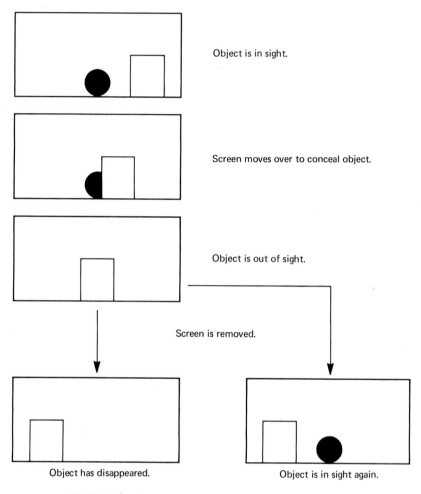

Object is in sight.

Screen moves over to conceal object.

Object is out of sight.

Screen is removed.

Object has disappeared.

Object is in sight again.

FIGURE 7.4
How will a stage-III infant respond to these two events?

Suppose we present an infant with an object and then drop a screen over the object so as to make it vanish. We then remove the screen, either revealing the object or revealing an empty place where the object had been. (See Figure 7.4.) What responses would be predicted by the two alternative explanations? If infants indeed think that an object no longer exists when it is out of sight, they should hardly expect to see the object again when the screen is removed. Following this logic, they should be more surprised by the reappearance sequence than by the nonreappearance sequence. On the contrary, if infants believe the object is still there, hidden behind the screen, then they should be more surprised by nonreappearance than by reappearance. Experiments of this kind have been done by Bower (1966c) and Charlesworth (1966).

In my own experiment, change in heartrate was used as a measure of surprise. I found that infants too young to be able to pick up a cloth were more surprised by nonreappearance than by reappearance. The indication is that the infants did believe that the hidden object still existed even though it was out of sight. If heartrate change can be taken as a fair measure of cognitive upset, it would seem that this is a clear disproof of the standard explanation of stage-III behavior. If infant subjects actually do believe that an object still exists after it has been covered by a screen, then their belief should also manifest itself in other behaviors. If presented with a moving object which they can track, the infants should be able to track the object and anticipate its reappearance when the object goes behind a screen. In other words, if an infant sees an object move behind a screen, he should expect the object to come out on the other side of the screen—provided he really believes the object continues to exist when out of sight. Experiments like this have also been done (Gardner, 1971; Bower, Broughton, and Moore, 1971). The results indicate quite clearly that infants as young as eight weeks of age will anticipate the reappearance of an object that has gone behind a screen. That is to say, they will turn their eyes to reach the exit side of the screen just before, or just as, the moving object emerges from behind the screen. It is not the case that the object is looked at after it emerges. Rather, the infants' eyes are at the exit point just as, or just before, the object appears. This indicates anticipation of emergence rather than reaction to emergence.

This result, together with data on infants' surprise at nonreappearance, would seem to prove conclusively that quite young infants—infants still in the age range of Piaget's stage II—know that objects still exist after they have been occluded by a screen. They can manifest this knowledge in their eye movements but not in hand and arm movements. Clearly, the implication is that the stage-III deficit is really a deficit in the motor system—not a deficit in the infant's knowledge of the world. However, that implication can only be admitted if we accept that the eye-movement behavior unambiguously indexes a belief in the continued existence of hidden objects. Such a belief could produce the observed behavior; however, the behavior could also be generated in other ways.

The simplest possible reason for the behavior would be inability to arrest an ongoing head movement. If the infant was moving his head and eyes in pursuit of the moving object and was unable to stop his moving head, then he would continue to "track" the object even if he thought it no longer existed after it had disappeared behind the screen. Simple inability to arrest an ongoing head movement could thus result in apparent anticipatory behavior with no real anticipation or belief that the object was still moving behind the screen.

This counter explanation was easily tested; infants were presented with an object that moved toward a screen but stopped before it reached the screen. If the infants were "anticipating" because of an inability to stop their head movements, they should also "anticipate" in this situation. Indeed, this is just what happened. Infants who were presented with a moving object that stopped while still in sight continued to look along the path the object had been traveling; they ignored the stationary object sitting there in full view. This kind of result obviously casts doubt on any statement that young infants believe in the continued existence of objects that have gone out of sight; yet it is a result that does not fit with the surprise data gathered with stationary objects. Those data could hardly be accounted for by supposing some inability to arrest an ongoing action.

Closer analysis of the tracking data showed that the continuation of tracking did not in fact result from inability to arrest head and eye movements. A frame-by-frame analysis of videotape records showed that the infants—even the youngest (12 weeks)—all stopped when the object stopped; and then, after an interval of a few hundred milliseconds, they continued to move their eyes along the path the object had been following before it stopped. In other words, the infants could arrest their head movements, but after doing so they again began to "track," ignoring the visible, stationary object.

There are several possible explanations for these bizarre behaviors. For example, one could argue that infants have learned something to the effect: "A movement on one side of a screen will be followed by movement on the other side of a screen." The infants might well have learned that movement of an object toward a screen is usually followed by movement of an object away from the other side of the screen. This kind of learning would explain the bizarre continuation of tracking behavior, as well as the seemingly intelligent anticipation behavior. Unfortunately for this explanation, continuation of tracking after the tracked object has stopped occurs when there is *no* screen in the visual field at all. An infant between 12 and 20 weeks of age, if presented with a moving object that stops, will continue to track along the path that the moving object was following—even if he has stopped momentarily with the stopped object and even if there is no screen in the visual field. This odd continuation of tracking behavior is thus not peculiar to the screen situation but rather represents a general response to moving objects.

What is it that produces this seemingly aberrant behavior? One possible explanation is that the infants do not realize that the object, once stopped, is the same object that had been moving. The infants might think that the object which stops is a new stationary object; they then continue to look for the moving object which they had been tracking. This sort of explanation at least makes sense of the continuation behavior. We are saying that infants do not realize that a moving object is the same object when it becomes stationary. If this is true, then the converse must also be true; the infants should fail to recognize that a stationary object that begins to move is still the same object after it starts moving. In other words, they should see the moving object as a new object.

If this is the case, what behaviors might we expect to see? We might expect infants to continue staring at the place where an object had been resting before it started to move. Piaget reports that this is indeed the case. However, such observations cannot be conclusive, for one could always argue that the infant is merely slow to respond to movement. One might also expect that an infant who is tracking a moving object will look back to where the object had been—a behavior analogous to the continued "tracking" of an object that has stopped moving. This kind of behavior has also been observed; it is not reliable, however, perhaps because a moving object is intrinsically more interesting to an infant than is a stationary object.

A more complicated experiment was done to test the predictions. Infants were presented with an object (a toy train bedecked with flashing lights); the train remained stationary in one place (A) for ten seconds before moving to another place (B), where it stopped for ten seconds before returning to A, where it stopped for ten seconds before moving off again to B. This A-B-A-B sequence was repeated a number of times. How would an infant see this sequence if he does not know that a stationary object is the same object when it moves, and vice-versa? He should see initially an object stationary at A. After ten seconds, this object will disappear, and a new moving object will appear. The moving object will then disappear, and a new stationary object will appear at B. After ten seconds, that object will also disappear, and yet another moving object will appear. It in turn will disappear, and the stationary object will reappear at A, and so on. Infants who are presented with this kind of sequence between 12 and 16 weeks of age initially show continuation of tracking after the object has stopped. However, within a few trials, they settle down to track the object from A to B and back again with no overshooting beyond the place where the object actually stops. The infants look as if they are indeed tracking an object from place to place. If the analysis given above is correct, the infants are really looking at four objects, largely ignoring the moving ones and concentrating on the stationary objects. Rather than having learned to track a single object from place to place, the infants have learned something of this sort: "An object at place A will disappear and an object at place B will appear; the object at place B will disappear, and the object at place A will appear." This kind of learning would also produce the smooth tracking that is actually observed.

Suppose now that the object stationary at A, instead of going off to B, moves to a new location, C. What should the infants do in this situation? If the infants are in fact tracking a single object from place to place, they should simply track the object to its new location. If, on the contrary, the infants are operating with the rule: "Object at A disappears; object at B appears"—then the infants should not track the object to C, but rather should look for it in its familiar location, B. This is what actually happens. The infants ignore the clearly visible object at location C and look steadfastly for it at B—often looking surprised and puzzled that the object is not to be seen at B (Figure 7.5).

It thus would seem that infants fitting into Piaget's stage II do not identify a stationary object as being the same object when it moves; nor do they identify a moving object with itself when it becomes stationary. The question that immediately springs to mind is: how do infants in this age range identify objects? Under what conditions do such infants think that an object remains the same object? This is a different problem from the one we have been considering so far. The problem up till now has been to specify whether an infant thinks that an object still exists after it has been occluded from view. We are now asking under what conditions an infant thinks that an object is the same object. It seems that the transitions from being stationary to assuming motion, and vice-versa, are enough to make an infant believe that he is dealing with two objects.

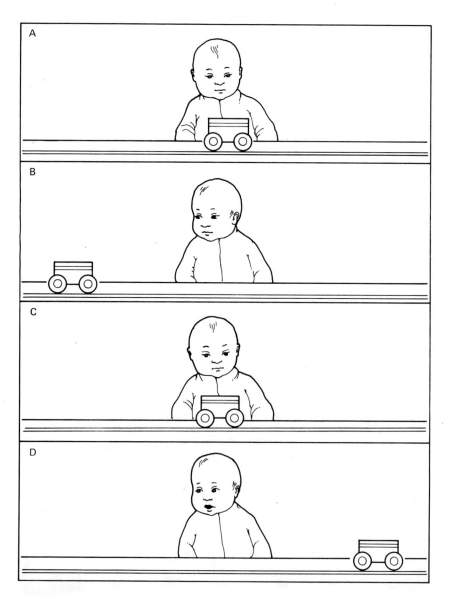

FIGURE 7.5
On the catch trial, instead of looking to the left where the train is now sitting, the infant typically looks to the right where the train had stopped on all previous trials. (From T. G. R. Bower, "The Object in the World of the Infant." Copyright © 1971 by Scientific American, Inc. All rights reserved.)

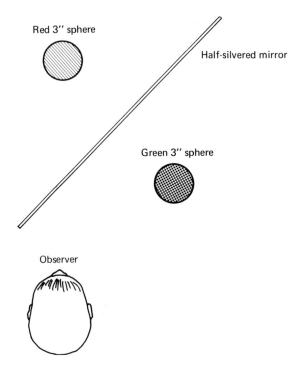

FIGURE 7.6
When the green three-inch sphere is in darkness, the subject sees only the red three-inch sphere on the mirror. If the illumination is changed instantaneously to the green three-inch sphere (leaving the red three-inch sphere in darkness), it is seen to appear at the place where the red object was on the mirror, and it looks as if the red object has turned into a green object.

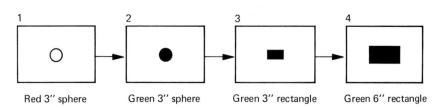

FIGURE 7.7
On seeing this sequence of transformations, adults maintain that they have seen only one object that has undergone a series of changes.

Is it the case, then, that an infant thinks an object is the same as long as it stays in the same place? And, similarly, does he think an object is the same as long as it continues on the same path of movement? We are really asking for the infant's definition of object identity. There seem to be two possible definitions: an object is the same object as long as it stays in the same place; and an object is the same object as long as it continues on the same path of movement.

How can we test whether the infant actually uses these definitions? Fortunately, similar problems have been tested in adults (Michotte, 1962). Michotte presented adults with an object of some given size, shape and color—let's say a red, three-inch sphere in a particular place. After some time, the object was changed, this time becoming a green three-inch sphere. The way in which this was done is shown in Figure 7.6. Subjects were then asked to describe what had happened. They usually said that the object had been changed but was still the same object. Further one-step changes (into a green three-inch cube) elicited the same response. In fact, subjects would watch a red three-inch sphere turn by stages (Figure 7.7) into a green six-inch cube, while maintaining that they had seen only one object undergo a series of changes. If two aspects were changed at the same time (a red three-inch sphere became a green six-inch sphere) while staying in the same place, subjects were likely to say that the original object had been *replaced* by *another* object. If three aspects were changed (the red three-inch sphere became, in one step, a green six-inch cube), subjects said unanimously that the object had been replaced by another object. Continuity of place is thus not enough to produce object identity in adults, although place is still important.

In another set of experiments, the object disappeared from one place, and an identical object appeared in a different place. Subjects agreed that it was the same object that had moved. If however the object which appeared in the different place differed in one other aspect—say size—subjects were more likely to say that the original object had been replaced by another object in a different place. Adults thus seem to define identity by some kind of addition of place, size, shape, and color. If there is overlap in any three of these features, subjects will say that no new object has been introduced. If any two features are changed, subjects will tend to say that some kind of substitution has taken place. Place therefore has no privileged part to play in the adults' definition of identity.

Michotte has done similar experiments with a moving object. In his experiments, an object moved behind a screen and then reemerged on course but with some of its features changed. Some of the transformations he used are shown in Figure 7.8. Movement appears to be a more powerful determinant of identity than is place, since more extreme changes could be tolerated by subjects before they would say that a new object had been introduced. With the more extreme changes, however, the subjects gave peculiar responses such as: "It looks as if it is the same object that has changed, but I *know* that you must have introduced another object somehow." In other words, it seemed as if these subjects had a cognitive criterion of identity that could override the evidence of their senses.

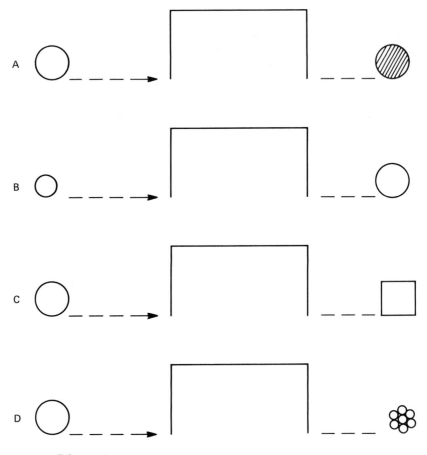

FIGURE 7.8
Transformations used in Michotte's experiment: four examples of the object reemerging from behind the screen with some of its features changed.

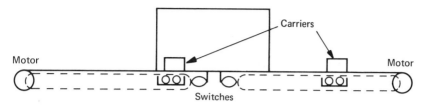

FIGURE 7.9
The carriers on the two track segments were driven by two independent,
separately controlled motors. Two solid state timers provided precise control of
the intervals between movements. The center segment was screened by a
15 cm. white screen. The background was black velvet. (From Bower,
Broughton, and Moore, "Tracking Behavior of Infants." *J. Exper. Child Psych.*
Vol. 11, No. 2, April 1971.)

These experiments depend heavily on verbal reports which are, of
course, not available from infants. However, one can use other indicators.
Bower, Broughton, and Moore (1971) performed an experiment that was
directly modeled on the movement experiments of Michotte. Infants
watched an object approach and then move behind a screen. When the
first object should have reemerged from behind the screen, a different
object came out and continued along the original path at the original
speed. The apparatus used to accomplish this is shown in Figure 7.9. The
infants' eye movements were observed. It was thought that, if the infants
saw the new object as a new object, their tracking might be disrupted as
they looked back for the original object. This change in looking pattern
was seen in infants of about 20 weeks of age or more. The younger infants, however, continued to track as if nothing had happened—even
when the transformation was as gross as that shown in Figure 7.10. A
gross change in size, shape, and color made no difference to those infants.

One might argue that the response demanded too much from the
younger infants; and they could not organize a looking-back response.
However, these responses were observed in the same infants in a different
experimental condition. In that condition two identical objects were used.
One object disappeared behind the screen, and a second one emerged
immediately from the other side of the screen. This second object emerged
much sooner than the original object could have emerged while maintaining its original speed. The object that did appear was identical to the
first in all of its features; however, it was on a different path of movement.

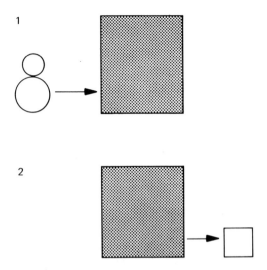

FIGURE 7.10
The tracking of infants in the Bower, Broughton,
and Moore (1971) experiment was not disturbed
by the reemergence of a completely different object.

In this condition, the infants typically made a rapid eye movement to catch the new object but then went back to the exit point; they then jump-tracked to catch the new object again and then returned again to the exit point. The younger infants would typically refuse to look at more than one or two presentations of this sequence—evidence that they found it odd and disturbing.

Lest one think that the observed behavior was a function of the screen, the experiments were repeated, using an enlarged tachistoscope to change objects (Figure 7.11). The results were exactly the same. As long as the object continued on the same path of movement—even though all of its features were changed—the infants were not disturbed, and their tracking was not affected. As soon as the movement path was changed—even though everything else was left the same—the smooth tracking disappeared, and the infants gave some evidence of disturbance. It thus seems that three- to four-month-old infants define the identity of a moving object solely in terms of movement. The other features are not taken into account. We know from work described in Chapter 5 that infants of this age can tell that there has been a change. However, the change is interpreted as a change in the object—not as the introduction of a new object.

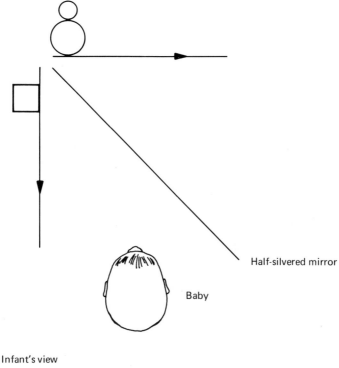

Infant's view

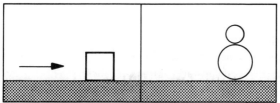

FIGURE 7.11
Both objects move at the same speed, starting from the same point
on the track. If only the small object is illuminated, when the
illumination is switched to the large object, the small object appears
to have changed into a large object on the same path of movement.
(See also Figure 7.6.)

The behavior of the older infants, by contrast, indicated that they took
other features into account—not just movement.

Attempts to demonstrate the existence of a place criterion for identity
have also been made. It would seem that the same response measure could
be used. If one object is substituted for another, and the infant perceives
this as a substitution rather than as a change occurring in the same object

—then we might expect the infant to look for the object that has been replaced. If, on the other hand, the infant perceives a change in the same object, then we would not expect to see any searching behavior at all. Experiments have used tachistoscopic devices to produce event sequences with objects retaining the same place but changing in every other way or with objects changing place while retaining all their other features (Bower, 1974b). The results were less clear than were the results from infant tracking. When an object changes place, the younger infants (three to four months) do look back and forth between the two locations. This behavior is not seen in five- to six-month-old infants. If the substitute object is put in the same place as the original object, younger infants do not look for the original object but continue to stare at the place where the original object was. Older infants—even up to one year of age—also show this concentration on the place where the objects are put (for most objects). If a very significant object such as the infant's mother is used, however, then five- to six-month-old infants will look for their mother after a replacement object has appeared in the place where she was. Younger infants do not show this behavior. Thus, on the criterion of looking for an object (provided that the object is as significant as the mother) place loses its exclusive role in defining the identity of stationary objects around the time when movement loses its privileged role for moving objects.

Infants roughly between the ages of 12 and 20 weeks equate an object with its place or with its path of movement. They seem to think that an object will remain in its place—even after the object has been occluded by a screen. Likewise, their responses indicate an awareness that the path of movement continues behind the occluding screen. They do not seem to be aware that place and movement are linked—that a single object can move from place to place without becoming a whole series of different objects. By the end of this period (around 20 weeks), the infants' behavior has changed, indicating that they have coordinated place and movement. When presented with a moving object that stops, the 20-week-old stops tracking and remains stopped. When presented with a stationary object that proceeds to move, the 20-week-old can follow it no matter where it moves or has moved. These infants seem to be aware that an object can go from place to place along movement paths. They also seem to know that movement links spatially disparate places. We are arguing then that infants have learned the coordination between place and movement; this argument explains the change in the tracking behaviors already described.

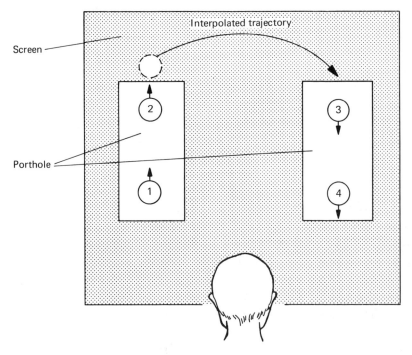

FIGURE 7.12
Mundy-Castle apparatus.

Coordination is an inference or a construct to explain something else. However, Mundy-Castle and Anglin (1969) have done an experiment which seems to show the coordination directly. The experimental set-up is shown in Figure 7.12. Mundy-Castle observed the eye movements of the infants as they looked at his display. Infants around 12 weeks of age showed a simple side-to-side, place-to-place tracking. These infants were able to anticipate the appearance of the object in each porthole, but this was done by simple eye movements in the horizontal plane. Some time later a completely new behavior appeared. The infants began to interpolate a trajectory between the two portholes: rather than going directly from one porthole to the other, the infants began to go up and over, *as if following the trajectory they thought the object must have been following to get from one place to the other.* This trajectory interpolation is visible evidence of the coordination of place and movement within the mind of the infant.

The trajectories that are interpolated reveal a surprising degree of knowledge about the world. Thus, if the interval between disappearance from one porthole and subsequent reappearance in the other porthole is long, the interpolated trajectory is high and rather steep. If the interval is short, the interpolated trajectory is low and rather flat. This shows that the infants know not only that objects move from place to place along trajectories, but also *how* they must move to get from one place to another at a particular speed. Indeed, this is a degree of sophistication we would not have dreamt of attributing to infants a few years ago.

Coordinating place and movement responses has obvious advantages for the infant. It will markedly improve the success of his tracking. However, this advance will also create new problems for the infant—most obviously in the realm of object identity. The infant at around 12 weeks seems to think that an object is the same object as long as it is in the same place and that all objects in the same place are the same object, or that an object is the same object as long as it continues to move on the same path of movement and that all objects on the same path of movement are the same object. It follows that these infants think that a single object seen in different places is, in fact, a number of different objects. This error should disappear after place and movement are coordinated.

Indeed, this does occur for at least one object, and it can be demonstrated with a simple optical arrangement which allows one to present infants with multiple images of a single object (Figure 7.13). If one presents the infant with a multiple of his mother—say, three mothers—the infant of less than five months of age is not disturbed at all but will, in fact, interact with all three mothers in turn. If the set up provides one mother and two strangers, the infant will preferentially interact with his mother and still show no signs of disturbance. However, past the age of five months (after the coordination of place and movement), the sight of three mothers becomes very disturbing to the child; at this same age, a set up of one mother and two strangers has no effect. I would contend that this in fact shows the young infant (less than five months) thinks he has a multiplicity of mothers, whereas the older child knows he has but one. That one mother can no longer be identified merely by a place or a movement. Her other features must also have become critical.

Identification by features is no problem in the case of the mother, since the mother is unique. However, most objects in the world are not unique in terms of their features. Thus, if the infant were to rely on fea-

FIGURE 7.13
Multiple mothers. A very simple optical arrangement allows one to present
infants with multiple images of a single object.

tures alone, he would identify many different objects as one object. There
is evidence that identification of objects remains a problem for a long time
after infancy (Piaget, 1945). There is no problem as long as an object
stays in one place or is seen to move from one place to another. If the
movement is unobserved (an invisible displacement) the infant then has
a problem. How is he to know whether this is the same object that has
moved or a new object that has just appeared? Obviously this is a problem
that cannot be solved in any deductive fashion. The best anyone can do—
even an adult—is make an educated guess. As we shall see, the infant's
guesses become progressively better as he grows up.

The tremendous conceptual development that has gone on in these
first five months is summarized in Table 7.2. At this point in time the
infant, as judged by his eye movements and his startle responses, knows a
great deal about objects. The infant knows that objects exist when occluded by a screen. He also knows how to identify objects by their features as well as by their location. He knows that seen objects are tangible,
and he can infer how an object gets from one place to another. Still, the
infant at this age cannot solve the standard object-permanence problem:
when presented with a desirable object that is covered with a cup or cloth,

TABLE 7.2

Conceptual Development in the First Five Months of Life (As observed in tracking, Mundy-Castle, and multiple-mother experiments)

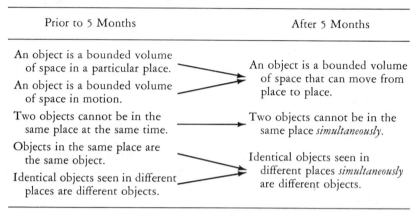

Prior to 5 Months	After 5 Months
An object is a bounded volume of space in a particular place.	An object is a bounded volume of space that can move from place to place.
An object is a bounded volume of space in motion.	
Two objects cannot be in the same place at the same time.	Two objects cannot be in the same place *simultaneously*.
Objects in the same place are the same object.	Identical objects seen in different places *simultaneously* are different objects.
Identical objects seen in different places are different objects.	

the infants make no attempt to recover the object. They act as if the object no longer exists; and yet we have learned from their eye movements and startle responses that they know out-of-sight objects are still there, behind the occluding object, the screen. Surely this can only mean that they are lacking in motor skill.

Some time ago, I tested this hypothesis by selecting infants who had failed the standard object-permanence test with opaque cups and retesting them with transparent cups (Bower, 1967b). When the transparent cup is used, the infant can see the object inside the cup. Thus, there can be no reason to believe that any failure to obtain the object is due to lack of information about its whereabouts; and the motor skills required to remove a transparent cup are exactly the same as those required to remove an opaque cup. If an infant fails to remove the opaque cup because of lack of motor skill, then the same lack should produce failure with the transparent cup. The initial results were very promising. All of the infants tested sat helplessly before the transparent cup, just as they had before the opaque cup. Since the object was clearly visible inside the transparent cup, their behavior could only have been due to a motor difficulty. Unfortunately for the hypothesis, the results did not hold up when a longer time was given to obtain the object (Bower and Wishart, 1972). After a lag of three minutes on average, infants who had failed with opaque cups managed to get the object under the transparent cups. No matter how long they were given, these infants still failed the test with the opaque cup. Concentrated practice in removing transparent cups did not transfer to opaque cups. It thus seemed that lack of motor skill alone could hardly account for the failure to obtain an object covered by a cup. It is the transparency of the cup that is important.

One possibility of explaining away object permanence has been considered by Piaget (1937) and is perhaps supported by these results. That explanation is attributing the behavior to a failure of memory. Even in the case of the transparent cup, it takes a very long time to organize a response. Is it not possible that, in the time taken to organize a response, the infant forgets what is under the opaque cup and so loses the goal of his response? Since the object is continuously visible under the transparent cup, memory would no longer be a factor. Perhaps the opaque cups demand more of memory than it can deliver at this age.

This hypothesis is attractively simple; however, common observation —rather than systematic experimentation—would suggest that it is probably wrong. The memory span of the five- to six-month-old infant is much greater than five minutes. Infants brought into the laboratory at this age often reveal that they remember what happened on a previous visit a day or more ago. Thus, infants brought in for the Mundy-Castle experiment will look at the portholes straight away without waiting for an object to appear. Infants brought in for object-permanence testing will rehearse the behaviors they display with the toys used in the test. Infants who have previously been fooled in the virtual-object situation will not reach again for virtual objects in that situation. None of these observations are systematic, but they do suggest a longer memory span than would account for failure on the standard object permanence test.

Theoretically speaking, there is a more interesting way to link development of the object concept prior to five months with development after five months. This is using the theoretical concept of *décalage*. As we have noted before, behaviors do recur in development. Walking and reaching are two examples. Piaget has argued that processes of conceptual development recur as well, whenever a concept must be used on a different level. This is particularly obvious once language begins. In Piaget's theory, this repetition of sequences of conceptual development is called *décalage*. It is possible that the development of object concept observed after five months is such a *décalage*. The conceptual knowledge that controls eye movements may have to be reformulated at a different level in order to control hand movements. There is, after all, a striking formal similarity between the errors made before five months with eye movements and the errors made after five months with hand movements. Thus, a three-month-old will look for an object where he has been accustomed to see it, regardless of where he has seen it go; and a nine-month-old will search for an object where he has previously found it, regardless of where he has seen it placed. The error seems to be formally the same, which might support the idea that what we observe between five and eighteen months is a repetition at the eye-hand level of organization already completed at the eye-movement level. The knowledge which an infant can display in his eye movements is not available to him at the level required to control his hand movements.

Many writers have argued that the concept of *décalage* is empty, a mere verbal device to cover ignorance in a causal cloak. Bruner (1966) in particular, has argued that—no matter what formal similarities we may find between behaviors occurring at different ages—if the behaviors are different, they must be treated as different behaviors with different, independent developmental histories. With this view, it makes no sense to try to connect eye movements and hand movements in terms of the knowledge required to control them. The behaviors are different and must be treated differently. This is certainly a valid point, and it reiterates arguments made in previous chapters of this book. As we have seen, there are ways of showing the presence or absence of an ancestral relation between behaviors. But first let us examine the behaviors in question in more detail.

There is an apparent contradiction between the knowledge available to the infant to control his eye movements and the knowledge available to the infant to control his hand movements. As far as eye movements and startle responses are concerned, the evidence thus far presented indicates that "out of sight is not out of mind." The standard reaching situation, by contrast, indicates that "out of sight is out of mind"—as far as the part of the mind which controls hand movements is concerned. If we look at the minutiae of the two situations, however, the contradiction perhaps lessens. "Out of sight" in the eye-movement experiments means "out of sight *behind* a screen." In the hand-movement situation, "out of sight" means "out of sight *under* a cloth or a cup."

Behind versus *under* might seem a very trivial distinction. However, we should recall one item of knowledge we inferred was in the repertoire of the five-month-old—that is, the item which states that two objects cannot be in the same place at the same time. An object as we saw in the previous chapter is a bounded volume in space, located in up-down, near-far, and right-left coordinates. When we place a cup over another object, the cup occupies the whole space that was occupied by the object now under the cup. The infant is thus presented with a new object in the same place as the previous object. The infant knows that two objects cannot be in the same place simultaneously: where can the original object be? With the knowledge currently available to the infant, no answer can be given. The old object has disappeared and has been replaced by a new object in the same place. The same analysis applies to covering with a cloth. As long as the infant knows that two objects cannot be in the same place at the same time and does not know that one object can be *inside* another, the standard object-permanence test must be seen by him as replacement—not occlusion.

This analysis, if true, sets aside the problems of *décalage* and separate behaviors. The infant's failure in the standard test situation stems from the very knowledge that leads to success in the eye-movement tasks. The analysis, if true, suggests that five-month-old infants should be able to obtain objects that are out of sight—provided the objects have not been hidden by being placed under another object. There are two studies which suggest this is the case. Bower and Wishart (1972) studied the behavior of infants who had failed the standard object-permanence test in a some-what different hiding test. These infants were shown an object; but, before they could reach for the object, the room lights were extinguished so that object and everything else vanished. The infant's behavior was recorded by means of an infrared-sensitive vidicon camera. All of the infants were able to reach out and grasp the object they had observed but could no longer see (Figure 7.14). In other words, out of sight was not out of mind as long as the transition to out of sight was accomplished by plunging the entire room into darkness. All of these infants were tested again in the standard object-permanence situation when the transition to "out of sight" was accomplished by placing the desired object under another object. Again, all of the infants failed to obtain the object. Apparently then the *nature of the transition* from "in sight" to "out of sight" is what determines or prevents successful hand and arm search.

A similar result was obtained in a study by Brown (1973). A group of infants who had failed a standard object-permanence test were shown a desirable object that was then occluded by a screen (Figure 7.15). The

FIGURE 7.14
Infant reaching for an object in the dark. This infant had failed the standard object-permanence test; yet he was able to reach out and grasp the object which he had seen but could no longer see. Apparently, the nature of the transition to "out of sight" determines the infant's success or failure.

screen was obviously between the infant and the object, rather than in the same place as the object. All of the infants without exception, were able to remove the screen to get at the object. In a subsequent test, all of them, without exception, failed even to attempt to remove a cup that was covering an object. Once again, it is the *nature of the transition* to "out of sight" rather than the mere *fact* of being out of sight that appears to be important.

These studies seem to remove the apparent contradiction between the eye-movement data and the eye-hand data. The same items of knowledge are responsible for the success of the one behavior and the failure of the other. The implication is that the infant cannot succeed in the standard object-permanence tests until he comprehends the relation "inside." He must reformulate his rule, "Two objects cannot be in the same place at the same time," to read, "Two objects cannot be in the same place at the same time unless one is inside the other."

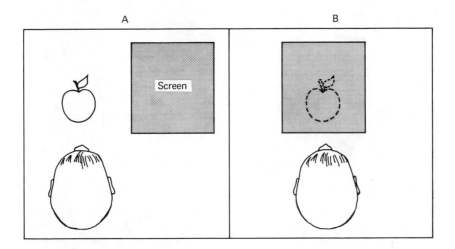

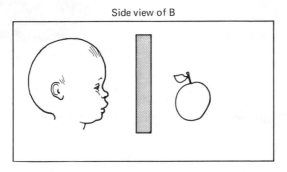

FIGURE 7.15
Here a screen is being used to hide the object instead of the cloth used in the standard object-permanence test.

On this hypothesis development after five months is development of understanding the relation "inside." The main landmarks of the development have been sketched out already. One question is: do we gain anything from placing the burden of development on comprehension of the relation "inside"? I think we do, although the evidence is far from systematic. At the end of stage III, before the child begins to remove cloths and cups from objects, the infant will often lift the cloth and object together. If we are lucky, we can then observe the infant's reaction if the object falls out of the cloth. The reaction is one of stunned amazement,

FIGURE 7.16
Having picked up object and cloth together, the infant is amazed when the object falls out of the cloth; he does not pick up the object for some time.

with prolonged orientation to the object and the cloth in the hand; this may last for many seconds before the object is picked up (Figure 7.16).

This kind of observation can be interpreted as the infant accepting object-with-cloth as a new object. When the object-with-cloth turns into object *and* cloth, the child is surprised—hardly an amazing result considering the conceptual knowledge the infant can bring to the situation. It is possible to set up a similar situation more easily if one covers a toy with a cup that is intrinsically attractive. The infant will pick up the toy by itself, or the cup by itself, and play with either. If, however, the cup is used to cover the toy and the cup is then picked up, the sight of the toy is surprising enough that neither may be played with for a long time.

Of course the infant eventually reaches the stage where he will routinely remove a cup or a cloth that covers a desirable toy. This does not imply that the infant necessarily understands the relation "inside." It is much more likely that the infant has learned an S-R rule of the sort: "When one object replaces another, pick up the replacement object, and the original object will reappear." There is no causality in such a rule—no comprehension of the relationship "inside." In fact, this rule is far too specific to describe the behavior of the stage-IV infant. These infants can find an object that has been hidden in view. If however they are allowed to find an object in one place after having watched while it was hidden there, they will look for the object again in that same place even after seeing the object hidden somewhere else.

This second behavior—which we will refer to as the *place error*—could not be accounted for by the rule just outlined. This behavior would require a rule such as: "When a desired object is not in sight, search for it where it has previously been found." This is a bizarre rule, and we must wonder where it came from. Even though we can only speculate, there are nonetheless some pointers in our previous discussion of identity. The problem posed by invisible displacements has been mentioned. If an object moves or is moved while the infant is looking away from it, and is out of sight when the infant looks back to the place where it was, what can the infant do to retrieve the object? He has no perceptual information at all about the location of the object.

Infants under six months of age in fact show no attempt at retrieval. Over this age, we do see behaviors which include looking for an object where it has been found before (Bower, 1974b). The behavior is a perfectly valid answer in this context. Where there is no perceptual information about the location of an object, it makes sense to look for it in places where it has been seen before. If we are correct in saying that covering one object by another is a totally mysterious transition to a stage-IV infant, then perhaps it is not surprising that place errors also appear in the standard object-permanence test where looking at an original object site is a completely inappropriate behavior.

These two behaviors (removing a cup or cloth and place error) characterize stage IV. At the end of stage IV, they are amalgamated so that the infant seems to have a conditional pairing of responses; if an object is seen to disappear when its place is taken by another object, the infant will pick up the replacement object to obtain the original object. If the original object disappears, but is not seen to disappear, then the infant will look for the object where it has previously been found. This pair of behaviors leads naturally to the errors as well as the successes characteristic of stage V. Consider the following observation from Piaget (1937):

OBS. 55. At 1;6 (8) Jacqueline is sitting on a green rug and playing with a potato which interests her very much (it is a new object for her). She says "po-terre" and amuses herself by putting it into an empty box and taking it out again. For several days she has been enthusiastic about this game.

I. I then take the potato and put it in the box while Jacqueline watches. Then I place the box under the rug and turn it upside down thus leaving the object hidden by the rug without letting the child see my maneuver, and I bring out the empty box. I say to Jacqueline, who has not stopped looking at the rug and who has realized that I was doing something under it: "Give papa the potato." She searches for the object in the box, looks at me, again looks at the box minutely, looks at the rug, etc., but it does not occur to her to raise the rug in order to find the potato underneath.

During the five subsequent attempts the reaction is uniformly negative. I begin again, however, each time putting the object in the box as the child watches, putting the box under the rug, and bringing it out empty. Each time Jacqueline looks in the box, then looks at everything around her including the rug, but does not search under it.

II. At the seventh attempt, I change the technique. I place the object in the box and the box under the rug but leave the object in the box. As soon as I remove my empty hand Jacqueline looks under the rug, finds and grasps the box, opens it and takes the potato out of it. Same reaction a second time.

III. Then I resume the first technique: emptying the box under the rug and bringing it forth empty. At first Jacqueline looks for the object in the box, and not finding it there searches for it under the rug. Hence the attempt has been successful. This occurs a second time but from the third attempt on, the result becomes negative again, as in I. Is this due to fatigue?

What are we to make of this sequence? At first the infant searches for the object in the box where the potato disappeared. When it is not there, she has no information about its location—not even information about its usual place because the only place the object has been found before is in the box. During the second procedure, the object is "given" a location where it has been found, so that as soon as the third part begins the child can apply the appropriate behavior—that is, look for an object that has vanished in places where it has been found before. This behavior still shows no comprehension of the relation "inside," as is made clear by other behaviors. One behavior which can be observed in infants of this age and which seems particularly bizarre occurs after the infant has found an object several times under the same cup. If the object is then placed to one side of the cup in full view, the infant will still pick up the cup, examine it, and shake it, as if expecting objects to pop out. The cup is seen as a cornucopia rather than as a container—something that objects can emerge from without first having to go into. The same lack of comprehension produces the error we have taken as most typical of this stage— the *switching error*. If the infant sees an object hidden under one of two cups and the cups are then transposed, the infant will search for the object at the place where it was last seen, ignoring the transposition. There is thus no awareness that the object is out of sight *inside* the cup. Eventually, of course, the relationship is discovered. The child becomes aware that two objects can be in the same place—provided that one is inside the other. At this point, the development of the object concept (as this is conventionally understood) is almost over. What is still to be attained is the arrangement of all of the information acquired up to this point into a coherent whole. This allows the infant in some circumstances to deduce the location of an object that has been invisibly displaced. Piaget has described the classic circumstance:

OBS. 59. Lucienne at I;I (4) finds a watch chain in my fist. I then replace the chain in my hand and slip this hand under a pillow. I leave the chain under the pillow and bring my hand out closed.

I. First attempt: Lucienne looks in my hand, then finding nothing, looks at me, laughing. She resumes searching, then gives up.

Attempts 2–5: Same reactions. I use the watch instead of the chain to increase her interest; same difficulty.

Sixth attempt: This time, sudden success. Lucienne opens my hand as soon as I take it out from under the pillow. After having examined it a moment she stops, looks around her, then suddenly looks under the pillow and finds the watch.

Subsequent attempts: Same reaction.

II. Then I resume the experiment with a quilt which is on the child's right. Lucienne begins by looking in my hand which I have removed closed from under the quilt. After having opened and explored it for a moment Lucienne searches under the quilt without hesitation.

Subsequent attempts: Same success (Piaget, 1937).

The baby here has seen the object disappear into the hand; she has seen the hand with the object inside it (as she now understands) move under a cloth and come out again. She has inspected the hand and found nothing there. Her success reflects an ability to order these facts and deduce that the object that was in the hand *must* be under the cloth.

The sequence of development is laid out in Table 7.3, which incorporates the observed sequence of behavior and the hypothetical rules and concepts that are supposed to underlie it. One must remember that these rules and concepts *are* hypothetical. Since there are as many rules as there are observed behaviors, it is no more economical at this point to talk of rules than it is to talk of behaviors.

The rule/concept terminology can only be justified if it illuminates the process of development. One may ask whether it is necessary here. There are a variety of ways to account for the development of the object concept. If we go back to the earliest stages of development (development of tracking behaviors), we can see that there are ways to account for the development which do not rely on hypothetical internal mechanisms. The 12-week-old infant will continue to track along the path of a moving object after the object has stopped moving; the same infant will look in the place where a stationary object had been resting before it was moved—ignoring the seen movement of the object. We interpreted this as the result of a conceptual failure—a failure to identify a moving object with itself when stationary and vice-versa. When these errors disappeared, we interpreted it as the removal of the conceptual block. Even though this argument was hopefully a plausible one, it is not necessarily the explanation.

The development could be generated in other ways: the change in one case is a change from continuing along the object's path of movement after the object stops moving. Even from the very beginning of this segment of development, the infants can stop when the object stops. Eventually, by the end of the segment, the infants stop with the object and do not continue. This change has been explained in terms of a coordination of two hypothetical rules: "An object is the same object as long as it

TABLE 7.3   215
Hypothetical Sequence of Development

Stages I and II

Rules	1. An object is a bounded volume of space. (See Chapter 5.)
	2. All objects in the same place are the same object. (See text.)
	3. Two objects cannot be in the same place. (See text.)
	4. All objects on the same path of movement are the same object. (See text.)
	5. Two objects cannot be on the same path of movement. (See text.)
Behavior	To find a stationary object, search for it in the place where it usually is.
	To find a moving object, search for it along its path of movement.

Stage III

Rules	1. An object is a bounded volume of space that can move from place to place along trajectories.
	2. Two objects cannot be in the same place simultaneously.
	3. Objects are identified by their size, shape, color and location.
Behavior	If an object is replaced in the same place by an object of a different size, shape and color, do nothing.

Stage IV

Rules	Same as Stage III.
Behavior	Same as Stage II, plus:
	If an object is replaced in the same place by an object of a different size, shape and color, search for the original object where it has been seen before.

Stage V

Rules	Same as Stage IV.
Behavior	Same as Stage II, plus:
	If an object is replaced by another object, search for the replaced object where it was last seen.

Stage VI

Rules	Same as Stage III–V, except that rule 2 becomes:
	Two objects cannot be in the same place simultaneously, unless one is *inside* the other.
Behavior	See text.

stays in the same place," and "An object is the same object as long as it continues on the same path of movement." Obviously, it is not necessary to speak of coordination. Each of the two behaviors could develop independently through learning with reinforcement. Thus, the infant could cease to follow the path of an object after the object had stopped simply because (1) there is no reinforcement of the following behavior and (2) there is reinforcement for stopping with the object. Continued tracking means losing sight of the object, whereas maintaining the stop fixation means maintaining sight of the object. If sight of an object is taken as reinforcement, then a very simple learning model could account for the development. A similar learning model could be used to account for development from looking for an object where it has previously been seen to looking for an object in the direction it has been seen to move. Both behaviors are in the repertoire of the youngest infants studied, but only the latter will be likely to lead to the behavior of keeping an object in view. The former behavior, in fact, will quite often lead to failure. It is no wonder that the latter behavior should replace the former behavior in the course of development.

Is there any good reason to abandon this simple learning model? The learning model proposes two independent learning processes underlying the two observed changes in behavior. The pattern of change in both behaviors is in fact exceedingly similar, however, which might lead one to believe that a single process underlies both sets of behavior changes (Figure 7.17). The similarity, of course, could be dismissed as coincidence; but how would we then explain the Mundy-Castle trajectory-interpolation effect? (See Figure 7.12.) We have argued that this effect reflected the same change process as that which reduced the tracking errors to zero. Obviously, if two independent learning processes account for the reduction of the tracking errors, nothing can be said about the Mundy-Castle effect. It must remain on the sidelines, as a curious effect that has nothing to do with learning or reinforcement; certainly, no reinforcement theory could explain why the useless trajectory is interpolated in that situation.

What alternative account of the change process can we offer? We have talked about development as coordination of rules or concepts, but we have not specified any mechanisms to explain what produces the coordination. The major virtue of the learning model is that it does offer an explanation of the processes producing change, rather than give a mere description of the effects of the processes.

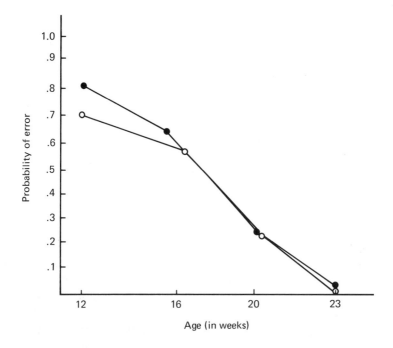

● = Probability of continuation when object has stopped moving
○ = Probability of searching for a stationary object that has moved
        in the place where it has been

FIGURE 7.17
The pattern of development in both tracking tasks is very similar.
This might be taken as a suggestion that a single process
underlies both of them.

Piaget's dynamic model for development also has these virtues, but it
is quite different from a simple learning model. The key concept in
Piaget's model is the idea of *conflict* or *contradiction*. Piaget proposes that
cognitive development occurs only when the infant or child is made aware
of a conflict between two rules, concepts, or modes of coping with the
world when applied to the same situation. The rules for maintaining contact with stationary objects characteristic of the 12-week-old contradict
his rules for maintaining contact with moving objects. Indeed, the concepts underlying these rules are fundamentally incompatible and must

TABLE 7.4
An Example of the Equilibration Process

	1. Conflict		
Concept	An object is a place.	vs.	An object is movement.
Rule	To find an object look in its usual place.	vs.	To find an object look along its path of movement.
Behavior	Place error described in text.	vs.	Continuation of tracking described in text.

	2. Amalgamation
Concept	An object is a *thing* that can move from place to place along trajectories.
Rule	To find an object that has been seen to move, follow the path of movement; to find a moving object that no longer moves, look for it stationary.
Behavior	Cessation of place and movement errors and incorporation of Mundy-Castle trajectory interpolation.

result in conflict whenever they are applied to any situation involving objects that move or stop. As long as place and movement are not co-ordinated, a conflict must be generated whenever a stationary object moves or a moving object stops. This kind of conflict between two partially valid rules or concepts is the necessary condition for cognitive development. The existence of such a conflict triggers processes aimed at resolving the conflict or contradiction. These processes are (confusingly) labeled *equilibration* processes. The end product of equilibration is formulation of new concepts and rules which amalgamate the elements in the conflict. Thus the conflict for the three-month-old can be resolved by the amalgamation shown in Table 7.4. According to Piaget, equilibration itself must be a regulated process so that—given the elements of a conflict—one should be able to predict the outcome of the amalgamation. Unfortunately the rules for equilibration are not well specified; prediction is possible in principle, but it is not yet possible in practice.

This theory and the simple learning model could hardly be more different. The learning model assumes that there is development within a

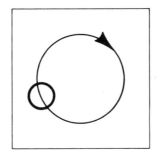

FIGURE 7.18
Circular training.

single behavior. Piaget's model asserts that development is not possible until there is conflict between behaviors or between the rules controlling the behaviors. The learning model asserts that development is specific to a behavior. Piaget predicts that development occurs in all behaviors generated by a concept or rule, including behaviors that may never have appeared before.

The differences between these theories can produce differential predictions, particularly about the effect which special experience has on development. The learning model clearly cannot predict any transfer from one tracking task to another. Piaget, by contrast, predicts that any equilibration sufficient to improve performance on one task will also improve all of the other tasks employing that same concept. This was tested in a specific training experiment. Two groups of infants were matched for age, sex, and initial performance on the Mundy-Castle task. Mean age at the beginning of the experiment was 80 days, so it was not surprising that the average performance was reactive looking from side to side, with little anticipation and no interpolated trajectories. One group of infants was given intervening practice in following an object moving in a circular trajectory as shown in Figure 7.18. The extremes of its arc were the same distance apart as the portholes used in the Mundy-Castle situation. The eye movement required to track the object would have counted as a trajectory interpolation, if elicited in the Mundy-Castle situation. The object was never seen as stationary by the infant, so the situation did not elicit any conflict. It provided training in circular tracking with no conflict. According to Piaget's view, then, it might be expected to improve the

220

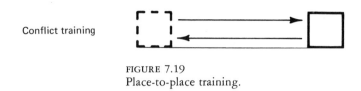

FIGURE 7.19
Place-to-place training.

actual process of circular tracking; but it should not produce any conflict and, therefore, should produce no development of trajectory interpolation or place-movement amalgamation. Since the movement at the horizontal ends of the arc are similar to the movements seen in the portholes in the Mundy-Castle task, one might strain the learning model to predict some kind of generalization of the circular tracking behavior from one situation to the other.

The other group of infants was exposed to a simple place-to-place movement of an object in the horizontal plane (Figure 7.19). The object was stationary in one place first and then moved to the other location, where it stopped for a while, before returning to its original location. The cycle was repeated several times. This situation is a rich conflict situation in Piagetian terms. Every time the object begins moving or stops moving, it induces a conflict between the two, partial object concepts which the child has in his head. Exposure to this situation should therefore produce development on a wide front, including development of trajectory interpolation in the Mundy-Castle situation. This is the last thing one could expect on a simple learning model, since there is no basis for stimulus generalization and no commonality of response between this situation and the Mundy-Castle situation. The results most definitely favored the Piagetian hypothesis. Infants shown the conflict situation produced four times as many trajectory interpolations as the infants trained in the circular-tracking situation. The situation which elicited the conflict also elicited the development—a result entirely in accord with Piaget's predictions.

Further support for Piaget's hypothesis can be found in studies on the age when training can produce development. In the development of tracking ability, an *asynchrony* usually takes place between the two modes of coping with objects that stop and start; these modes are later amalgamated. Usually, though not always, anticipatory responses to a moving object appear sooner than do anticipatory responses to a stationary object seen in different places at different times. Thus, it is possible to present the infant with a training situation where only one behavior can be applied. The alternative behavior is not yet in the infant's repertoire and so cannot be brought into conflict with the first behavior. The situation looks like this: if the infant in this stage is presented with an object which moves from place to place, no conflict will be induced since the response to movement is the only one in the infant's repertoire.

Would the presentation of this situation lead to accelerated development of the behavior in question, or must there be conflict before development is possible? According to the learning theory model of development, the shaping of a behavior could begin at any time after the behavior appears. Thus, if an infant continues to follow the trajectory of an object which stops, the subsequent lack of contact with the object should lead to extinction of the behavior.

A test was made by comparing two groups of infants on just that task. One group began at 8 weeks, the other at 12 weeks. Each was tested weekly for a response to an object which moved in a circular path and stopped occasionally. At 16 weeks, neither group made any errors to speak of. Neither group continued tracking after the object had stopped. However, after the 8-week-old group had had 4 weeks of training, they did worse on the test than did the naive group—not in errors but in terms of successful following. The experienced group would not track the target object; indeed, they seemed to find the situation aversive. Apparently, then, if experience is introduced to correct a behavior at a time when there is no alternative way of coping, the experience does not lead to improved behavior, but rather to its complete extinction—a result quite in accord with Piaget's theory but wholly in contradiction to any simple learning model.

Another way that Piaget's model differs from simple learning models concerns the issue of *stages* in development. Piaget explicitly describes development as proceeding through a series of stages. A stage is defined as a period during which development is stationary for a period—one stage terminating when a new stage begins, with no intermediate periods. This concept is quite contrary to the standard predictions of learning theory. Learning theory standardly predicts that behavior change is cumulative and gradual. Piaget's stage theory predicts that behavior change is all or none: the infant responds in a way typical to one stage or in a way typical to the next stage—with no intermediate modes of response. Normally, learning theory would claim that performance on a task improves

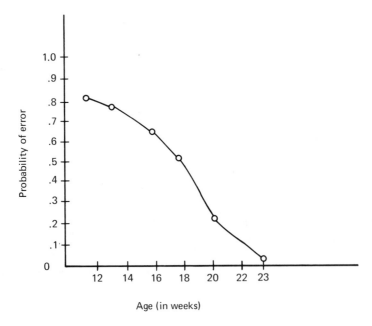

FIGURE 7.20

Smooth change in average performance on a tracking task of infants between 12 and 23 weeks. If, however, we look at each individual record, performance in terms of reduction of errors is much more likely to be discontinuous than a smooth decline.

gradually. Stage theory, by contrast, would predict no improvement in a task until errors simply disappear—all at once, with no slow change.

The stage is a very controversial concept. Indeed, the idea of sudden discontinuities in development upsets our standard ideas of how these processes occur. Perhaps, because physical growth is so obviously continuous, we find it very difficult to think of mental growth as proceeding by way of a series of discontinuities. Certainly, there are enormous problems in establishing the hypothesis that development is stage-like. If, for example, the performance of a number of infants at the same age is averaged and then a range of ages is compared, one usually obtains a smooth change in average performance with age, like these shown in Figure 7.20. If one examines an individual infant, one is much less likely to observe such a smooth change and more likely to see discontinuities. However, the question that is always asked is whether these discontinuities are genuine.

Suppose one sees a child at age 20 weeks and the child makes 100 percent errors. Suppose one then sees the child at 21 weeks of age, and performance is 100 percent correct. Does this change indicate a discontinuity? It might, but there might, on the other hand, have been a gradual change in the intervening week. The same argument can be applied if the interval between tests is only a day or even an hour. In order to demonstrate a discontinuity, there must be a gap between tests, and it is impossible to prove that an intermediate level of performance would not have been observed had one tested during the gap.

Fortunately this need not be a barrier to using the concept of a stage. There are other ways to demonstrate that development is stage-like. Let us again use the transition of the object concept from stage II to stage III. Piaget would argue that the transition is accomplished by the amalgamation of rules governing responses to stationary objects and rules governing responses to moving objects. Prior to this amalgamation, the infant can respond to a moving object or to a stationary object, but he cannot respond to an object that moves and stops. Presented with an object that moves and stops, the infant can either deal with it as a moving object, (which leads to one type of error) or deal with it as a stationary object (which leads to other types of error). Either mode of response is possible; in a situation where both are possible, we should not expect one mode of response to predominate completely. (We would never expect to find 100 percent errors of any one kind.) Thus, in a situation where an object is moving and then stops, we can expect continuation of tracking if the infant is using the movement strategy of coping. If he is using the place strategy, then we would not expect a "continuation of tracking" error.

We might ask what determines which strategy will be used at any particular instant. If the strategies are equally probable, then a random process will decide which strategy is employed at any arbitrary point in time. If the strategies are not equally probable, then the more probable strategy is, of course, more likely to be employed. All this is banal enough. It nevertheless allows us to make very precise predictions on the stage theory and to contrast them with predictions from the continuous learning model. Suppose the infant is at a stage where each strategy is equiprobable. The movement strategy has a probability of occurrence of 0.5, and the place strategy has a probability of occurrence of 0.5. Thus when presented with a moving object that stops, the infant might employ his strategy for dealing with moving objects; in this case, he will continue tracking after the object has stopped, thereby making an error in this

TABLE 7.5
Expected and Obtained Distributions of Errors in
Last Error Trial of Tracking Task

N Errors	f Expected	f Obtained
1	.38	1
2	1.32	4
3	2.63	2
4	3.28	2
5	2.63	0
6	1.32	2
7	.38	0
8	.05	1

$$\chi^2 = 1.32 \qquad .3 > p > .2$$

situation. On the other hand, he might employ his strategy for dealing with stationary objects; in that case, he will stop and remain stopped with the object, making no error in the situation. We would thus expect the error rate in this situation to be 50 percent, reflecting the strategy probabilities.

The converse of this is true in the case of the transition between stationary places. How will the error rate change during the transition to stage III? According to Piaget's theory, it will not change at all. Performance will not improve but will remain at a level determined by the strategy probability (0.5) until it changes completely. Then the single strategy probabilities will drop to zero, and the amalgamated strategy will be applied whenever the infant has to cope with an object that changes position. On a continuous learning model, the probability of movement errors and place errors should decline continuously. This latter condition has never been found in any experimental investigation. Table 7.5 shows the distribution of results obtained from a group of infants in a tracking task. The session shown was the last session on which any of the infants showed any errors. On the next and all succeeding sessions, performance was without error. On this last session with errors, performance was exactly as predicted by Piaget: the error probability was 0.5 on average, and there was no indication of any decline at all.

It thus seems that Piaget's dynamic model of contradiction and equilibration has even more going for it—at least as a description of the transition of the object concept from stage II to stage III. Conflict can accelerate development; practice without conflict does not produce development; and development is discontinuous—a conceptual revolution rather than a gradual evolution.

Can Piaget's model similarly illuminate the later stages of object-concept development? I have suggested elsewhere (1967) that conflict was necessary to generate the beginnings of search for objects which have vanished incomprehensibly, whether under cups or in some other way. The infant of five months has begun to identify objects by their features rather than by their position in space. This means the infant can recognize an object as being the same when seen in different places at different times— even if he has no idea how the object got from place to place. When infants younger than five months are presented with an incomprehensible disappearance, they genuinely act as if the object no longer exists. They make no attempt to look for the object. When the object is presented again, they act as if it were a new object, as gauged by latency of response data and the like. Adults presented with similarly incomprehensible disappearances (by Michotte) tended to say: "It looks as if it has vanished into thin air but I know it must be somewhere." The young infant has not yet acquired the "but." However, soon after the appearance of identification based on features, the infant does begin to search for objects that have vanished incomprehensibly. The search is not well guided—how could it be—but it is a search. When the object reappears it is treated as the same object. I have previously argued that the new behavior was produced by conflict between the two original responses—the response to disappearance ("The object has vanished into thin air and no longer exists anywhere") and the response to reappearance ("This is the same object as that which vanished"). The conflict induced by these two strategies can only be resolved by introducing a new rule: "Objects which have vanished still exist somewhere." This is a rule which produces the poorly oriented search behavior characteristic of the stage.

The main outlines of an argument supporting the importance of conflict in generating transition from stage-IV to stage-V behavior have already been outlined. The infant in stage IV seems to have two "magical" rules for finding objects that have vanished imcomprehensibly: "Look for them at the place where they were last seen," and "Look for them where they usually are." If simultaneously available to the infant, these two rules

TABLE 7.6
Expected and Obtained Distributions of Errors on
Last Error Trial of Stage IV to Stage V Transition
Test (Table shows the distribution of errors on the
last day on which infants made an error and the
expected distribution based on the assumption of
random responding. As can be seen, the difference
was not significant.)

N Errors	f Expected	f Obtained
6	0	1
5	5	6
4	13	14
3	18	14
2	13	12
1	5	7

$$\chi^2 = 2.09 \qquad .90 > p > .75$$

Source: Bower and Paterson, 1972.

would necessarily produce a conflict every time he was presented with an incomprehensible disappearance. Direct evidence is not yet available on this point since no one as yet has attempted to produce acceleration of development by maximizing the conflict. However, two other predictions from Piaget's theory have been tested and confirmed. These are that development is discontinuous and that the mean probability of application of either rule stays at 0.5 until amalgamation of the rules occurs (Bower and Paterson, 1972). Table 7.6 shows results of the last session of testing prior to the beginning of errorless performance. As can be seen, the pattern of errors is very close to that predicted on the assumption of stationary performance with a 0.5 probability of adopting an erroneous strategy. Such data are in accord with Piaget's theory. Thus, even though conflict has not been established here as the driving force in development, the pattern of development fits with the conflict theory of cognitive growth.

What about the last major transition from stage V to stage VI? We have argued that this transition is accomplished by the amalgamation of the concept "inside" with the general object concept; after this amalgamation the child understands that two objects can be in the same place if one is inside the other. The utilization of the relationship "inside" appears late in the behavior of the infant. The ability to put things inside other things or take them out is something that appears late in behavior development—later than the skill requirements of the task would suggest. Piaget's observations suggest that the "inside" relation is highly mysterious even to a one-year-old. The relationship between the goal ("one object inside the other") and the means for obtaining it are obviously not clear to the infant until well after the requisite motor skills are attained. Two of Piaget's observations may show this.

OBS. III. From 1;2 (28) to 1;3 (6) Lucienne systematically puts grass, earth, pebbles, etc., into all the hollow objects within reach: bowls, pails, boxes, etc.

At 1;3 (6) her finger explores the surface of a spade and discovers that the metal handle is hollow: she puts her finger inside and immediately looks for grass to put in the opening.

The same day she puts bowls (of identical dimensions) inside each other; she does it delicately, carefully examining the interrelations of objects.

At 1;3 (7) she has four or five pebbles before her. She puts them into a bowl one by one and takes them out in the same way. Then she empties them from one bowl into the other, still one by one.

At 1;3 (9), on the other hand, she discovers the possibility of emptying the entire contents of a receptacle at one stroke; she piles into a basket the metal molds she has at hand, some stones, blades of grass, etc., then turns the whole thing upside down.

At 1;3 (12) she puts her five molds into a big strainer and takes them out one by one. Sometimes she puts two or three in a pile, sometimes one, then she takes it out, puts in a second one, takes it out, etc.

Afterward she puts a little spade in the strainer, then lifts it up and turns it upside down until the spade falls out.

At 1;3 (14) she puts her molds in a watering can and empties the whole thing at once.

At 1;4 (11) for the first time she is presented with nested boxes. She immediately tries to take out those which are inside. Not succeeding, she purposely turns the whole thing upside down and the contents spread out on the floor. Then she tries to replace them, but hastily and naturally without order.

OBS. 112. At 1;3 (28) Jacqueline for the first time sees the same boxes to be nested but now scattered on the floor. She takes one of them (I), turns it in all directions, and puts her index finger inside it. She rejects it and takes a second (II), same behavior (this time she puts her whole hand inside). In throwing aside the second cube she drops it accidentally into a much larger one (III); she immediately takes it out and puts it in again. Then she takes another (IV), which she also puts into the big one (III). She takes them out and puts them both in again, several times in succession.

After this she takes a big one (V), almost as large as the one she has heretofore used as a container (III), and immediately tries to put it inside. She does not succeed and merely places it askew across the opening of the other one. Then she manages to put it in but not to take it out. It does not occur to her to reverse the big one (III) in order to make the smaller one (V) fall out. Finally she discovers an adequate procedure by sliding her finger against the inside wall of the little one.

Then she chooses a much smaller cube (VI) and puts it into the big one (III). She takes it out and puts it in again about ten times. Then she takes the big one (V) which she puts back and takes out right away. Then she takes a little one (VII) which she puts in and takes out many times.

Then comes a curious experiment: she takes one of the largest cubes (VIII) which she tries to put into a smaller one (VI); she gropes a moment and then gives up quite soon. Same reaction a second time.

Then she picks up cubes V and III and tries to put the first into the second. She succeeds in putting it in but has great difficulty in getting it out again. As soon as she has achieved her goal she repeats the procedure ten times, through functional assimilation.

Finally, when cube V is in cube III, she grasps a smaller cube (IV) and puts it into V. She takes it out and puts it back in, sometimes performing this operation with her left hand, sometimes with her right.

OBS. 113. Around 1;2 (18) Laurent has begun to put pebbles, small apples, etc., into various pails, etc., and to turn them over. This behavior pattern becomes increasingly frequent during the following weeks. Between 1;3 and 1;6 the sight of a hollow object almost automatically arouses in Laurent a desire to fill it, to displace it, and to empty it shortly afterward. At 1;3 (17), for example, he fills a metal cup with grass and pebbles and empties it at a distance, etc. [Piaget, 1937]

OBS. 174. These kinds of apprenticeship can be further complicated by requiring the child to correct the position, not only of the object to be put in, but also of the container. So it is that at 1;1 (23) Lucienne sees me put a ring into half of a case for eyeglasses. She looks at the object inside the case, shakes the case and lets the ring fall out. She then tries immediately to replace it but the apprenticeship is accomplished on two occasions.

During a first phase, Lucienne tries four sequential maneuvers, all unsuccessful. (1) She first presses her three fingers holding the ring against the opening of the case and drops the ring. The ring falls to the side because her fingers prevent it from entering. (2) She presses the ring against the closed end of the case and lets it go. (3) She holds the case upside down and puts the ring into the opening but without tilting it up. The ring falls out at the first movement of the case. (4) She places the ring on the floor and presses both ends of the case against it, alternately, as though the ring would enter it by itself.

During a second phase, on the contrary, Lucienne learns to correct her attempts. First, she no longer places the case on the ring as though the latter would enter by itself. Then when she presses the ring against the wrong end of the case, she does not let it go but turns the case over in order to slide it into the opening. She holds the case almost vertically and, when it is too slanting, she straightens it before letting the ring go. Finally, she learns only to drop it inside the case by first sliding it to the end of her fingers instead of letting it fall when the fingers still obstruct an opening of the case.

At 1;1 (24) after having disengaged the ring from her thumb around which it fell by chance, Lucienne sees me put it around a stick. She then tries to draw it toward her without putting it along the wood. Then she shakes the stick and the ring falls. In order to put it around the stick again, she simply presses it at a certain place and lets it go. Same reaction six times in succession. Then she tries to put it on at the end, but lets it drop. That afternoon she succeeds twice in putting it on the stick but she merely presses it several times against the stick. The following days both reactions subsist without excluding each other, but the attempts to put it on the stick prevail increasingly above the others. [Piaget, 1936]

These observations suggest something of the difficulty an infant has in putting one object inside another, and some of the fascination the act has for the infant once it can be accomplished. The perfection of this act is an excellent example of the assimilation-accommodation-equilibration process discussed in the last chapter, operating at a higher level. Here, the sight of one object inside another defines the end point or purpose of the schema to which the separated objects are assimilated; the child having seen a ring inside a box tries to reinstate this relationship when presented with the ring and the box separately. Accommodation here consists in trying a range of possible behaviors to discover whether they can produce the desired end. Equilibrium is attained by the discovery of the appropriate means to achieve the end.

Once an infant has achieved the behavioral skills necessary to put one object inside another object, he has a piece of information that can correct his erroneous object concept. He thinks that two objects cannot be in the same place simultaneously, but he now knows that one object can be inside another. Somehow the infant must amalgamate these two items of information and discover that two objects cannot be in the same place at the same time unless one object is inside the other. He must become aware that two objects—one inside the other—are like one object insofar as movement is concerned. Container and contained move as one, but they remain two objects, potentially separable into two independent objects. The discovery can be made at any time after the baby finds out how to put one object inside another, but it is not made immediately. In the case of Piaget's daughter, there was a delay of three months between the discovery of the relation "inside" and its amalgamation with the object concept.

There is at this time no explanation of how the amalgamation is accomplished. We do not know that conflict between the belief that two objects cannot be in the same place at once and the information that one object can be inside another is important. However, there is an obvious possibility of conflict, and we must agree that conflict is an important motor force in development. It seems highly likely that the potential conflict is critical in the final attainment of the object concept.

What about attaining the ability to deduce the location of an object that has vanished invisibly? Can that be fitted into the conflict model? It would seem not at first sight. Deduction becomes possible after all the information gathered during the course of development is organized into a coherent whole, with general principles which can be coordinated and applied in specific situations. In a sense, this is amalgamation, but it does not seem to require the kind of subordination typical of amalgamation after conflict. Piaget seems to argue that deduction at this level is irreducible—a basic process whose existence we must accept. Certainly, the primitive deductions of the infant seem to spring inevitably from his acquired knowledge; no further events are necessary to force deduction from this corpus of information.

The object, as we have analyzed it thus far, is an object in space. We have been concerned with change in the infant's responses to objects moved around in space. The relationship "inside" is itself a spatial relationship. The discovery of the properties of objects in space does not exhaust the development of the object concept. The abstraction of the quantitative properties of objects is at least as important—although as yet very little studied.

By quantitative properties I mean dimensions of difference between objects, such as size or weight. Our analysis of the infant's treatment of weight, based on the work of Mounoud & Bower (1974), was begun in the last chapter. We saw how differentiated responses to different weights gradually emerged, with anticipation of weight coming later. The infant learns that the same object weighs the same each time it is picked up; this allows him some measure of prediction. He also learns that weight covaries with the visible dimensions of objects, so that, other things being equal, the longer an object is, the heavier it will be; this allows the infant an even greater degree of anticipation. In the last chapter, we left our infant facing a puzzle that brought these two behaviors into conflict. How should the infant respond to an object he has already picked up but has then seen transformed—made longer? On the one hand, it is the same object, so it should weigh the same; on the other hand, it is longer, so it should weigh more. We might think the infant would instantaneously solve the problem by noting that, although the object was longer, it was also narrower. This is not what happens, however. Mounoud and Bower found that the infant initially responds as if he expects the object to be heavier; conversely, if the object is compressed to become shorter (and wider) the infant responds as if he thinks the object has become lighter. Weight at this point is not an independent dimension of objects; it is equated with length. In time (in the second half of the second year), the infant is able to respond appropriately, ignoring the increased length and expecting the changed object to weigh the same. At this point, we can say that the infant has abstracted the dimension of weight from the visible properties that covary with it. This attainment does not affect the infant's ability to use dimensions correlated with weight, such as length, to predict the weight of an object that has not been handled.

Curiously enough, prediction is not in fact enhanced by consideration of dimensions other than length that covary with weight. The infant seems to know two things: that weight is correlated with length, and that weight is also simultaneously independent of length, so that an object weighs the same regardless of deformations of its shape. Thus, if the infant is presented with a series of objects such as that shown in Figure 7.21, he will respond to object C entirely on the basis of its length. If he has previously picked up the object and then seen it bent in two (C¹), he will ignore the new length and respond on the basis of the information acquired in his prior contact with the object. This is a perfectly satisfactory state of affairs from a practical point of view. It will be years before the child's cognitive development forces him to modify these empirical rules. For the moment, the child's inherently contradictory concept of weight as something related to, but independent of, visual dimensions serves him well enough.

Size is a more easily attainable dimension of objects than is weight. One might think that by the age of six months the infant has discovered all there is to know about sizes. The infant at this age can adjust his hand

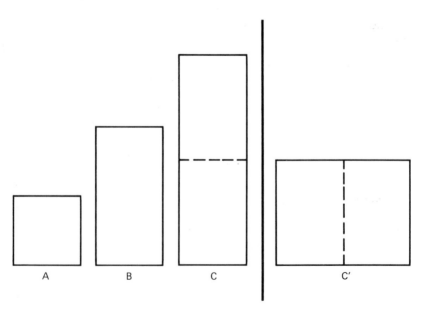

FIGURE 7.21
Object C can be bent in two to produce C'.

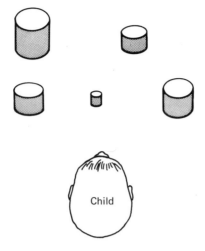

FIGURE 7.22
The set of objects used in the
experiment of Greenfield
et al. (1972).

to the size of an object, perceive it as constant during displacements in space, identify various sizes, and so on (see Chapter 5). The discoveries of a five-month-old are, however, very far from a concept of size. The deficiencies of the young infant's size concept is shown in a simple, ingenious experiment performed by Greenfield, Nelson, and Saltzman (1972). Infants of one year were shown a set of objects like those shown in Figure 7.22. The experimenter showed the babies how to make a nested structure out of the cups, and then they left the infants to stack the objects on their own. All of the infants made some attempt at stacking but failed to do much more than get one object on top of or inside another. Having placed one smaller object on top of a larger object, they might then place a yet larger object on top of the previous two, undoing the whole structure. One-year-olds and even two-year-olds simply cannot organize these objects according to their size. These infants can perceive the size of the objects relative to their own hands, for they can reach out and pick up the objects with perfect success. What they cannot do is organize the sizes of the objects *relative to one another*. "Size" at this stage is something relative to the infant; it is not yet a relation between objects. Size is still egocentric.

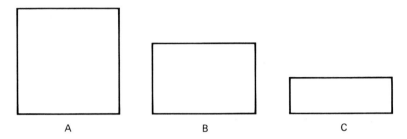

FIGURE 7.23
B can be big or little, depending on whether it is paired with A or C.

The first signs of development come when the infant dichotomizes objects into big and little. When this occurs, the infant consistently makes pairs of objects with a little object on top of a big one; he does not try to add an inappropriately sized object to his two component structures. This degree of classification does not permit a very high level of success, and it invariably leads to conflict, since the same object can be big or little depending upon whether it functions as a supporting object or a supported object. What, for example, would the infant make of the situation shown in Figure 7.23, where the center object can be big or little depending on which object it is paired with? We may speculate that this conflict produces the concept of size as a dimension along which objects may be ordered, so that they are not merely big or little, relative to the infant. Certainly, the infant's two-item structures (little object on top of big object) soon give way to ordered piles of five objects, each object progressively smaller than the one beneath it.

It must be emphasized that the concepts of size and weight thus far described are the merest beginnings of quantitative concepts. The development of true number concepts takes many years. The nature of the development has been intensively described by Piaget and his coworkers in a long series of books such as *The Child's Conception of Space* (1948), *The Child's Conception of Geometry* (1948), *The Child's Conception of Number* (1941). These can hardly be summarized here. The major point is that the development of the concept of number begins in infancy, long before speech or formal instruction play any part. The child is forced to generate number concepts by the requirements of his everyday activities—activities so commonplace that the fondest parent barely thinks them worthy of comment. They are worth mentioning because these are the simple be-ginnings from which the whole structure of mathematical thinking takes root.

Mounoud (1972) has argued that conservation and all other mathe-matical capacities have behavioral as well as verbal/symbolic manifesta-tions. The behavioral symptoms of these concepts are continuous from birth onward, and it is only by studying them that we can truly grasp the continuity of the development of mathematical thought. Most research on the development of mathematical thinking has concentrated on the ages between four and seven years and has ignored the beginnings of mathematical reasoning in the sensory-motor period. It seems to me that this is a perilous strategy. Only when we understand the beginnings of a process, when it is still simple and relatively undifferentiated, can we hope to understand its more complex manifestations.

Cognitive Development: An Overview. Although we have skimmed only a few of the topics that could fall under the rubric of cognitive develop-ment, perhaps we have seen enough to draw an outline of the processes which produce change. One key idea that has been emphasized again and again is conflict. We have followed Piaget in arguing that conflict is the motive force in development. Conflict arises whenever the infant has two incompatible ways of dealing with the same situation. The conflict thus engendered produces the step to the next stage of cognitive functioning. However, there is a great deal about conflict that we have left unclear. In particular, we have left unclear just what it is that is in conflict or is in-compatible. During the stage when an infant comes to know that an ob-ject may move from one place to another along a trajectory (the be-ginnings of the object concept), the conflict is between two possible eye movements—a continuous movement in pursuit of the trajectory, or a jump-like movement between two separate places. Both of these responses could not be performed simultaneously; there was thus a conflict between behaviors at a very peripheral level of functioning.

The conflict invoked to instigate search for an object that has vanished incomprehensibly or invisibly was quite different. The infant has an initial response of no search for an impossibly vanished object. We have taken this as evidence that the infant believes the object no longer exists. Along with this, the infant initially treats the object as a new and different object when it reappears. The conflict arises when the infant begins to identify objects by their features; he then realizes that the object which has reappeared is not a different object. If it is the same object, then it must have been somewhere while it was out of sight. Thus, objects that vanish are to be found somewhere. Surely, the conflict here is not between behaviors but between two different sets of rules for dealing with objects. The conflict is not a behavioral one but is entirely inside the infant's head between two incompatible ways of understanding an event.

The transition from stage IV to stage V of the object concept is accomplished as the result of a conflict which initially seems to be behavioral. The infant can search for an object that has vanished in a way that the child cannot comprehend by going to the place where the object was last seen or by going to the place where the object was found before. When these two locations are separated, as in the standard test procedure, there is a behavioral conflict since the infant cannot, or is not allowed to, perform both responses simultaneously.

The transition from stage V to stage VI, by contrast, does not seem to involve a straight behavioral conflict. The infant's behavior in stage V is comprehensible if he believes that two objects cannot be in the same place simultaneously; the infant can however put objects inside one another. At some time, the infant must realize the conflict between the belief and the behavior, or realize that the behavior produces an outcome that contradicts the predictions of the belief.

The conflict involved in conservation of weight is perhaps the most specifically behavioral conflict of all. At the moment of picking up the object, the infant has the choice of applying one pressure or another; these are, of course, mutually exclusive.

In all of these cases of conflict between behaviors, it is possible that the true conflict is between the rules that control the behaviors. The behavioral choice might function simply to signal to the infant an incompatibility between two rules, with equilibration operating on the rules directly. It is possible that equilibration operates at an even more abstract level, within the concept that generates the rules. Ockham's razor is probably twitching in his hand at this point! Behaviors! Rules! Concepts! Why all these terms when the only observables are the behaviors? The answer lies partly in the concept of stage and partly in the nature of the behavioral changes observed during cognitive development. The behaviors we have chosen to focus on are only a few of those typical of an infant in a particular stage. If the stage concept is valid, when one of these behaviors changes, then all of the behaviors typical of that stage should also change. This is a theoretical prediction that has not really been tested, but it could be. It seems to have some face validity at least for the transition of the object concept from stage III to stage IV. At this transition point, the infant changes his responses to a wide variety of situations more or less synchronously. At this point we simply do not know how precise the synchrony is. If a large number of behaviors do change simultaneously, however, it is more parsimonious to assume change in an underlying concept which generates all of the behaviors, than to assume separate independent changes in each behavior. Although there is insufficient evidence for us to accept or reject the hypothesis that change occurs at a level which is more abstract than behavior, I am disposed to accept it as a working hypothesis to be tested in the future. It is certainly an hypothesis that could be tested rather easily.

One reason for believing that development does not occur at the level of behavior itself is the obvious fact that no single behavior seems to be critical for the development of the object concept. Infants of the appropriate age perform at the appropriate level regardless of whether they have been tested before or whether they have ever performed any of the specific behaviors required in the test. The most striking example of this comes from a study of limbless thalidomide infants carried out by Gouin-Décarie (1965). She found that the sensory-motor intelligence of these infants, tested around the age of two years, was approximately normal. To perform the tests, the infants would lift cloths with their teeth, to discover where the experimenter had hidden the object. Such a finding must raise the possibility of a maturational account of the development. This is not necessary if the development we are discussing is conceptual development. The thalidomide infant like the normal infant tracks objects with his eyes and so should develop normally up to stage IV. After that his search behavior must diverge from that of the normal infant. Even so, there is no reason why his concepts should be different. His ways of testing them, however, will be very different. Where the normal infant can manipulate screens or cloths with his hand, the thalidomide infant can only look with his eyes. The normal infant can discover "inside" in the course of his manipulative play. The thalidomide infant can only discover it by watching. However as soon as cup feeding begins, the infant can hardly help observing the relation. Gouin-Décarie's data indicate that this kind of discovery is almost as effective as discovery through manipulation.

In this context it is extremely interesting to observe the unstructured play behavior of infants. One can observe babies inventing object-permanence test situations for themselves. Picking up cloths or covers becomes a fascinating game at around the age of six months. Throwing cloths over objects and removing them again becomes a constant preoccupation. Any toy that includes disappearances and reappearances will produce rapt attention; perhaps, that is why the jack-in-the-box is such a useful toy. Those infants who have toy boxes and tidy mothers are almost bound to hit on the rule, "Search for an object that has vanished incomprehensibly in the place where it usually is"—the place being the toy box. One can observe infants throwing a toy away, crawling to the toy box, then crawling away again empty handed, to search for the toy elsewhere. If they succeed in finding the object, the whole routine may become a game.

Piaget's son was surely typical in finding the relation "inside" fascinating, and he seized every opportunity to exercise it. Getting the contents of a glass from inside the glass to outside it, on the floor, is probably a cognitively important activity for the child. One of my own daughters spent the best part of one night placing small objects in my hand, closing my hand on them, moving my hand to a new location, and then opening it up to see if the objects were still there. This kept her happy and busy till nearly 4 A.M. Any parent could multiply instances of this kind of behavior. Play has not yet been studied for the light it could throw on cognitive development—a lack I hope will soon be remedied. The point I would like to make in connection with play is that the infant can hardly help discovering the problems posed by objects in the course of his everyday activities. The conflicts that we abstract and put in the formal test situation are bound to be discovered by the infant as he copes with a normal environment. In any normal environment, there are moving objects; objects do disappear incomprehensibly; things are placed in containers, and the containers are moved away. Standard object-permanence test situations are merely refined instances of everyday situations, reflecting the same cognitive problems, often with completely different behaviors. It is the vicarious nature of cognitive development—the fact that the same concepts may be arrived at through completely different means— which argues most forcibly that the development is conceptual rather than simply behavioral.

Another critical question about conflict is when conflict situations can affect development. We have already argued that the kind of conflict which induces development can only occur if there are two alternative ways of coping with a situation. If the infant has only one way of coping with a situation, and we change the situation so that this method becomes invalid, we do not engender development but rather an aversion from the situation which may hinder development. Some evidence to this point has already been given (p. 221). Similar effects can easily be demonstrated if we present a stage-IV infant with the stage-VI task—finding an object under a cup that has been transposed with another cup. The infant's available strategy gives him no success in this situation at all. The result is a very rapid disgust with the situation.

Similar bad effects can arise if we introduce too much confirmation of one method of coping with a situation. An example of this was given in one well-intentioned attempt to accelerate the attainment of stage VI of the object concept (Brunskill, 1971). Infants in stage IV of the object concept were presented with stage-V problems—not in the usual way, but with two totally different cups serving as covers (one plain white, the other bright red). After the infants solved the stage-V problem with these cups, they were introduced to the stage-VI problem, in which cups are transposed. They passed this very quickly—so quickly, in fact, as to be suspicious. Examination of their behavior showed that they paid little attention to the transpositions and often looked away. After several sessions of practice, the infants were given a standard test using plain cups. They failed this completely, doing worse than a comparison group which had been given no practice at all. Apparently, these infants had learned to go to the cup where the object disappeared; they identified the cup by its color, which enabled them to ignore the transpositions and the problem posed by them. The other infants did not have this inappropriate hypothesis to discard and so were more readily able to formulate an appropriate answer to the problem posed by the transposition task.

It thus seems that conflicts may be introduced too early or too late—before two modes of coping exist, or after one has been so strengthened that the other cannot redirect it.

The last general point I would like to make about cognitive development in infancy is that it is truly progressive. Despite surface reversals and repetition, cognitive development—like the development of motor skills and the development of learning itself—is truly progressive. Superficially similar errors are never the same error. Each advance incorporates and reorganizes that which has preceded it. All of these properties of cognitive

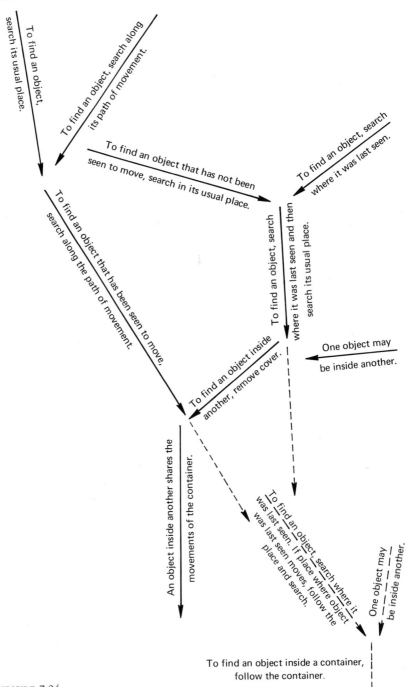

FIGURE 7.24
A modified epigenetic landscape.

development can be expressed in a modified epigenetic landscape as shown in Figure 7.24. The epigenetic landscape is an abstract model for structural development. We used it before to discuss motor development. In the present context it reminds us that the development of hypotheses, concepts, and rules—just like the development of motor skills—is based in structural changes within the nervous system, presumably akin to directly observable structural changes, sharing the same basic mechanisms. The major causal factors in motor development are environmental events interacting with maturationally generated behaviors. The major causal factors in cognitive development are behaviors interacting with other behaviors in their application to environmental events.

Bibliography

Ahrens, R.
  1954. Beitrage zur entwicklung des physiognomie—und mimikerkennes. *Zeitschrift für Experimentelle und Angewandte Psychologie, 2.*

Alt, J.; Trevarthen, C.; & Ingersoll, S. M.
  1973. The co-ordination of early reaching with visual fixation in infants. Manuscript in preparation.

André-Thomas, & Dargassies, St. A.
  1952. *Etudes neurologiques sur le nouveau-né et le jeune nourrisson.* Paris: Masson.

André-Thomas, & Autguarden.
  1953. Les deux marches. *La Presse Médicale,* **61**, 582–584.

Aronson, E., & Dunkeld, J.
  1972. Unpublished data, Edinburgh University.

Aronson, E., & Dunkeld, J.
  1973. Effect of visual assymetry on eye-hand co-ordination in infancy. Unpublished manuscript.

Aronson, E., & Rosenbloom, S.
  1971. Space perception in early infancy: perception within a common auditory-visual space. *Science,* **172**, 1161–1163.

Ball, W., & Tronick, E.
  1971. Infant responses to impending collision: optical and real. *Science,* **171**, 818–820.

Berkeley, G.
  1923. Essay towards a new theory of vision. In *Theory of vision and other writings by Bishop Berkeley.* London: Dent.

Boring, E. G.
  1942. *Sensation and perception in the history of experimental psychology.* New York: Appleton-Century-Crofts.

Bower, T. G. R.
    1965. Stimulus variables determining space perception in infants. *Science*, 3, 323–324. (a).

Bower, T. G. R.
    1965. The determinants of perceptual unity in infancy. *Psychonomic Science*, 3. (b).

Bower, T. G. R.
    1966. The visual world of infants. *Scientific American*, 215, 80–92. Offprint No. 502. (a).

Bower, T. G. R.
    1966. Heterogeneous summation in human infants. *Animal Behavior*, 14. (b).

Bower, T. G. R.
    1966. Object permanence and short-term memory in the human infant, Unpublished manuscript. (c).

Bower, T. G. R.
    1967. Phenomenal identity and form perception in infants. *Perception and Psychophysics*, 2. (a).

Bower, T. G. R.
    1967. The development of object permanence. Some studies of existence constancy. *Perception and Psychophysics*, 2, 411–418. (b).

Bower, T. G. R.
    1972. Object perception in infants. *Perception*, 1, No. 1.

Bower, T. G. R.
    1973. The development of reaching in infants. Unpublished monograph.

Bower, T. G. R.
    The evolution of sensory systems. In R. B. Macleod and H. L. Pick (Eds.), *Essays in honour of J. J. Gibson*. New York: Cornell University Press, in press (a).

Bower, T. G. R.
    Reality and identity in the development of the object concept. In J. Mehler (Ed.), *Handbook of Cognitive Psychology*, in press (b).

Bower, T. G. R.; Broughton, J. M.; & Moore, M. K.
    1970. Infant responses to approaching objects: an indicator of response to distal variables. *Perception and Psychophysics*, 9. (a).

Bower, T. G. R.; Broughton, J. M.; & Moore, M. K.
    1970. Demonstration of intention in the reaching behavior of neonate humans. *Nature*, 228, No. 5272. (b).

Bower, T. G. R.; Broughton, J. M.; & Moore, M. K.
    1970. The coordination of vision and touch in infancy. *Perception and Psychophysics*, 8. (c).

Bower, T. G. R.; Broughton, J. M.; & Moore, M. K.
   1971. The development of the object concept as manifested by changes in the tracking behavior of infants between 7 and 20 weeks of age. *Journal of Experimental Child Psychology*, 11, No. 2.

Bower, T. G. R., & Dunkeld, J.
   1973. Perceptual development. Unpublished manuscript.

Bower, T. G. R., & Paterson, J. G.
   1972. Stages in the development of the object concept. *Cognition*, 1, No. 1.

Bower, T. G. R., & Wishart, J. G.
   1972. The effects of motor skill on object permanence. *Cognition*, 1, No. 2.

Bower, T. G. R., & Wishart, J. G.
   1973. Development of auditory-manual co-ordination. In preparation.

Brown, I.
   1973. A study of object permanence. Unpublished final honors thesis, Edinburgh University.

Bruner, J. S.
   Organization of early skilled action. *Child Development*, in press.

Bruner, J. S.; Olver, R. R.; Greenfield, P. M.; et al.
   1966. *Studies in Cognitive Growth*. New York: John Wiley.

Brunskill, A.
   1971. Some studies of object permanence with children and monkeys. Unpublished honors thesis, Edinburgh University.

Brunswik, E.
   1956. *Perception and the representative design of psychology experiments*. Berkeley, Calif.: University of California Press.

Charlesworth, W. R.
   1966. Persistence of orienting and attending behavior in infants as a function of stimulus-locus uncertainty. *Child Development*, 37.

Cruickshank, R. M.
   1941. The development of visual size constancy in early infancy. *Journal of Genetic Psychology*, 58, 327–351.

Dennis, W.
   1940. The effect of cradling practices upon the onset of walking in Hopi children. *Journal of Genetic Psychology*, 56, 77–86.

Duncker, K.
   1938. Induced motion. In W. H. Ellis (Ed.), *Source book of gestalt psychology*. London: Routledge/Harcourt Brace.

Dunkeld, J.
   1972. Unpublished data, Edinburgh University.

Elkind, D., & Sameroff, A.
  1970. Developmental psychology. *Annual Review of Psychology*. **21**, 191–238.

Engen, T.; Lipsitt, L. P.; & Kaye, H.
  1963. Olfactory responses and adaptation in the human neonate. *Journal of Comparative Physiology and Psychology*, **56**, 73–77.

Fantz, R. L.
  1961. The origin of form perception. *Scientific American*, **204**, 66–72. Offprint No. 459.

Fraiberg, S.
  1968. Parallel and divergent patterns in blind and sighted infants. *Psychoanalytic Study of the Child*, **23**, 264–299.

Fraiberg, S., & Freedman, D. A.
  1964. Studies in the ego development of the congenitally blind infant. *Psychoanalytic Study of the Child*, **19**, 113–169.

Fraiberg, S.; Siegel, B. L., & Gibson, R.
  1966. The role of sound in the search behavior of a blind infant. *Psychoanalytic Study of the Child*, **21**, 327–357.

Freedman, D. G.
  1964. Smiling in blind infants and the issue of innate versus acquired. *Journal of Child Psychology and Psychiatry and Allied Disciplines*, **5**, 171–184.

Gardner, J. K.
  1971. Unpublished doctoral dissertation, Harvard University.

Gesell, A., & Amatruda, C. S.
  1941. *Developmental diagnosis*. Hoeber.

Gesell, A., & Thompson, H.
  1929. Learning and growth in identical infant twins: an experimental study by the method of co-twin control. *Genetic Psychology Monographs*, **6**, 1–124.

Gesell, A.; Thompson, H.; & Amatruda, C. S.
  1934. *Infant behaviour: its genesis and growth*. New York: McGraw-Hill.

Gibson, J. J.
  1950. *The perception of the visual world*. Cambridge, England: Riverside Press.

Gibson, E. J.
  1969. *Principles of perceptual learning and development*. New York: Appleton-Century-Crofts.

Gibson, E. J., & Walk, R. D.
  1960. The "visual cliff." *Scientific American*, **202**, 64–71. Offprint No. 402.

Gouin Décarie, T.
  1969. A study of the mental and emotional development of the thalido-
    mide child. In B. M. Foss (Ed.), *Determinants of infant behaviour.*
    Vol. IV. London: Methuen.

Graham, C. H.; Bartlett, N. R.; Brown, J. L.; Hsia, Y.; Mueller, C. G.; &
  Riggs, L. A.
  1965. *Vision and visual perception.* New York: John Wiley.

Greenfield, P. M.; Nelson, K.; & Saltzman, E.
  1972. The development of rulebound strategies for manipulating seriated
    cups: a parallel between action and grammar. *Cognitive Psychology,*
    3, 291–310.

Gregory, R. L.
  1966. *Eye and brain.* New York: World University Library.

Gregory, R. L., & Zangwill, O. L.
  1963. The origin of the autokinetic effect. *Quarterly Journal of Experi-
    mental Psychology,* 15, 4.

Guilford, J. P., & Dallenbach, K. M.
  1928. A study of the autokinetic sensation. *American Journal of Psychology,*
    40, 91–93.

Harris, C. S.
  1965. Perceptual adaptation to inverted, reversed, and displaced vision.
    Psychological Review, 72, No. 6.

Hay, J. C.
  1966. Optical motions and space perception: an extension of Gibson's
    analysis. *Psychological Review,* 73, No. 6.

Hebb, D. O.
  1949. The organization of behaviour. New York: John Wiley.

Held, R.
  1965. Plasticity in sensory-motor systems. *Scientific American,* 213 (5),
    84–94. Offprint No. 494.

Held, R., & Bauer, J. A.
  1966. Visually guided reaching in infant monkeys after restricted rearing.
    Science, 155.

Held, R., & Hein, A.
  1963. Movement-produced stimulation in the development of visually
    guided behavior. *Journal of Comparative and Physiological Psychology,*
    56.

Helson, H.
  1933. The fundamental propositions of gestalt psychology. *Psychological
    Review,* 40.

Henderson, N.
    1969. Developmental slant perception. Unpublished doctoral dissertation, Tufts University, Medford, Mass.

Hershenson, M.
    1965. Form perception in the human newborn. Paper presented at 2nd Annual Symposium, Center for Visual Science, University of Rochester, New York, June.

Humphrey, T.
    1969. Postnatal repetition of human pre-natal activity sequences with some suggestions of their neuroanatomical basis. In R. J. Robinson (Ed.), *Brain and early behaviour*. New York: Academic Press.

James, W.
    1890. *The principles of psychology*, Vol. 2. New York: Holt & Company.

Johansen, M.
    1957. The experienced continuations. *Acta Psychologica*, 13.

Katz, D.
    1911. Die erscheinungsweisen der farben. *Zeitung Psychologie Erbildung*, 7.

Kohler, I.
    1964. The formation and transformation of the perceptual world. *Psychological Issues*, 3 (4, Monograph No. 12).

Lashley, K. S., & Russell, J. T.
    1934. The mechanism of vision. A preliminary test of innate organization. *Journal of Genetic Psychology*, 45, 136–144.

Lee, D. N.
    Visual information during locomotion. In Pick, H. L. and R. B. McLeod (Eds.), *Essays in honour of J. J. Gibson*. New York: Cornell University Press, in press.

Lee, D. N., & Bower, T. G. R.
    1969. Unpublished data, Harvard University.

Lenneberg, E. H.
    1967. *Biological foundations of language*. New York: John Wiley.

Lewis, M.
    1965. Exploratory studies in the development of a face schema. Paper presented at the meeting of the American Psychological Association, Chicago, September.

Lipsitt, L.
    1969. Learning capacities of the human infant. In R. J. Robinson (Ed.), *Brain and early behaviour*. London: Academic Press.

Mach, E.
    1959. *The analysis of sensations*. New York: Dover Publications. (Original edition, 1885).

Mack, A., & Bachant, J.
1969. Perceived movement of the after-image during eye-movements. *Perception and Psychophysics*, **6**, 379–384.

Mann, I. C.
1928. *The development of the human eye.* Cambridge, England: Cambridge University Press.

McGraw, M. B.
1940. Neural maturation as exemplified by the achievement of bladder control. *Journal of Pediatrics*, 580–590.

McKenzie, B. E., & Day, R. H.
1972. Object distance as a determinant of visual fixation in early infancy. *Science*, **178**.

Michotte, A.
1962. *Causalité, permanence et réalité phénoménales.* Louvain: Publications Universitaires Belgium.

Michotte, A.; Thines, G.; & Crabbé, G.
1964. Les compléments amodaux des structures perceptives. Louvain, Belgium: Publications Universitaires.

Mounoud, P.
1972. Développement des systèmes de représentation et de traitement chez l'enfant. *Bulletin de Psychologie Scolaire et D'Orientation*, **25**, (296), 5–7.

Mounoud, P., & Bower, T. G. R.
Conservation of weight in infants. *Cognition*, in press.

Mundy-Castle, A. C., & Anglin, J.
1969. The development of looking in infancy. Paper read at Society for Research in Child Development, Santa Monica, California, April.

Munn, N. L.
1965. *The evolution and growth of human behaviour.* Boston: Houghton Mifflin.

Papousek, H.
1965. The development of higher nervous activity in children in the first half-year of life. In P. H. Mussen (Ed.), *European research in cognitive development*. Society for Research in Child Development Monographs, **30** (2).

Papousek, H.
1967. Experimental studies of appetitional behavior in human newborns and infants. In H. W. Stevenson, E. H. Hess, and H. L. Rheingold (Eds.), *Early behaviour*. New York: John Wiley.

Papousek, H.
    1969. Individual variability in learned responses in human infants. In
    R. J. Robinson (Ed.), *Brain and early behaviour*. London: Academic
    Press.

Peiper, N.
    1963. *Cerebral function in infancy and childhood*. New York: Consultations
    Bureau.

Piaget, J.
    1951. *Play, dreams and imitation in childhood*. New York: W. W. Norton
    & Co. (Original French edition published in 1946.)

Piaget, J.
    1953. *The origins of intelligence in children*. London: Routledge & Kegan
    Paul. (Original French edition published in 1936.)

Piaget, J.
    1954. *Origins of intelligence*. New York: Basic Books.

Piaget, J.
    1955. *The construction of reality in the child*. London: Routledge & Kegan
    Paul. (Original French edition published in 1937.)

Piaget, J.
    1956. *The child's conception of space*. London: Routledge & Kegan Paul.
    (Original French edition published in 1948.)

Piaget, J.
    1961. *Les mécanismes perceptifs*. Paris: Presses Universitaires de France.

Piaget, J.
    1967. *Biologie et connaissance*. Éditions Gallimard.

Piaget, J.; Inhelder, B.; & Szeminska, A.
    1960. *The child's conception of geometry*. New York: Basic Books. (Original
    French edition published in 1948.)

Piaget, J., & Szeminska, A.
    1952. *The child's conception of number*. New York: Humanities Press.
    (Original French edition published in 1941.)

Prechtl, H. F. R.
    1965. Problems of behavioral studies in the newborn infant. In D. S.
    Lehrman, R. A. Hinde, and E. Shaw (Eds.), *Advances in the study of
    behaviour*. New York: Academic Press.

Rice, C. E., & Feinstein, S. H.
    1965. *Sonar system of the blind: size discrimination. Science*, **148**, 1105–1107.

Rock, I.
    1966. *The nature of perceptual adaptation*. New York: Basic Books.

Rock, I., & Harris, C. S.
  1967. Vision and touch. *Scientific American*, 216, No. 5. Offprint No. 507.

Rock, I., & McDermott, W.
  1964. The perception of visual angle. *Acta Psychologica*, 22.

Royce, J. R.; Stayton, W. R.; & Kinkade, R. G.
  1962. Experimental reduction of autokinetic movement. *American Journal of Psychology*, 75.

Salapatek, P.
  1966. Personal communication.

Schweizer, G.
  1909. *Uber das sternschwanken.* Referred to in H. F. Adams, The auto-kinetic sensations. *Psychological Review Monograph Supplement*, 14, No. 2, 1–45.

Siqueland, E. R., & Lipsitt, L. P.
  1966. Conditioned head-turning in human newborns. *Journal of Experimental Child Psychology*, 3, 356–376.

Sperry, R. W.
  1959. The growth of nerve circuits. *Scientific American*, 201.

Stevens, S. S., & Newman, E. B.
  1936. The localization of actual sources of sound. *American Journal of Psychology*, 48, 297–306.

Stoper, A. E.
  1967. *Vision during pursuit movement: the role of oculomotor information.* Doctoral dissertation, Brandeis University, Waltham, Mass.

Tronick, E.
  1971. *Stimulus control and the growth of the infant's visual field.* Unpublished manuscript. Center for Cognitive Studies, Harvard University, Cambridge, Mass.

Tronick, E., & Clanton, C.
  1971. Infant looking patterns. *Vision Research*, No. 11.

Urwin, C.
  1973. The development of a blind baby. Unpublished manuscript read at Edinburgh University, January.

Von Békésy, G.
  1969. *Sensory inhibition.* Princeton: Princeton University Press.

Waddington, C. H.
  1957. *The strategy of the genes.* London: Allen & Unwin.

Walk, R. D.
  1969. Paper given at the Eastern Psychological Association's Annual Conference, Philadelphia.

Wallach, H.
   1968. *Informational discrepancy as a basis of perceptual adaptation*. In S. Freedman (Ed.), *The neuropsychology of spatially-oriented behaviour*. Homewood, Ill.: Dorsey Press.

Walls, G. L.
   1942. *The vertebrate eye and its adaptive radiation*. Cranbrook Institute of Science, Bulletin 19.

Watson, J. S.
   1965. Evidence of discriminative operant learning within thirty seconds by infants 7 to 26 weeks of age. Paper presented at Society for Research in Child Development, Minneapolis, March.

Watson, J. S.
   1966. The development and generalization of "contingency awareness" in early infancy: some hypotheses. *Merrill Palmer Quarterly of Behaviour and Development*, **12** (2).

Watson, J. S.
   1967. Memory and "contingency analysis" in infant learning. *Merrill Palmer Quarterly*, **13**.

Wertheimer, M.
   1961. Psychomotor co-ordination of auditory-visual space at birth. *Science*, **134**, 1692.

White, B. L.
   1963. Development of perception during the first six months. Paper read at the American Association for the Advancement of Science, December.

White, B. L.
   1971. Human infants—experience and psychological development. Englewood Cliffs, N.J.: Prentice Hall.

White, B. L.; Castle, P.; & Held, R.
   1964. Observations on the development of visually directed reaching. *Child Development*, **35**, 349–364.

White, B., & Held, R.
   1966. Plasticity of sensory-motor development in the human infant. In J. F. Rosenblith and W. Allinsmith (Eds.), *The causes of behaviour*. 2nd ed. Boston: Allyn and Bacon.

Wolff, P. H.
   1969. Motor development and holotelencephaly. In R. J. Robinson (Ed.), *Brain and early behaviour*. London: Academic Press.

Index